Post-Katrina Brazucas: Brazilian Immigrants in New Orleans

❖

Annie McNeill Gibson

UNO PRESS

Printed in the United States of America

Annie McNeill Gibson

Post-Katrina Brazucas: Brazilian Immigrants in New Orleans

ISBN: 978-1-60801-070-7

Library of Congress Control Number: 2011937523

UNO PRESS

University of New Orleans Press

unopress.org

Managing Editor: Bill Lavender

Book Design: Lindsay Maples and Allison Reu

Acknowledgements

I would like to dedicate this book to the memory of Aldin Valerio, a great friend and a heroic rebuilder of the city of New Orleans. May you rest in peace and may this book be a small reminder of the mark that you left in the lives of so many. New Orleans will forever be grateful to you.

This book is a result of the love and patience of many people. First of all, I would like to thank everyone in the Brazilian community in New Orleans who was so willing to open their homes to me and share their stories. The most important result of this book is not the finished product, but the people, relationships and experiences that I have encountered along the way. I would like to especially thank Jackson de Sousa Santos for all the love and fond memories. Thank you to Jacaré, Geamom, Luis, Nalu, Rogerio, and Kelson for helping me make connections with people in the Brazilian community. These friendships have made the sacrifices of writing worthwhile. Thank you Lucien Bruno for accompanying me on parts of my research trip in Brazil, and for offering your solidarity, your observations, and your company on long bus trips. I am also eternally grateful to Chicão, Alberto, Vazinho, Raquel, Vilela, Kelson, Jacson, Cristiano, Reginaldo, Edilson, Diogo, Markinhos, Ibrahim, Fabio, Jackson, Junior, and Vanderley for letting me stay in your houses and share intimate moments with your families during my time in Brazil. Thank you for all the care that you took to make me feel at home and to share with me your culture and your lives. And thank you for teaching me how to eat piqui fruit, fish for piranhas, milk cows, skin a goat, ride a motorcyle, make *canjica*, and play the *berrante* (instrument used to call the cows). Thank you Fabrício, Marcos, and Zumbi for hosting me in Kansas City, Boston, and New York. You were wonderful tour guides into the Brazilian communities in which you live.

I would like to thank the Stone Center for Latin American Studies, FLAS, and the Research Grant for the Global South for providing the financial support for my Tulane graduate study which provided the time and space for the research for this book. I would like to send a special thank you to Jimmy Huck for always being approachable and open to conversation. Also, thank you, UT Austin, for taking me in for the Hurricane Semester while Tulane was closed. Because of the kindness shown to me in Austin, I will always have very fond memories of the good friends that I made through that traumatic time period. Thank you, Capoeira Evolução of Austin for being a second family for me when I moved to Texas. I quickly felt right at home. And thank you to Marcelle for being my roommate and confidant during that time.

I would like to thank Christopher Dunn, Adeline Masquelier, and Dan Sharp for providing feedback throughout the writing process. Without your help I could never have gotten through it. I would especially like to thank Christopher Dunn for all the attention and support that he has provided me through every stage of this project. Thank you for believing in me as a student and for supporting my decisions to choose topics and work styles that others saw as being less than conventional for the academic setting. Also, thank you for hiring me as your assistant to work on the BRASA conference. It was an amazing opportunity to understand the academic world and to converse with other Brazilianists.

I am grateful to Curtis and Carol Pierre for providing me with a support group and an adopted family in Casa Samba. I could not have stayed sane during the writing process if it were not for the creative outlets provided to me through Brazilian dance and music. Thank you for supporting me, developing my dancing skills, and teaching me how to be a professional performer. Moments spent with Casa Samba have been highlights of my graduate career both intellectually, by providing me with a fascinating site for my ethnography, and physically by keeping me of sane mind, body, and spirit.

I would like to thank all of my collegues, especially Xela Korda and Aaron Lorenz for providing emotional support and listening to me during the lonely moments of writing a dissertation. And Adam Frick and Ryan Mass for their conference paper at Harvard University on Brazilians in New Orleans that illustrated to a community of migration scholars this new migration corridor to New Orleans.

Finally, I would most like to thank my family (Mom, Dad, Josh, Shambhavi, and Kavi), especially my mother, Gail Gibson, for being a constant sounding board, for reminding me of dangling modifiers, and for encouraging me to always follow my heart, even when it was the path less taken. I hope that one day I will be as amazing a mother, as brilliant a scholar, and as kind a person as you are. Without the help of all those mentioned above and others whose names I have unintentionally left out, this book would never have been written.

Contents

Post-Katrina Brazucas: Brazilian Immigrants in New Orleans

CHICO BUARQUE DE HOLANDA
"IRACEMA VOOU"

Iracema voou
Para a América
Leva roupa de lã
E anda lépida
Vê um filme de quando em vez
Não domina o idioma inglês
Lava chão numa casa de chá
Tem saído ao luar
Com um mímico
Ambiciona estudar
Canto lírico
Não dá mole pra polícia
Se puder, vai ficando por lá
Tem saudade do Ceará
Mas não muita
Uns dias, afoita
Me liga a cobrar

É Iracema da América

CHICO BUARQUE DE HOLANDA
"IRACEMA FLEW"

Iracema flew to America,
She wears wool clothes and walks joyfully,
She sees a movie every now and then,
Does not speak English,
Washes floors in a tea house,
Has gone out when the moon rises with a mime,
Dreams of studying lyrical voice,
Doesn't fret the police,
If she could, she would stay there,
Though she longs for Ceará,
But not too much,
After a few days she hesitantly calls me collect.

She is Iracema of America.

Introduction: Brazilian Immigrants' Imaginings of Place in New Orleans

August 29, 2005 is a date that is forever etched in the memories of people from New Orleans. As Hurricane Katrina ravaged the city, the winds and the water brought changes beyond the devastating destruction of lives, communities, and infrastructure. Hurricane Katrina also marked a shift in local cultural imaginings, which now include the collective memory of the storm and its aftermath. Not only did the aftermath of Hurricane Katrina call for a rethinking of the New Orleanian community that was displaced by the storm, but the need for reconstruction was a pull factor for a large wave of Latino immigration to the city that has changed the local demographics and, thus, the local culture of New Orleans. Immigration to New Orleans is now a significant factor in the creation and recreation of New Orleanian culture in the post-Katrina age. The aftermath of Hurricane Katrina has been a laboratory for understanding both the patterns of transregional and transnational immigration and the processes of cultural creation and reproduction that have occurred in the localized space of New Orleans.

Among the many Latino groups that moved down to New Orleans post-Katrina, Brazilian immigrants moved down to work in reconstruction. This book is about the Brazilian immigrant network to New Orleans after Hurricane Katrina: How it was established, how it has progressed from 2006 to the present, and how Brazilians invented their sense of place in New Orleans. Because this book is a vignette of the Brazilian community in New Orleans, I have not incorporated stories from other Latino groups in the city, though it should be noted that there are many parallels between the communities in terms of the types of jobs they were performing, their roles in reconstruction, and their access (or lack thereof) to resources. But even though there are obvious similarities between Brazilians and other Latino groups in the city, their language, culture, and racial differences have tended to keep Brazilians divided from their Hispanic counterparts. In 2006-2007, at the height of rebuilding efforts, I estimated through surveys conducted at the visiting Brazilian consulate, by looking at the number of Globo satellite dishes installed in the greater New Orleans area, and through personal interviews within the Brazilian community that between 7,000 and 9,000 Brazilians lived in the greater New Orleans area. The majority of these hailed from the states of Minas Gerais, Rondônia, Pará, and Goiás. Now, in 2010, I would estimate that this number is closer to 3,000-4,000, but Brazilians remain a sizeable immigrant community in New Orleans.

As in other parts of the country, Brazilian culture in the context of New Orleans has in many ways been "invisible." Few people are aware of the extent of their presence because they are an enclave community that tends to be lumped under the label "Hispanic," a label by which few, if any, Brazilians self-identify. A critical root of the problem Brazilians meet in the U.S. is that they are either conflated or elided by the Hispanic/Latino rubric; that is, they are either misinterpreted as "just another Latino" or they are assumed to not exist at all. The experience of being Brazilian in the United States, or being "Brazuca" as it is often termed in academic literature on the subject (and usually used to define undocumented Brazilian immigrants in the U.S.), means learning to become part of this elusively invisible community. In short, the subjugation of identity to public categorical claims complicates Brazilian social categorization and compartmentalization by outsiders. The Brazilian immigrant community in New Orleans proves to be no exception. My own analysis of the everyday decisions made by Brazilians as they establish an enclave in New Orleans takes as a given that Brazilians deal with their status as an "invisible minority."

Beyond their invisibility, the Brazilian immigrant's understanding of place in New Orleans is inextricably linked to the city's mythic Katrina past constructed through media flows, pioneer migrants' personal experience, and finally the stories that those pioneers told about their "Katrina time" to other immigrants. Brazilians began to arrive in New Orleans and defined the city based on the opportunities for work generated by the hurricane. The work that immigrants did in New Orleans, especially during the first two phases of reconstruction, have set the tone for how Brazilians have imagined their place in New Orleans from then until now. Memories of Hurricane Katrina have perpetuated Brazilian immigration to New Orleans for the years immediately following the storm, regardless of the economic reality now that the recovery work has slowed.

The Author

Deciding to write a book on Brazilian immigration after Katrina is in some ways autobiographical. It is a way of documenting my own migration down to New Orleans (three weeks before Katrina) to begin my graduate career; my months of exile in Austin, Texas; and my becoming reunited with a city and two diverse cultures (those of the city of New Orleans and those of the nation of Brazil) that are dear to my heart. My decision to move to New Orleans in the first place was motivated by my love for Brazilian culture. I had previously been living in New Jersey, where I was very involved with the Capoeira Senzala Group. I traveled around the New Jersey/New York area taking capoeira classes and doing performances with other capoeiristas. In fact, I was so involved that I decided that I wanted to go back to graduate school to write my Master's thesis on the globalization of capoeira. Tulane has strengths in Brazilian Studies, and I had always been attracted to the musicality of New Orleans. I applied to graduate school and, when I learned that I had been accepted, the first thing that I did was call up Curtis Pierre, the capoeira angola teacher in New Orleans, to see if there was a sizeable capoeira group for me to get involved with. Once I knew that I could be in a lively city like New Orleans and surrounded by people devoted to Brazilian culture, I was ready to make my move.

Hurricane Katrina was devastating to me. When I first arrived at UT Austin two weeks into their semester with nothing but two changes of clothes, I was distraught by my uprooting. But unlike many residents of New Orleans, I was lucky that things soon turned out for the best for me. I got an apartment with another woman from New Orleans who was to begin the same Tulane program in Latin American Studies. And, again, one of the things that helped me regain some sense of normalcy in my life was finding the Brazilian community in Austin. I first met the local capoeira group when I went to a benefit party held in Austin to raise relief money for Casa Samba, the samba school/capoeira group in New Orleans that I had become involved with, mere days before Hurricane Katrina. When I started training capoeira with Grupo Evolução in Austin, there was an outpouring of support to help me feel at home in their community. They even donated capoeira clothes to me as an offering of solidarity so that I could begin training right away. From those contacts I soon learned where I could go to hear Brazilian *pagode* music on the weekends. When my semester at Austin ended and both the city of New Orleans and Tulane reopened their doors, it was a difficult decision to leave the friends that I had made in Austin to begin again in New Orleans, a city that I was still unsure about after the devastation of Hurricane Katrina. Would it have the same culture and vibrancy that I had first been attracted to?

The short answer is that I made the right choice. Being part of the reconstruction effort was both healing and a learning experience for me, not to mention the eventual topic of my dissertation and now the topic of my first book. Fittingly, some of the first people that I met after returning to the city were Brazilians. I went to the opening graduate student reception at the house of my graduate student advisor at Tulane University, Jimmy Huck. He invited his neighbors to the party, a group of ten Brazilians who had moved into the Uptown neighborhood near Tulane soon after the storm to work in reconstruction. As my friendship with those neighbors grew and I found myself spending more and more Sunday afternoons at Brazilian *churrascos*, I also got to watch intimately as the Brazilian community in New Orleans began to grow, change, and establish itself in New Orleans.

When I first arrived after Hurricane Katrina in January 2006, the city was struggling even to provide basic services for its citizens, much less for the migrant workers who had flocked to the area. A support system for Brazilians was nearly non-existent. Because I spoke both English and Portuguese, I began getting involved translating and assisting with housing, work, and law enforcement issues for these recent immigrants. I accompanied them to Western Union to send checks and to the stores to eat *salgadinhos* (Brazilian finger foods). I took them to the hospital when they were sick or when their appendix burst. I went to bingo games to help them earn money for friends in need. And I drove people to the airport when they decided to return home to Brazil. I interviewed Brazilians in New Orleans who arrived days after the storm, who came down accompanying family members months later, and who were in New Orleans prior to Katrina. I interviewed Brazilians who are still in New Orleans today but will not be here tomorrow, who hope to be here for the rest of their lives, who were in Brazil and are thinking about moving to New Orleans, who had returned to Brazil from New Orleans, and who had moved from New Orleans to another city in the U.S. after the rush for construction jobs ended. I interviewed architects in Brazil building projects for Brazilians still in New Orleans, family members of Brazilians who had not seen their son or daughter for years, and family members who watched their son or daughter arrive in Brazil at that moment that I stood there with them. I talked to an *atravessador* and a *coyote*[1] who organized trips for Brazilians to cross the border, Brazilians who lived in New Orleans but were stuck in immigration jail, and Brazilians with legal residency. I talked to Brazilian musicians, Americans obsessed with Brazilian culture, and Brazilians who shy away from it. Needless to say, the network linking Brazilians to New Orleans is complex and diverse. This book is an attempt to sort through and organize how these different relationships form an immigrant network and, thus, an immigrant enclave.

When I first became involved with the Brazilian community in New Orleans, my work translating and advocating for them was simply what I did with my free time from graduate school. It was my escape from the library and the theoretical discussions of globalization and modernity. I helped them because it was fun and hanging out with Brazilian migrant workers was challenging and enlightening for me on a personal level. It made me question who I was, what advantages I had been born into, and what was really important to me about the life that I am living.

I had no idea that the friendships that I built would end up being the groundwork for my graduate studies. Three years later, as I debated possible dissertation topics, (and I had three radically different ideas),

---

[1] The *atravessador* is the name given to the person in Brazil who organizes the trip to Mexico to cross into the United States undocumented. The *coyote* is the person who will actually guide immigrants across the border.

I decided that I write best when I write about what I care about most. I also realized that, through serendipity, I was in a unique position; no one I knew could tell the stories about Brazilian immigration to New Orleans that I could tell. And these stories were meaningful, not only as portraits of life in New Orleans post-Katrina, but also to the same theoretical debate on globalization that I thought that I was escaping when I had left the library those evenings to hang out with the Brazilians. Besides my direct involvement with Brazilian workers, I have also been constantly involved with the Brazilian cultural performance scene in New Orleans since 2005. My connection to this scene began through my love of capoeira, but I soon found myself performing as a samba dancer for New Orleans' samba school, Casa Samba.

Once I decided that I wanted to tell the stories of these immigrants who meant so much to me, I needed to understand not only why Brazilians had decided to stay in New Orleans, but also their motivations for leaving Brazil in the first place. I then went to Brazil to visit the sending communities. I visited Belo Horizonte, Governador Valadares, Ipatinga, Manhuaçu, and Padre Paraíso, Minas Gerais; Goiânia and Turvânia, Goiás; Colorado do Oeste, Rondônia; and Conceição do Araguaia and Redenção, Pará. These are all towns in which between three to eleven people had returned to Brazil after living in New Orleans. I was interested in asking migrants about their motivations for going to the United States as well as their reasons for returning. And I was also interested in hearing their perspectives on the time that they lived in New Orleans. Had their experience in New Orleans been any different from other cities where they lived in the United States? What were their most poignant memories about New Orleans in the aftermath of Hurricane Katrina? How did they describe that experience to their loved ones?

The three months that I spent in Brazil conducting these interviews was life-altering for me in that it revealed a Brazil that I had not been familiar with before. Daily routines there involved milking cows bought in Brazil with money earned in New Orleans, fishing for piranhas, skinning goats, feeding chickens, picking mango to sell at the market, and making periodic trips to the local bank to see if needed cash had arrived from a family member working in the United States. During my research trip, I explored towns and villages in Brazil's vast interior; my travels to Brazil in the past had always taken me to the coastal cities for which Brazil is better known.

Figure 1: Researcher milking cows bought with NOLA remittances

The subjects of my interviews in Brazil were friends and acquaintances that I had known in New Orleans. I had met them either through social occasions around the city or because I had helped them at some point by providing translation services. My long-term and personal relationships with my interview subjects granted me access to very sensitive information as an insider-outsider. I visited returned migrants from New Orleans who had been back in Brazil for anywhere from a year to less than a day. They opened up their lives to me, and, for this, I am very grateful. I was able to stay in their homes and spend time with their families. I experienced the daily routines that they fell into after arriving home. I was able to see all stages of their readjustment process. I watched touching reunions with family members who hadn't seen each other for over seven years, and I spent hours talking to others who had been back home for a longer time, some of whom were very happy to be reunited with their families, while others felt that they had made the wrong decision in returning to Brazil. Along with my research in New Orleans and my research trip to Brazil, I conducted a three-week research trip to Kansas City, Boston, and Newark to interview immigrants who lived in New Orleans at some point post-Katrina, but who had subsequently moved on to their respective cities. These experiences strongly influenced my interpretation of how

Brazilians in New Orleans imagined their place in the city in relationship to other Brazilian communities in the U.S.

When I traveled to Brazil and to other Brazilian communities in the U.S., I took with me photographs of family members of Brazilians who are still living in New Orleans. And while I travelled, I took pictures of family members to bring back to immigrants still living in New Orleans. Some of these people had not seen their families for more than seven years. One immigrant took that CD of photographs of his hometown that I had taken in Brazil and turned it into a slide show in his Chalmette home, which he played on his widescreen TV as background during a *churrasco* party at his house. As the pictures of Brazil flashed by, they reminded him of those absent loved ones and also became a way for him to bridge his two worlds. He identified for friends in Chalmette the persons in each picture and asked me to give descriptions of my trip over and over so that he could feel closer to his family, especially his mother, vicariously, through my brief encounters with her. My presence in Brazil brought similar experiences with mothers. They brought out photo albums to share with their families, asking me to explain the nuances of cultural traditions or the destruction of Hurricane Katrina from my American perspective. Were there really cars in the trees as in the picture? And did the wind really do that? This was a way for them to feel closer to the experiences of their sons and daughters in the U.S.

Research, Methods, Assumptions

The research for this book was based heavily on participant observation along with a compilation of interviews in New Orleans and in the communities in Brazil that sent those Brazilians who would later end up in New Orleans. I conducted over 150 unstructured recorded interviews with Brazilians who were in some way connected to the Brazilian immigrant network in New Orleans. In most cases, interviews were with immigrants themselves, but I also interviewed family members in Brazil and important leaders in the Brazilian cultural community in New Orleans. A few of those people whom I interviewed work with Brazilian culture in New Orleans but are not themselves Brazilian. Their opinions and the work that they do in representing Brazil, however, is important in understanding the place of Brazilians in New Orleans.

Over the course of writing this book, the demographic numbers of Brazilians in New Orleans have constantly fluctuated, currently leveling out at what I think to be between 3,000-4,000 Brazilians in New Orleans in 2010. However, this may not be the case by the time this book reaches publication, or even by tomorrow, for that matter. But the spaces where Brazilian national and regional cultures are performed reflect a demographic presence of Brazilians in the city. Jacques Attali notes that we should judge a society more by its sounds, art, and festivities than by its statistics (Attali 3). This statement is especially applicable to the case of Brazilians in New Orleans; the status of the Brazilian community in New Orleans is often more visible through the interactions within the spaces Brazilians mark as their own rather than through the mere facts of their demographic numbers. Many Brazilian immigrants in New Orleans are undocumented, leading to hesitancy in their willingness to be counted. When I began doing research in 2006, the phenomenon of undocumented Brazilian immigration to the U.S. was growing at a rapid rate. Yet, the number greatly abated during the course of this research, largely in response to the economic crisis in the U.S. and the strengthening Brazilian economy. (I think we will see this trend continue, especially with Brazil hosting the World Cup in 2014 and the Olympic Games in 2016.)

While my research uses New Orleans as a focus space, interviews and research were done in a transnational and a transregional setting, taking into account Brazilian immigrant mobility as a key factor in Brazilian imaginings of their identity in New Orleans. Brazilians' understanding of their place in New Orleans almost always involves a reference with other places of contact, both in Brazil and in the United States. My interviews reflected not only a Brazil/New Orleans comparison, but also a New Orleans/other U.S. city comparison. An immigrant who arrives straight from Brazil to New Orleans may be more inclined to focus on the differences between Brazil and New Orleans, while those who have lived in another city in the U.S. first may be inclined to see more similarities between Brazil and New Orleans in contrast to the other U.S. city where they previously lived. I was able to follow some of my interviewees as they moved away from New Orleans and to conduct interviews after they returned to Brazil (36 people) and in other cities in the United States (11 people). Along with these interviews of migrants, I was also able to interview family members and friends of immigrants in New Orleans whose life had been affected by the migration of their loved ones.

There is a disproportionate number of male voices to female voices in my interviews throughout this book. This is because I concentrated on the recovery time period immediately post-Katrina when the number of men in the city was proportionately larger. I have done my best to include female voices, but it should be noted that the vast majority of my informants were men. This dictated in subtle (and not-so-subtle) ways the types of relationships that I developed with my interviewees. On the one hand, being a female allowed me quicker access into a community of men who were lonely for their wives, mothers, and girlfriends back home. My female voice was called upon to console worried mothers or to provide a female presence in parties and gatherings that often had unequal male and female attendees. On the other hand, there were often times when immigrants hesitated to reveal to me certain information (their exploits of the weekend, for example). Even in their absence in numbers, however, women represent an important dimension of the migrant experience to New Orleans. The socially patterned relationships between sexes has greatly influenced the immigration experience of Brazilian immigrants as they have interacted with each other and with the greater New Orleanian community and I have tried to keep gender issues in mind when analyzing the relationships that Brazilian men and women built in the city post-Katrina. An in-depth gender analysis, however, necessarily lies outside the scope of this book. (Gender issues are mattering more as we move farther away from that initial moment of migration; the number of Brazilian females, in fact, seems to be growing at a faster rate than that of Brazilian males within the community today.)

A few of my interviews went unrecorded when the information that I was being told was very confidential. This was the case when I interviewed a *coyote* in Minas Gerais and an *atravessador* in Rondônia. I also did not record several interviews with undocumented immigrants who were involved in some sort of illegal business in the U.S. Some of these businesses are considered criminal activity (forging passports, destroying cars to collect the insurance money) and some are simply the inevitable consequence of trying to make a living as an undocumented immigrant (opening businesses when they were not a legal citizen or buying a false social security number or work visa).

Obviously these examples are not equal in import or in "illegality." I believe that no human being should be labeled an "illegal" person, but these examples are all reasons why some interviewees opted to speak to me without the recorder present.[2]

In this study, the names of interviewees as well as the companies that they work for have been changed in order to preserve their anonymity. The exception to this is that a few interviewees made a particular point of saying that they wanted their names published in this book as their claim to fame in "America." But in order to protect these people as well, I do not distinguish between the real names and aliases. They know who they are. You, the reader, do not. I have also purposefully left out the names of companies for which these immigrants worked to protect companies from any penalties for knowingly employing undocumented workers.

The purpose of this book is to tell stories of hope, dreams, and perseverance of the Brazilian immigrants who made unbelievable sacrifices and took incredible risks in order to make a better life for their families, and ended up rebuilding one of America's most unique cities along the way. The stories told about Hurricane Katrina (by residents and immigrants alike) are heart-wrenching. And along with the stories of sadness and loss are the stories of new emerging communities. Brazilians have made a physical mark on New Orleans through their work in reconstruction: Tulane University, Loyola University, the Riverwalk, the Superdome, several famous BBQ restaurants along St. Charles, and numerous bars along Bourbon Street were rebuilt by mostly Brazilian construction crews, not to mention the thousands of homes that Brazilians rebuilt so that New Orleanians, dealing with the trauma of their lost lives, could move back home. Even the private security companies, FEMA and Blackwater, hired to keep the city safe in the first weeks of the disaster, were fed by the hands of Brazilian workers.

---

[2] The immigration experience is a complicated mixture of both economic opportunity and exploitation. The term "illegal immigrant" is not precise, nor descriptive enough to be profitably used in the political debate surrounding immigration because it does nothing to describe the situation through which the person immigrated. If a writer must use the term "illegal," it is the act and not the person that should be labeled as such. For example, an immigrant could cross the border illegally, overstay a tourist visa illegally, or sneak into the country without documents. But to lump all the complex circumstances and life experiences of undocumented immigrants under the general term "illegal" is a disservice to the immigration debate.

These contributions should not be left unrecognized. Anyone who has found solace in a rebuilt New Orleans must be thankful for the workers who made it possible for the city to be reborn after Hurricane Katrina. These workers were the real first responders to the city. These are the people who invented ways to help, to work, and to live when there was no infrastructure to do any of these things.

There are two main questions driving the research for this book: First, how was the Brazilian immigrant network to New Orleans established? With this question, I am taking into account transnational flows, not just of people, but also of philosophies and images of Brazil. And the second question: How did Brazilians construct the beginnings of a cohesive Brazilian community in New Orleans post-Katrina? This question speaks to the possibility that a permanent and settled Brazilian enclave can exist in New Orleans, though its shape and context change with time and circumstance.

Transnational Relationships as Everyday Interactions

I would like to call attention to the difficulty of conducting this fieldwork when the field site was not contained. I have found myself constantly struggling as I try to decide how key narratives, often located in spaces far removed from New Orleans, should be included into a study that is supposedly grounded in post-Katrina New Orleans. In truth, this book bridges two nations and many diverse communities of Brazilians and aficionados of Brazilian culture. These narratives located in distant spaces are important, however, because they become part of the complex story of how Brazilian immigrants contextualize the benefits and drawbacks of living in New Orleans. The narratives in these chapters address Brazilian culture in the specific time and spatial moment of Hurricane Katrina in New Orleans. Yet, this moment is inextricably linked to networks of people and spaces that are located outside of New Orleans, in Brazil and in other parts of the U.S. It is also important to note that years from now, because culture is a process, the articulations of a Brazilian enclave identity in New Orleans will most likely reveal differences from this study since transnational connections will change along with the local context of New Orleans.

The transnational experience is a liminal experience. It does not exist as a finished product because it is defined based on the imagination of the person living (or observing) it. The concept of liminality comes from the Latin word, "limen," which means threshold or doorway. Victor Turner has described liminality as a constant state of becoming, always being redefined. Whether those influences are transnational flows such as media, television, or migration, or whether they are the localized constructions of spatial interaction, a person's sense of belonging mutates as he or she comes into contact with different information, people, and institutional systems that organize society across borders.

The immigrant's imagining of self identity is often located in a transnational relationship with at least two different locales and ideas of "home" that coexist. Imagination is particularly important because Brazilians may be physically and socially located in the space of New Orleans, but they construct a present picture of their home city in, say, Governador Valadares, which coexists with them during their residency in New Orleans and perhaps in another location of residency in the United States as well. Brazilians are often involved in the distant home city in the present daily context by sending remittances, following news of that place over the web or on TV or radio, and staying connected with friends and loved ones there through a Webcam, Orkut, or MSN. These everyday transnational connections lead to a *saudades*[3] for the present, a longing for something that still exists in the present but that is located in a transnational space, betwixt and between.

The transnational space (inevitable in migration and in global capitalism in general) exists as an amorphous idea that has direct consequences for the creation of Brazilian cultures in New Orleans by providing a space for cultural recreation that does not happen between walls, on streets, or in buildings, but in the imagination of the im-

[3] *Saudades* is one of the most frequent emotion words in the Portuguese language. This word, which has no direct translation in English, is part of Brazilian culture and especially part of migrant culture. *Saudades* is a desire to be in another time or in another place, at times simultaneously, because it does not necessarily represent a desire to change the current state of things. The migrant may not want to return, though his *saudades* persist. It is a deep and heartfelt longing for the place and the people who are absent. The word expresses the state of your soul, a deep sense of anguish and nostalgia caused by distance or absence. Yet, this anguish is sweet and delicate, unlike mere expressions of homesickness that do not usually focus on people the way that *saudades* does in Portuguese. "Sinto saudades de você" could be translated as "I feel nostalgia for the times that we spent together," "I feel longings of you," and "I miss you." Yet each of these lacks the full meaning of *saudades* unless you could somehow combine these phrases together into one English word. (Farrell 310)

migrants who dream about the physical space that is absent everyday (dreaming of the U.S. while in Brazil and of Brazil while in the U.S.). The transnational and transregional flows of people, skill sets, and institutions, which poured out at a heightened intensity to New Orleans in reaction to Hurricane Katrina, call for an understanding of the links between global processes and local happenings.

Brazilians finding reasons to celebrate alongside New Orleanians, especially during the surreal moments following Hurricane Katrina, reveal a transcultural dialogue that happened because of the particular setting of the disaster. Space and social interactions were democratized because there were not enough official spaces open to pay much attention to hierarchies. Through bbq's in backyards where gestures, miming, and perhaps a shared dance became ways of communicating, Brazilians began to feel a part of the social fabric of the city by tying home experiences of the *churrasco* with the local lived experience. Brazilian cultural practices became reappropriated and re-rooted in the new cultural terrain of New Orleans, often acquiring new characteristics, yet still being ways that Brazilians expressed being Brazilian in the enclave of New Orleans.

In the Brazilian community in New Orleans, we find that transnational processes have allowed Brazilian migrants to recreate Brazilian cultural experiences in localized space. *Festas Juninas* (The Brazilian June Festivals) are now performed in backyards in Kenner, La.; Brazilian *Carnaval* music is now blared from pickup trucks sitting on the parade routes of Mardi Gras; roofers from Goiânia are now fixing the roofs in New Orleans; and Brazilians swing to zydeco and stomp their feet to the rhythms of the second line. These processes can be seen as partial Brazilian acculturation to New Orleans through the creation of hybrid Brazilian-New Orleanian experiences. Yet it is not viable to claim these hybrid transnational experiences as inauthentic or any less Brazilian. In fact, these are often moments when Brazilians in New Orleans find themselves feeling the most Brazilian. During these moments immigrants communicate Brazilian dreams, songs, fantasies, myths, and stories that root them to certain imagined places and experiences remembered in Brazil, images that are paramount in defining how the enclave claims a sense of being that can unite people across spatial divides while simultaneously grounding them to their local environment.

Inventing a Brazilian Enclave in New Orleans

The Brazilian enclave in New Orleans has, thus, become a hybrid representation of lived experiences in Brazil and lived experiences in New Orleans. Most of the first responders post-Katrina were young immigrants themselves who had had little time in the U.S. New Orleanian culture and the culture of Katrina marked them deeply. The concept of cultural hybridity is a slippery slope. In many ways, hybridity is a universal description of culture. What culture is not hybrid in some way? Although similar to terms such as *mestiçagem*, syncretism, or even creolization, hybridity is useful exactly because of its ability to capture a broader meaning, but it is always dependent on the context of its existence. Hybridity becomes useful through contextualizing within the local space the processes, the spaces, and the cultures that merge to create a new way of understanding identity.

As I use the term, hybridity refers to a diverse Brazilian enclave culture as it unfolds with a constant dialogue between the diverse cultures of New Orleans. Implied in this meaning are the residual meanings of the terms mentioned above: creolization, *mestiçagem*, and syncretism. Brazilians tend to approach these processes with a sense of cordiality, with a national culture that has expounded an idea of Brazilians as "cordial people." For example, Sérgio Buarque de Holanda theorized cordiality as a central aspect to Brazilian culture, Gilberto Freyre emphasized the flexibility of the Portuguese as well as the African roots of Northeasterners, and Roberto da Matta explored the ways in which Brazilians have used their flexibility and spontaneity to come up with their own characteristic solutions and self-expressions. A Brazilian in New Orleans commented, "Gosto de New Orleans porque é uma cidade alegre." (I like New Orleans because it is a happy city.) Brazilians in New Orleans find themselves not only getting along with New Orleanians, but also connecting to a city culture that defines itself on principles of cordiality and harmony, even when the actual reality on the streets is often quite chaotic.

The experience of finding similarities and contrasts with the local that prides itself on the specificity of its culture (defining the city as "a happy place," for example), creates Brazilians' own unique hybrid enclave in New Orleans. I argue that a sense of a hybrid identity of a Brazilian immigrant living in New Orleans inevitably differs from a compatriot who is living in Boston because of the local context of New

Orleans and, more specifically for this particular study, because of the post-Katrina environment in which Brazilians began to arrive. Brazilians in New Orleans developed different tactics of survival and success based on the local context and the particular time.

Brazilian immigration to New Orleans provides a unique context for studying the formation of an enclave community because, on the one hand, it was mostly a secondary economic migration bringing immigrants from established enclave communities in other parts of the country drawn by the usual economic lures of job opportunities. On the other hand, these everyday activities of enclave formation (finding jobs, making friends, learning to navigate the new city) happened in the surreal post-Katrina environment, an environment that necessarily influenced access to resources, labor options, and social and gender interactions between Brazilians and the devastated local community and among Brazilians themselves in unusual ways.

This book engages with the everyday movements of Brazilians in New Orleans: what they did for work and for enjoyment, where they chose to go (or not to go), and how they imagined themselves in relationship to all that they saw and felt during these experiences. These everyday interactions happened within the crisis context of post-Katrina recovery, a far from ordinary time and space in New Orleans. Brazilian everyday interactions happened with increased intensity in this cataclysmic environment that immigrants would come to call their new home.

By performing daily acts as a community, or with interests that are in common with one's community, so a community is established. The methods by which Brazilians found work, the type of work that they performed, the groceries that they bought, the music that they chose to listen to, the bars that they frequented, the clothes that they wore, the television channels that they watched, and the park where they gathered for *churrascos* (bbqs where meat is grilled) were all spaces where Brazilians began to define their community. The space of New Orleans was ultimately "used" and consumed in the way that Brazilians decided to use it, though Hurricane Katrina affected all these decisions by dictating the resources available for Brazilian interaction with the city.

The aftermath of Katrina was a special moment: First came disaster and then came ongoing identity performances that happened "out of time and out of place" from the regular rhythm of New Orleans. (The construction industry was manned and often run by a new immigrant labor force, Brazilian enclave spaces struggled to take root, Brazilians watched Americans perform their representations of Brazilian identity on stage, and Brazilians watched Mardi Gras take over the city.) Yet, no matter how spectacular their surroundings and the local events may be, immigrants go about their daily lives and daily routines. The meeting point between the lives of immigrants who are following the quotidian norms (the ebbs and flows of survival) within an immigrant network and within the spectacular post-Katrina environment provides the very framework for understanding how Brazilian immigration to New Orleans is unique.

The Everyday, Power Structures, and Identity

The concept of the everyday has been explored by various scholars since the late nineteenth century as a space that is both ordinary and spectacular in its function. The everyday truly began to be thought of as an important intellectual tool for discussing culture and society with the influences of theorists such as Henri Lefebvre, Roland Barthes, Maurice Blanchot and Michel De Certeau. In this book, I will be focusing specifically on Lefebvre and De Certeau's discussion of the everyday as a space of social reconfiguration, the concept that I find most applicable to the Brazilian community in New Orleans. According to Lefebvre, the fact that the everyday can subvert authority or reconfigure space is due directly to its indeterminate qualities. Lefebvre views the everyday as being so invasive in its familiarity that it then becomes pervasive and meaningful.

Everyday life is, in a sense, residual, defined by "what is left over: after all distinct, superior, specialized, structured activities have been singled out by analysis, must be defined as a totality... Everyday life is profoundly related to all activities, and encompasses them with all their differences and their conflicts; it is their meeting place, their bond, and their common ground." (Lefebvre 69)

For Brazilians in the U.S., the different force fields that make up hegemony (that is, the pervasive ways in which social, cultural, and political systems exert dominance without direct force) are those institutions that dictate their migratory status. These fields manifest themselves in both state and civil society. Federal immigration policies and laws affect how immigrants perform their lives in the U.S. The local civil society (police, employers, local judiciary decisions) and the consumer markets and media influence how hegemony has acted upon Brazilians.

The Brazilian enclave in New Orleans is a particularly vulnerable community to these hegemonic forces for several reasons: First, Brazilians are persons grouped with Latinos, yet they do not self-identify with this group, giving them the status of an invisible minority as outlined by Maxine Margolis. Language becomes an important component of their relationship to the hegemonic structures. The majority of Brazilians who relocated to New Orleans post-Katrina had arrived relatively recently (within two years or less) in the U.S. They did not come with English skills and they did not speak Spanish. These facts diminished them even more, increasing their vulnerability to structural powers of hegemony. Their recent arrival in the U.S. also made them less familiar with how to access resources and about their own rights within the system. In the case of living in New Orleans, their language and invisibility also influenced their knowledge of evacuation plans (and their safety from immigration officials) should there be a future hurricane in which they should evacuate.

Second, a relatively small percentage of the Brazilians living in New Orleans are documented. Because of their irregular legal position, there is no one advocating to set up state services for them as could begin to happen in a place such as Massachusetts or New York (though in general it has not) where there are Brazilians who have been in the U.S. for a longer period of time, many of them now legal residents or second generation. This status contrasts to the Latino community in New Orleans that has members and leaders who established at least some cultural presence in the city pre-Katrina and could advocate for newer arrivals. The Honduran community, for example, has been in New Orleans since the 1950s when New Orleans was the base of operations for the United Fruit Company. The fact that there are few Brazilian spaces, not only in New Orleans but in the whole country, that are run by Brazilians promoting Brazilian immigrant rights, and that there are comparatively few spaces promoting Brazilian culture or cuisine, are testaments to Brazilians' relatively recent migration to the U.S. in comparison to other immigrant groups. There are few *coxinha* trucks in America, for example. (A *coxinha* is a Brazilian snack made from battered minced chicken and seasonings.) Here I am drawing a comparison to the ubiquitous taco trucks in New Orleans post-Katrina, which were seen as symbolic markers of the new Latino presence. Significantly, however, a Brazilian BBQ truck (modeled off the taco trucks) began to operate in New Orleans in 2010, marking the arrival of Brazilian community and the hybridity of cultural traditions for entrepreneurs in the post-Katrina world. There are also few Brazilian cultural spaces in New Orleans located in places where ordinary people walking around would have access to them. Brazilian spaces are, thus, spaces that are immigrant-based, participating in their isolation as an invisible community and intensifying the subjugation (and consent) to forces of hegemony.

For Brazilians in New Orleans, the tactics used to counter hegemony are ways by which they reappropriate their invisibility to work for their own advantage. For example, Brazilians may embrace their distance from Latino groups in order to shield themselves from the brunt of anti-immigrant discrimination. This may help them in the job market when employers or clients seem hesitant to hire a Hispanic but are more willing to hire a Brazilian because they don't know exactly how to place Brazilians. Brazilians may also form enclaves as a way of networking for needed resources among each other when they do not know how to do it themselves or when they are not allowed to access the hegemonic avenues for accessing resources because of legal status. Finally, they may actually use the fact that they cannot apply for certain state and federal benefits related to political discourses on civil rights to assume an identity that is "culturally" present. In the realm of culture they are both welcome and unthreatening to the civil society, perhaps providing them more social acceptance among local communities and more mobility than their status as undocumented workers would normally allow them in the political realm.

Brazilian "habitus" or habitation

The research in this book takes into account that the ways in which Brazilians choose to manipulate the everyday is dictated by what they already know, that is, by the social and cultural world that they carried with them from Brazil through their migration experience. It is impossible to speak of immigrant culture as an object because migration is a flowing process through which people leave one set of cultural norms to go to another. International migration creates international people, familiar and socialized in one set of cultural norms, but living the experiences of another set. The understanding of different cultural spaces, thus, invokes Bourdieu's concept of *habitus*, often talked about as "a feel for the game," or an embodied understanding of the social context in which one operates normally (Bourdieu 66). We are all predispositioned to interpersonal relations that we have learned since birth and that function as social products in the environment in which we self-identify. This *habitus* always acts as a reference by which we interpret other cultural spaces. Individual performers become, as Bourdieu describes it, "social agents" bound up by forces of culture, experience, history, and economics that they have grown up with (Ibid). By creating spaces in which immigrants can understand and function using their own social norms (*habitus*), immigrant populations increase their ability to access both social and economic capital. Similarly, by finding cultural spaces already in existence in New Orleans that can be "read" by Brazilian immigrants in the framework of their own cultural world, hybrid cultural experiences occur in which Brazilians have more opportunities for social and financial success because they will be more familiar with how to act, work, and behave in their surroundings.

The fact that the majority of Brazilians immigrate to New Orleans in order to accrue capital (whether it be economic or social) shows how a hegemonic idea of capitalism is embedded in Brazilian constructions of *habitus*. There is a willingness to "play the game" and invest in American capitalist ideologies. Yet, their immigration itself was motivated by the fact that the "rules" for the capitalist game were not set up equally for them. Thus, they undergo acts of what De Certeau would label as "tactics" in order to most successfully fulfill their goals preconditioned through *habitus*. Examples of such tactical practices among Brazilian immigrants begin even before Brazilians leave Brazil. Purchasing a ticket from an *atravessador* to come to the United States through Mexico, for example, is a way of tactically avoiding a social order that would deny them a visa. Once the immigrants have arrived in New Orleans, they can overcome the lack of legal documentation by purchasing a false driver's license or false social security card that will enable them to secure a more stable job. Also, tactically speaking, there are ways they can ally themselves with the local culture of New Orleans or with the Brazilian enclave community itself in order to increase both social and economic capital.

Miguel, from Minas Gerais, for example, printed his business cards with an American flag and an American eagle emblazoned across the front. When asked why he made such a decision, his answer was, "Because I love America." But this was also an obvious tactical decision to influence those customers who will be receiving his business card. The overt message is that, even though he is an immigrant, hiring him for your construction needs is a patriotic act. Miguel himself, however, is not an American citizen, nor even a holder of legal residency documents.

As another example of tactics for circumventing hegemonic social order, Wagner participates regularly in a "consocio entre amigos" (fraternity of friends) in which a group of Brazilians pools $100 apiece monthly. The pot then goes to a different member each month, allowing the pot winner access to a large sum of capital to enable him to make necessary investments such as buying a car for work in New Orleans or making a down payment on a project in Brazil. Although most Brazilians in New Orleans have limited resources and education, by pooling these resources as a community, they are able to gain greater access to the things that they need through everyday decision-making as a group. Likewise, daily social decisions such as who Brazilians befriend (both Brazilian and American) are ways of overcoming dominating strategies that simply reinforce the cultural norms. People act creatively and the reproduction of *habitus* is never a carbon copy as people move across space, time, and cultural continuums, acting in ways culturally relevant to their current situation.

Being Brazilian in the context of immigration to the United States and to New Orleans, in particular, also means having a certain amount of cultural and symbolic capital as part of what is imagined as the *habitus* of someone who hails from a country that is known for its spectacular cultural production. If Brazil is part of the cultural imagination of New Orleanians (and I say "if" because for many it is off the radar), more than likely, the Brazilian image is associated with representations of national culture: soccer, music, carnival. Innate music or dancing skills, an African diaspora population that is akin to that in New Orleans, or a tradition of celebrating carnival are all stereotypes of Brazil that can be transformed into capital when Brazilians express their alliance with these images of Brazil, whether they are true for the individual or not.

Everyday Space in New Orleans as Spectacular

My research in this book is also grounded in the assumption that Brazilians' everyday interactions and decisions engage with the unique physical and social space in which they find themselves. The everyday is framed by the urban space of New Orleans. A definition of "space," according to its conceptualization by Lefebvre, requires that it be understood not in terms of what it is, but in terms of how it is used. Space is action in the abstract because space stimulates certain behaviors. Human behavior is often, if not always, engaged in a power relationship with strategies of hegemonic control, and we should consequently view space as a constantly shifting dynamic of power relations. Space should not be read as an object. It is not a building or a street that makes up the separate elements of the city. Rather, it is an arena in which people display cultural expression, contest identities, and engage constantly in personal transformation. Space in this dynamic context is the effect that the buildings, walls, streets, or any other structures of a city have on the people who live there and the implications of how the people respond to this dynamic.

That being said, the structure of a city is hardly natural or without deliberate methods of construction and regulation. So, we have, on the one hand, hegemonic processes acting out in urban design (buildings, highways, traffic lights, business districts, police enforcing the status quo), and on the other the subjects of hegemony who are also affecting space through their response to urban design (going to some places and not others, working at the speed that they like, opening their own businesses, and evading both immigration and police surveillance). De Certeau argues that the revolt of the subject, for example, takes place to a large extent in the everyday, in subtle, unorganized practices in response to the "environmental context"—the city.

Not even taking into consideration the massive damage imposed by Hurricane Katrina, a subject that I will address later, New Orleans was always a "spectacular city." As revelers to New Orleans would argue, the everyday experience of New Orleans is not at all mundane because the city has always been imagined as anomalous in terms of American urban culture. As it rests in popular imagination, New Orleans is represented as Mikhail Bakhtin's "carnavalesque" city: the union of comedy and chaos. Characterized by its festivals, rowdy conventions, and the licensed carnival of Bourbon Street, New Orleans was also constantly on the brink of disaster. Katrina revealed this to the whole world.

There are tourists who visit the city year round searching for a type of cultural experience that they can "only find in New Orleans." It is a city with famous cemeteries and ghost tours that remember the carnavalesque union of the past and the present—bodies are sent off to the dead with jazz funerals. In the French Quarter, any day of the year, you can catch beads being thrown from a balcony window to party-goers roaming the streets whose bodies become the central spectacle of the show. Or you can drink a Hurricane, mocking the terror of natural disaster by carnivalizing its association with an alcoholic drink so strong that drinking it leaves you as disheveled as if you had been hit by a hurricane. New Orleans is culturally imagined as a space that suspends the rules and hierarchies of social structure by which the rest of the U.S. operates. People flock to "become someone else," masking themselves from their "other" lives, suspending the old world where they normally live.

Thus, in New Orleans, it is possible to find elements of the carnavalesque in the everyday, even though seeking out spaces like Bourbon Street may not be an everyday occurrence for locals. As Joseph Roach argues, the spatial logic of New Orleans is built to make certain powers and privileges not only seasonally visible, but also perpetually reproducible (14). At the same time, the speech, images, and gestures of the African-American community in New Orleans reveal an everyday doubleness, in which the "European" hierarchies that were historically imposed are only obliquely acknowledged (Ibid). I am admitting that even before Katrina, performances of a mundane, everyday in New Orleans (in their idiosyncrasies, comedies, and chaos) challenged the theoretical discussion of De Certeau's "everyday" as ordinary. After all, tourists flocked to New Orleans precisely because the everyday in New Orleans was (and is) conceptualized as being extraordinary. And, interestingly, in the context of Brazilian immigration to New Orleans, this city, which is so remarkable, holds unusual likenesses with Brazil (along with more salient differences). Brazilians come to see similarity between Brazilian expressions of individuality and collectivity and the comic tragedy that is part of the New Orleanian everyday expression.

Post-Katrina New Orleans: Devoid of "Normalcy"

Obviously, we must consider how these markers of the city that are based on historical constructions over the course of nearly three centuries have influenced the development of New Orleans everyday as carnavalesque, but we must also consider how the features of post-Katrina New Orleans have influenced the everyday performances of people and created an entirely new kind of spectacle of the everyday. In post-Katrina New Orleans, the power relations within space were and are subject to constant change and appropriation. In the aftermath of Hurricane Katrina, the physical and social stage of New Orleans revealed the constant mutation of the urban environment caused by the environmental chaos of the storm and the chaotic systems of control implemented during the city's reconstruction.

After the hurricane, the infrastructure of the city was in disarray—traffic lights were out, roads were not navigable, many neighborhoods were uninhabitable, and many basic services were unavailable. As reconstruction began, the fact that rebuilding happened more frequently in some areas of the city rather than others or that the reconstruction of Bourbon Street (the most conspicuous symbol of the carnavalesque) and the Superdome were priorities if the city was to return to its sense of normalcy are examples of how local government (and the tourism industry) regulate behavioral patterns in the city. Economic necessity dictated that New Orleans needed to be reconstructed as "festive" even in the face of disaster.

What happens to De Certeau's model when the everyday becomes canavalesque or even grotesque? With the destruction caused by Hurricane Katrina, any routines of normalcy were essentially destroyed. What is considered spectacular differs for different people at different times. Dealing with abandoned houses, poor infrastructure, and a chaotic living and working environment became part of the "spectacular everyday" that is New Orleans post-Katrina. But in this environment, people continued to carry out acts of mundane life in the face of the surreal.

The months following the storm saw a breakdown in hegemonic strategies because the political and economic structures had lost control of the physical environment of the city; communication systems were down, lights were out, people were stranded, stores were closed. "Resistance" through everyday practice in the context of post-Katrina refers mainly to survival tactics and, to use De Certeau's theorization of Levi Straus, to the *bricolage* ("poetic ways of 'making do' [De Certeau xv]) that Brazilian immigrants employ in order to deal with the breakdown of infrastructure caused by the storm as well as with their position as second-class citizen workers within this fractured environment. They invented clever ways of making do by sleeping in tents—or even in abandoned boats, in case the waters began to rise again—fitting ten people into a two-bedroom house, taking baths in the Mississippi, going door to door to find work, opening restaurants from home kitchens to feed workers, forging documents to open construction companies, and simply making comfortable homes and creating strong personal ties to the city.

Brazilian culture has its own translation of *bricolage: jeito. Jeito* is the MacGyver-like ability to creatively invent ways to survive. This practice was actively implemented in Brazilian constructions of their everyday space in the context of Katrina. I saw Brazilians using the everyday to exploit the fissures of the chaos. They moved into abandoned neighborhoods, they found themselves working in positions of power as subcontractors for work crews, and they converted warehouses into Brazilian churches and forsaken office spaces into their own restaurants.

In an article in the *Times-Picayune*, Rogerio Paiva, the Jefferson Parish owner of Rotolo's Pizzeria, remembered a moment when a Brazilian member of a painting crew asked Rogerio to telephone a homeowner with the purpose of undercutting his boss's bid on the reconstruction of the home. Rogerio explained that, "After years of living with economic turmoil and a fragile currency [in Brazil], '[Brazilians]... have to learn how to get away with things, how to survive... You have to hustle. You have to. There's no way you can sit around'" (Nolan 2).

Rogerio proclaims that, if Katrina had happened in Brazil, then "this city would have been rebuilt in three months. In Brazil you get no help from anybody. You've got to do it yourself" (Ibid). This attitude of *jeito* explained by Rogerio is an assumption that I have heard repeatedly among Brazilians when they explain their tactics for survival in the post-Katrina world. They used the everyday chaos of Katrina as opportunity to create a more established position for themselves within the emerging city structure. The goal of resistance in this act of *jeito* is not necessarily to assimilate or even to become a "New Orleanian" (the construction worker who was underbidding his boss, for example, was working entirely outside the strategies of hierarchy in order to better his own position within these same structures). It is merely a tactic of survival played out in everyday decision-making, developing innovative survival strategies when there is little access to resources.

Jeito is often linked to the Brazilian concept of *malandragem*, an inventive tactic of survival when the strategies are stacked against you. Roberto Da Matta undertook an important study of the culture of *malandragem* in his book *Carnivals, Rogues, and Heroes (Carnavais, Malandros e Heróis)*, arguing that the idea of the typical Brazilian as a *malandro* developed during the time of the Brazilian colony and in the earliest years of the empire. The idea is linked to popular resistance to the ruling elite; according to Da Matta, the common man became a *malandro* because it was the only way to perform popular resistance to the arbitrary systems of oppression of the ruling elite (Da Matta *Carnavais* 204).

Malandragem later comes to reference a very specific cultural context: the *carioca* samba world of the 1920s and 1930s. The *malandro*, a Bohemian figure, was often sung about in sambas: He lived off scams and invented ways to take advantage of the system. He was a ladies man, often supported by a wealthy woman, who spent his time dancing or playing music. The *malandro* figure was imagined in opposition to the the working fool (*otário*); the poor, working man is foolish precisely because he continues to work honestly in a system that will always exploit him.

Brazilians in New Orleans often described their own community as well as working-class New Orleanians as *malandros* because, even though they were workers, they invented ways to find jobs and make income outside of the typical institutional navigation. At first, this seems to be in opposition to the concept of *malandragem* in the cultural and historical context described above, since the *malandros* in the New Orleanian context, immigrants and natives alike, are workers pounding the pavement every day, rarely living a life of idleness, and also being exploited for their work. In this sense, they seem to fit the *otário* description more than that of the *malandro*. However, *malandragem* in its popular discourse is used to describe someone who invents creative ways to survive and to gain advantage in the system.

The *malandro* manages to enjoy life through difficult times because he prospers by refusing to use straight-forward and honest work alone as a viable method of living. The worker finds ways to take advantage of the working system, undercutting his boss or subcontracting to other workers, or even employing other workers (the *otários*) and not paying them. In this conceptualization, being a worker is not necessarily in opposition to the *malandro*.

The *malandro* figure, both in its historical context and its reconceptualization in New Orleans, is not someone who challenges to change the system, but who flexibly maneuvers himself into a position in order to take advantage of the current system. It is this conceptualization of the term that is expressed in Brazilian descriptions of their ways of coming to the United States, of finding work in New Orleans, and even of understanding the local working-class community as also possessing *malandragem*. Through creative acts of survival, Brazilians learned to exploit the fissures of the post-Katrina environment and formed special connections to the city, even if this agency arose because of the city's destruction. Brazilians' pivotal role in rebuilding provided a sense of personal allegiance to the city, an allegiance created through satisfaction in their inventiveness in seeking jobs, gratitude for those opportunities given because of the broken infrastructure, and a genuine pride in the product of their work.

We can imagine that Brazilians take advantage of the lack of structure in the post-Katrina environment to "poach" upon normal capitalist relationships of boss/worker and transform those relationships into something more beneficial for the immigrant. Antonio Ortiz, a Kenner insurance executive who sells general business insurance to many Brazilians, said he finds many Brazilians to be remarkably ambitious and entrepreneurial about launching their own businesses. "They remind me of the Vietnamese," Ortiz said. "They're not waiting around for anybody. They're going out and getting it" (Nolan 2).

The goal of the majority of Brazilians living in New Orleans is to earn enough money to be able to start their own small business, either in the U.S., or, more often, back home. Cattle raising and trading, real estate, car and car part dealerships, internet cafés, general stores, ice cream shops, and liquor stores are just a few of the businesses that Brazilians from New Orleans opened up in Brazil after returning home. For many, the aftermath of Hurricane Katrina provided the ready source of quick capital for them to do this. In New Orleans, Brazilians are often clandestine users of resources that they do not own (job markets, schools, healthcare), on territory that is not their own, in situations which would not immediately be equated to social alteration, but that inevitably change the social makeup of New Orleans and their own position within it. They are poachers in the most positive sense of the word, changing the status quo of the city but also rebuilding it. They may not be the legal owners of resources nor do they dictate the social organization of New Orleans, but they do have ways of reaping personal gain from such a position. New Orleans has likewise benefited and changed from their presence.

Leave-taking: Impacts of Emigration on Communities in Brazil

"What I accomplished in the three years in New Orleans, it would have taken me a lifetime to accomplish in Brazil," says a Brazilian immigrant as he packs his bags in New Orleans to return to Brazil. He will return to work for the same construction company that he worked for in Brazil before coming to the United States, and he will also begin working as an electrician, with skills that he learned during his time living in New Orleans. He plans to purchase a Brazilian electrician license so that he can begin practicing his new profession right away. "In Brazil, if you do not have a degree you are nothing. But if you have money, everything has a way of being resolved" (Field Notes 6 June 2009).

The desire to explore the unknown of the American experience, "fulfilling a dream," has been documented as inspiring migration to the United States and back again when immigrants become disillusioned to find that this dream is unfounded. In the context of Brazilian immigration, migration is thought of as a chance at economic prosperity for individuals and families. It is linked in complicated ways to other people, other communities, and to a nostalgia for two co-existing places, home and abroad, that truly exist only as imagined ideals. The decision to leave Brazil is complicated and different for each individual. But once leaving, each individual must confront his or her own rationalization for the decision to leave in order to understand the relationship to home in Brazil and to the new home abroad in New Orleans.

América: Migration as A Brazilian Cultural Experience

From March 14 to November 5, 2005, Brazilian TV Globo aired a *telenovela* called *América*, which focused on immigration (both legal and illegal) to the United States. In one of the opening scenes, Sol receives a glass snowball of New York City from a neighbor who has just arrived back in the Rio favela from the United States. As Sol receives the snowball, the neighbor explains to Sol what life is like in the United States and begins the construction of the United States as the land of opportunity.

> In the United States everything is beautiful. Everything works. Everyone is happy. There are no homeless people in the streets. Can you believe it! The United States is full of waiters who have become millionaires and housecleaners who became actresses. Everyone can afford their own house, good food, and the medical care is free.

The young Sol, who is 6 or 7 in the scene, listens intently and in this moment, her personal dream becomes a quest to go to the United States at all costs. As Sol battles to arrive in the United States, it becomes obvious that her dream, represented in the snowball of New York that she tirelessly carries around, is linked to the possibilities of a better standard of living and the possibilities to earn wealth for her family back home in a way that she could not if she was still living in Brazil. When her family implores her to give up her dream and go to college, she says that going to college will not guarantee her a better future in Brazil; it would only cause her to go into more debt. After receiving her degree, she found that the Brazilian job market could provide no guarantee that she would find a job. She dreams of a life that is much "better than what her mother lived."

I was watching this particular scene of *América* with Jacaré, a Brazilian immigrant who had crossed the border illegally seven years ago and now lives in New Orleans. As he watched the scene of the rich neighbor handing out toys to the neighborhood kids in the favela, he said, "This is exactly what it was like. This is what made me want to go to the United States. I knew people who went and then they would come back with lots of money and hand out gifts to us, things that we had never even seen before."

I asked him if he still felt the same way about the United States. His response was no. Things were much harder here than he thought they would be and the U.S. was not the dreamland that he imagined before immigration. (Especially the U.S. that he saw when he arrived in New Orleans only weeks after Hurricane Katrina had ravaged the city.) His friend who had returned back to Padre Paraíso, Minas Gerais, with money had gone in the 1980s when it was much easier to make money as an immigrant. But he said that his young cousins back in Brazil often talk with him about these same feelings. They want Jacaré to help them come to the United States because there is no future in their hometown in Brazil. Jacaré said that he tries to explain to them that things are not as simple in the United States as they imagine them, but he still believes that the U.S. offers his cousins a better opportunity than if they remain in Padre Paraíso.

The cultures of migration, expressed both in the telenovela *América* and in Jacaré's reaction to watching the novela, make apparent how the stories of immigration told by other migrants who return, whether those stories are positive or negative, influence and perpetuate future generations of migrants, who, living in an unsettled social or financial situation, continue to view the U.S. as a place to find economic prosperity. Even though *América* critiqued the image of the U.S. as a space where individual migrants can make their fortune (in *América*, immigrants are left homeless when they can't pay their bills; they are deported or killed in border crossing attempts; and Sol herself never manages to accrue the wealth that she had dreamed of), it still emphasized how migration was a powerful life choice for whole communities by making visible the interconnected transnational movements of people and media.

This *telenovela*, as a cultural space where pressing issues of the Brazilian nation enter into discourse in the realm of popular culture, highlighted the trend of increased Brazilian immigration to the U.S. and perhaps even transformed undocumented immigration into something more tangible and possible for Brazilians. This happened not because the *telenovela* glorified undocumented life in the U.S., but simply because it highlighted that it was a route that many Brazilians had opted to take, revealing the increased culture of migration in Brazil and the possibility of a Brazilian support network upon migrating. In *América*, migration was not represented as leaving Brazil behind; the happenings in Brazil constantly influenced happenings for migrants in the

U.S. and vice versa. Migration was imagined as a way to provide for families and communities back home, a reconfiguration of Brazilian social life where living outside of their home communities in Brazil actually helped migrants imagine themselves as being more strongly anchored to them.

The main plot of *América* revolves around the life of Sol, a *carioca* (a person from Rio de Janeiro) from the Vila Isabel neighborhood whose lifelong dream is to go to the United States; she is attracted by the promises of the American Dream that will provide her opportunities that she did not have in Brazil. In the *novela*, when asked by a fellow immigrant why she wants to go to the United States, Sol says, "I am going in search of my dream. In Brazil things were so difficult that there was not any room for me to dream." Having her visa denied on several occasions, Sol decides to make the journey illegally through Mexico. The journey is not easy and Sol must brave deportation, ruptures with her family and her love life caused by her departure, and the death of friends along the crossing. Eventually Sol arrives in the United States, after much trial and tribulation (including escaping from jail where she is imprisoned for unknowingly smuggling drugs), and she quickly realizes that life in the United States is not as easy as she had hoped. She washes dishes, sweeps the streets, cleans houses, and works as an exotic dancer on Ocean Drive, Miami Beach. Edi, the American man Sol marries in order to receive her green card and later falls in love with, asks Sol if she regrets coming to the U.S. She responds,

> Of course not! If I had to do it all over again, I would do it the same way. Well, not the same, because I made a few mistakes coming. But I don't have the slightest doubt that I would come. Here I have opportunities. There I never did. I thought that things would be easier, that things would be different than they are here. When I dreamed of coming, I imagined that America was like magic. Everything happened here, that when I arrived I would have a marvelous job waiting for me. That everything was going to be easy. It isn't like this, you know? Things are not easy, but they are possible.

Unlike soap operas in the United States that have a limited, daytime, viewing audience, Brazilian *telenovelas* are considered to be one of the great cultural expressions of the country and are the most expensive *telenovela* productions in all of Latin America (Gomes 12). Indeed, the cinematography and the production of the Brazilian *telenovelas* are impressive. Often referred to simply as *novelas*, they tend to broach controversial issues in Brazilian society. *América*, which aired in the 8 p.m. slot,[4] stirred national debates and alerted the news media about the number of Brazilians who die on the Mexican-U.S. border in pursuit of earning their dream.

Telenovelas provide a collective space for the nation by offering a specific vision of the historical and social development of the nation that can be shared by millions via the television. Characters of *telenovelas* become a sort of living history of Brazil, receiving important status by being referenced in other media forms as well. This intertextuality further reinforces the sense of a national story and identity that emerges from the *novela* experience. *Novela* watchers become part of a living history of a nation, in which, via television, everyone can take part.

According to Globo, *América* was one of the most widely watched *novelas* in Brazil's history with a median number of 49 points, each point representing about 56,000 households viewing the program. Writer of *América*, Glória Pérez, affirms that what has led *América* to be one of the most widely watched *novelas* in Brazilian history is the fact that the "Sonho Americano," the American Dream, really does exist, especially in Brazil's interior (Bartolomei).

TV Globo has reported that *América* was especially popular among the Brazilian poor. Though highly stylized in characteristic Brazilian *novela* form, *América* presents a complex and slightly anti-American view of undocumented immigration. The *novela* constantly alludes to the difficulties that immigrants face: unemployment, employer abuse, jail time, eviction when bills cannot be paid, having money stolen by unscrupulous Americans when trying to "buy" a marriage in order to get legal documents, immigration raids, and loneliness. Screenwriter Pérez emphasizes the enormous risks involved in illegal immigration

---

[4] Rede Globo is the main producer of novelas in Brazil. The productions are split into three different categories and organized by airtime: 6 p.m.: The "novela das seis" is usually romantic and kid friendly. Rarely is there violence, explicit sex or bad language. There is often an historic or religious theme. 7 p.m.: The "novela das sete" usually contains comedic plots with romance and some sex scenes allowed. This is the schedule in which new writers are tested. 8 p.m.: The "novela das oito" is considered prime time. These are the productions with the highest ratings. The plots are complex, mixing humor, romance, and thrilling action.

to the United States, the intricate networks of those involved in the smuggling industry, the prejudice against illegal immigrants in the United States, and the complexities of the differing world views between Americans and Brazilians. And Pérez insists that the border-crossing stories that she writes about in the *novela* were based on true cases. The American embassy sent Pérez photographs of a woman who was caught being brought across the border hidden in the dashboard of the car, for example, and she did a reenactment of this in the scene of protagonist Sol's first crossing (Bartolomei).

So if the *novela* is one of the great expressions of Brazilian national identity, what are the implications of having one of the most popular *novelas* of Brazilian history to be about Brazilian immigration to the United States? Brazil was once a country that saw itself as a receiver of immigrants, but if the *novela* is a cultural field in which Brazilians can explore a representation of themselves, then that suggests that Brazil is also a country of significant out-migration that needs to be taken seriously.

Rural Cultures of Migration

América also highlights the culture of Brazil's rural backcountry. Sol falls in love with a rodeo star, Tião, from the imaginary town of Boiaderos, located somewhere in the interior of São Paulo state. The *novela* explores the complexities of living in a small town in rural Brazil. In many cities in Brazil's vast interior, going to the United States becomes the new path of choice for earning money to invest in the rural lifestyle back home. Leaving the community is actually the way that the community sustains itself. In the *telenovela,* Tião comes from a very humble family that is threatened with being pushed off its land by a wealthy neighboring ranch owner. Tião's father died in a mining accident in Rondônia when Tião was a young boy. His father had gone to the mines to make money to support his family, because, as he tells us before taking a boat North, "there was no future being a cowboy if you don't have money to invest into it."

Just as Tião's father decides to go to the mines in search of a better future, migration journeys to the U.S. become modern versions of a similar story about a quest to better the living experience in the home communities. Both are equally dangerous (Tião's father dies in the mines and in migration to the U.S. many die in the border crossing).

Both show how migration becomes part of everyday community life through mass media, how financial investments from migrants living abroad fund entire communities, and how storytelling by returnees of migrant life, no matter how truthful these stories may actually be to lived experience, perpetuate future migration.

The vast interior of Brazil is sending many would-be cowboys to the United States in order to have the economic capital to be cowboys more successfully when they return. At the same time, the experience abroad changes the daily lives of the local culture and what it means to be a cowboy. For example, in the town of Turvânia (a suburb of Goiânia, located one and a half hours west of the city by bus), I interviewed returned immigrants who had lived in New Orleans post-Katrina. Bruno, a native of Turvânia, Goiás, who lived in New Orleans for two years and six months, invested all of his money in milk cows, two houses that he rents out for extra income, and a car (Bruno 23 January 2009). The migration chain from his home town had brought Bruno and his four friends from Turvânia to Marietta, Ga., in 2005. But since there was little work when they arrived, they went to New Orleans shortly after the hurricane, having lived in Marietta for less than two months before moving on to New Orleans.

The migration experience allowed Bruno to own his own cows once he returned, thus, allowing him to make a profit from their milk rather than having to earn a salary milking other people's cows as he had done before his immigration. His car and his house became prestige symbols. In the case of the houses, they also became generators of extra income through rent money. Bruno has no other job and, for now, he is able to live off his investments. This marks a shift in his daily lifestyle that he is still learning to adapt to. During my visit he had been home for less than 6 months. He admitted that he is often antsy about how to occupy his time, and said that he now spends most of that time at parties rather than on his farm, which is about five miles outside of town. Part of the draw of migrating is becoming a free agent, being able to work and consume in ways that the individuals themselves dictate. Yet there is also a tension in this lifestyle. Bruno told me he remembers the work he did in the U.S. with fondness because it gave him the power to consume. Working in Brazil as a "cowboy" only allows him to stay at status quo. He constantly battles with this situation now that he has returned. For return immigrants, the experience of migration inevitably transforms the way that they imagine their connection to their local rural culture. It gives them more autonomy if they invest wisely. But the experience abroad also opens their worldviews and becomes a constant point of comparison to their lives in their hometowns.

Brazilian immigration to the U.S. has seen a change in demographics from those immigrants who came to the US on a tourist visa and overstayed in the 1990s. The majority of immigrants during the 1990s came from more urban areas of Brazil, and they were middle to upper-middle class. Brazilians coming to the U.S. are now increasingly coming from rural and semi-rural areas of Brazil and tend to be of a lower socio-economic status; they come from a different Brazil and with a different conceptualization of Brazilian culture linked to their own, more rural, lifestyle in Brazil. Rural backgrounds also influence how they imagine their place in the U.S. as immigrants and how they conceptualize their return experience. Brazilians have commented to me, for example, that New Orleans is culturally similar to Brazil because of its proximity to rural Louisiana.

Figure 2: Whole cow roasting in a backyard in Somerville, Ma.

Weekend fishing trips, motorbike racing, and even alligator and armadillo hunting (though illegal) are activities that Brazilians have reported that they enjoy in Louisiana. These are activities culturally familiar to Brazilians from more rural areas of Brazil.

The photograph at left shows a Brazilian immigrant from Rondônia roasting a full cow on a skewer in a backyard in Somerville, Masssachusetts. (Many of the attendees of this particular party later relocated to New Orleans, La., after the hurricane.) The group of Rondônian immigrants had decided to buy a whole cow from a farm in New Hampshire for a birthday party. They were going to be charged an extra $500 for the butchering of the cow, so they asked if they could just do it themselves. Skeptical that these boys would know what they were doing, the cow seller nonetheless let them, and, in less than twenty minutes, to the amazement of the watching American farm workers, the Brazilians had the cow skinned and loaded onto the back of their truck. They took the carcass home to Somerville, put it on a skewer rigged to the motor of a car so that it would turn, and started a huge bonfire. The neighbors, seeing the entire carcass roasting in flames from their windows, called the police. When the police arrived, they didn't know quite what to do since the Brazilians had the legal papers of ownership of the cow. The police merely asked them to reduce the height of the flames. I find this anecdote particularly resonant and illustrative of how Brazilian rural migration to the U.S. complicates the narratives surrounding the modern migrant and their place making.

The following map, made by Heather Jordan of the Tulane School of Public Health, reveals a random sample of 96 Brazilians who came to the visiting Brazilian Consulate in New Orleans during March of 2009. While the sampling is small, it shows suggestively that a significant number of the Brazilians living in New Orleans come from the Central Western region of the country. The largest number of immigrants who showed up to visit the consulate was from Minas Gerais. However, the states of Rondônia, Goiás, and Pará are not far behind. Many of the Brazilians in New Orleans from Rondônia come from the Southeastern corner of Rondônia, near the city of Vilhena. In Goiás, there are many immigrants from the state capital of Goiânia and the surrounding towns. And the Brazilians from Pará come mainly from the Southern region of Pará, especially from the town of Conceição do Araguaia.

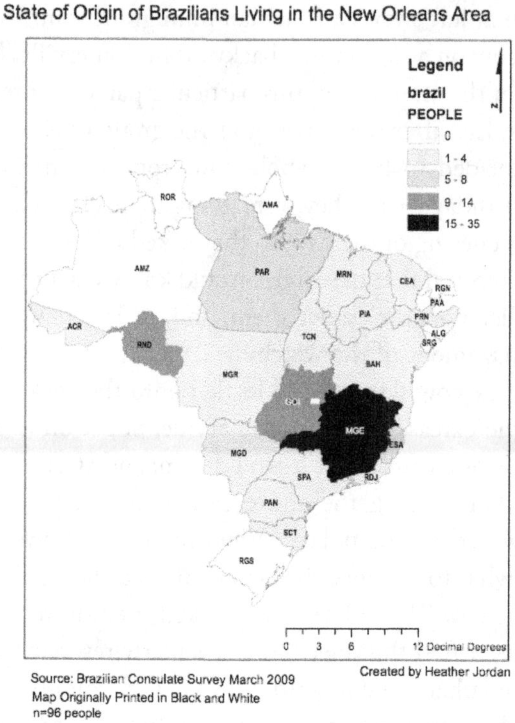

Figure 3: Brazilian Consulate Survey March 2009

Conceição do Araguaia as a Culture of Migration

In these areas of Brazil that are sending many migrants to the U.S., "cultures of migration" describes migration so pervasive in a community that it becomes a common aspect of local culture engrained in the everyday community aspects of social life and decision-making. The stories of migration are similar: Someone knew someone who had prospered by going to the United States. Witnessing the success of past immigrants motivated the next generation to make the journey. These stories founded the belief that, upon arrival in the United States, immigrants would encounter a rich and developed country where anything is possible; these imaginings permeated an entire generation of young people.

When I asked interviewees in sending communities in Brazil why going to the United States had become a common option for young people in their towns, no one could give me a clear answer, though all reasons seemed to be linked to the economic prospects that individuals felt their home town offered or did not offer them. Conceição do Araguaia, Pará, for example, is a beautiful town on the banks of the Araguaia River on the southern edge of the Amazon. A large number of Brazilian immigrants from Conceição do Araguaia migrated to New Orleans from Boston soon after Hurricane Katrina. When I went to Conceição to conduct research with returned migrants, the word traveled fast that there was a *gringa* visiting. The director of Fundação Bradesco, the best private school in the town, stopped by the house where I was staying and asked me if I would be willing to come talk with his students about the importance of learning English; the school was about to launch a new English curriculum and he hoped to motivate the students to study. I accepted and began my talk by asking the children to raise their hands if they had a friend or a family member living in the United States. All but three of the 250 students who had signed up for the program raised their hands. (Those remaining three students had a friend or a loved one in Europe.) Needless to say, the impact of immigration on Conceição do Araguaia is profound. The local identity is intertwined with the experience of community migration.

As another example of how migration marks the community of Conceição, Vanderley, a return immigrant from New Orleans via Boston and a native of Conceição do Araguaia said,

> In 2005 there was a fever in Conceição to go to the United States. Once a week, a *coyote* came to town to ask if there was anyone interested in going. He would even make special deals if you could get a package group together... Lots of people wanted to go to the United States because in a year you could earn what it would take you 20 years to earn living in Conceição (Vanderley 12 February 2009).[5]

[5] My interviews with immigrants from the Conceição do Araguaia and Xinguara region who immigrated between 2001 and 2005 confirmed that all seemed to go through the same *coyote* from Goiânia who was in charge of organizing trips to the United States from the region of Southern Pará.

Effects of History and Politics on Migration

Historical and contemporary political and economic trends in the home location influence how cultures of migration begin. Conceição is a city of great historical importance in Brazil as a place where Brazilian governmental policies have negatively affected the local community and provided little reason to believe in a successful future. Conceição do Araguaia is perhaps best known in Brazil because of the Araguaian War (*Guerilha do Araguaia*). In the late 1960s, members of the *Partido Comunista do Brasil* (Brazilian Communist Party, a maoist organization), fleeing the military dictatorship (1964-1985) in Southern Brazil, established headquarters in the Amazon region between Marabá and Conceição do Araguaia. The military dictatorship, though never reaching the "dirty war" level of Argentina, used systematic repression and torture to subdue those whom they thought to be subversives. Many of the guerilla organizers were students and young professionals who settled in villages among peasant farmers in remote towns such as São Geraldo, Xambioá, and Itaipavas. They sponsored literacy campaigns and medical care for the communities as a way to gain support for their political campaign against the military dictatorship (Schmink 72).

The group of guerillas never posed a significant threat to the government, but, in 1972, fearing an insurgency, the federal government issued a decree that gave the National Security Council jurisdiction to mobilize troops in a campaign to defeat the guerrillas. At first unsuccessful because the locals shielded the insurgents, the army began a war of terror on the local civilian population as a tactic to uncover the whereabouts of the guerillas. More than 10,000 soldiers were deployed in search of the guerillas living in hiding in the Araguaia region (Schmink 73).

Never, during my interviews with Brazilian immigrants from Conceição, was the guerilla movement directly acknowledged as one of the reasons for migrating. In fact, when I asked about the movement, few respondents could give me much information about it, saying only that the government had covered it up and they did not learn about it in school. Older members of the town, however, recalled the military occupation and even military tortures that occurred in their homes or in those of their neighbors, yet they were reluctant to provide details. While the Araguaian war was not a direct cause of mass immigration to the United States, it was a critical event in creating a sense of wariness about how the government treats civilians of the region. In the Southern Amazon region, in general, the Brazilian government is imagined as being a source of violence, conflict, or, at the very least, ineffectiveness, seeing the locals as expendable citizens to larger national projects. These sentiments can be motivators for cultures of migration. The full range of social and environmental problems that plague the Southern Pará region as a result of government policies have left many people who live there pessimistic about their future and perhaps more willing to migrate to places that will provide them more security.

The dictatorship is also important to mention as an aggravating factor in the cultures of migration not just in Conceição, but in all of Brazil because, after the military dictatorship, there was severe economic inflation that became one of the major causes of increased Brazilian immigration to the U.S. in the 1990s. Speaking about Brazilian immigrants to New York during the 1990s, Maxine Margolis writes,

> Brazilians in New York are primarily economic exiles, fleeing from conditions of hyperinflation that have gouged the middle class and made its standard of living harder to maintain. In 1990, Brazilian inflation reached 1,795 percent annually; by 1991, even after then-president Collor's much-heralded plan to slay inflation with 'a single bullet,' it was averaging 20 percent a month (*Little Brazil* 6).

Brazil underwent a period of liberalization, electing Fernando Collor de Mello in 1989. Yet, Collor's government was also accused of accepting bribes and doing little to help the poor. He was impeached in 1992 and succeeded by Franco Itamar. The plan to "slay inflation with a single bullet" is known as the "plano real," set into place as a way to stabilize domestic currency in early 1994 under the leadership of Collor and the direction of Minister of Finance Fernando Henrique Cardoso (elected president in 1994). But as Margolis notes, this plan did not trickle down fast enough to deter prospective migrants who were disillusioned with their economic prospects in Brazil. According to people I talked to in Conceição, the first migrants left for Boston in the 1990s, following the trend of cultures of migration that Margolis documents among immigrants in New York. And as more migrant networks were set up to the U.S., Brazilians who had lesser amounts of social capital had opportunities to migrate, supported by their compatriots who had immigrated in the 1990s.

The socio-economic contradictions that aided in increased cultures of migration in Brazil also helped Luiz Inácio Lula da Silva win the presidential election in 2002 by gaining the support of the poor and disenfranchised. Lula put himself forward as a conservative populist candidate, pledging to open Brazil's economy to a free market, to sell off unprofitable state enterprises, to cut down the size of the federal government, and to spend more on social welfare. Yet the largest wave of immigrants from Conceição to the U.S. happened after Lula was elected president. Migrants report that, in general, people in Conceição had already become too fearful of continued economic uncertainty to have much faith that Lula's plans would have much immediate effect on their local economic situation. Indeed, in Conceição do Araguaia, locals say that though they support Lula, there have not been sufficient changes to the local economy to deter future migration to the U.S. The current deterrent of massive migration is primarily the economic crisis in the U.S. rather than an increase in the standard of living for those in Conceição.[6] The Southern Pará region still seems to be particularly isolated from economic prospects that would begin to deter cultures of migration. In interviews in 2009, three return immigrants to Conceição had been unemployed for over a year since returning and are planning to try their luck in another city in Brazil (Goiânia is one of the prospects because of the growing construction industry there) or in Canada. The fact that return immigrants have negative experiences finding financially-viable lives in Conceição even after returning with capital from the U.S. encourages the culture of migration to continue. Immigrants from Conceição in New Orleans constantly tell me that they want to be able to return to Conceição to celebrate during the carnival season in July, the time period when the Araguaia riverbanks dry up, revealing a beach and marking a season of carnival and fun. The reality, however, is that the stability of the community and this period of carnival depend on the fact that many of its members are living in the U.S. in order to fund it.

Community Values Associated with Migration Beyond Economics

[6] This response is different from return immigrants from other sending cities. Those from Goiânia, for instance, seemed to feel that there were better prospects for a future than when they first decided to leave Brazil.

It is true that cultures of migration in Brazil are generated by a wish to "earn the dream," to become financially stable through the migration experience. But, in truth, the material benefits of migration obscure the more abstract meanings and values that working abroad represent. In the novel *Yes! Eu sou Brazuca* by José Victor Bicalho, the character Miro notes that there are many reasons that Brazilians decide to immigrate to the United States. He says, "There are few [immigrants] who are only looking for dollars. Behind the money there are many stories; many times the dollar is just an excuse, a trick that allows the change, the break [from Brazil]" (Bicalho 57).

Through migration, Brazilians gain the skills and agency to be self-sufficient and productive members of society in a way that they could not in their own hometowns because of lack of employment options. Having agency, gaining skills, and being productive members of their communities are the motivating factors represented by material investments; thus, migrants are motivated by much more than simple dollars. Edilson, an immigrant from Belo Horizonte who spent one year and six months living in New Orleans and who has now returned to Belo Horizonte, said, "I hope that the people that I know here in Brazil have the opportunity to go to the United States. It is worth it. Not just financially but as a life experience" (Edilson 30 December 2008).

What are these values associated with the act of migration that go beyond the mere financial benefits? It has been noted that in many communities those who choose to migrate are seen as highly motivated and productive members of the community (Massey "Why Does Immigration Occur?" 46). Migrants who make the journey to the U.S. are seen as hard workers and adventurers. These are the less tangible, often silent, motivators of migration. It is a symbol of prestige or even a coming of age choice for men and women, just as, for example, going to college would be in other communities.

In a conversation with a Brazilian who had decided to immigrate illegally to the United States when he was 19 years old, the immigrant told me that, while his main goal was making money, the adventure of traveling, going somewhere new, and the adventure through Mexico were all motivating factors for him as well. When asked if he would do it again, he said that if he could rethink his decisions at the time, he thinks he may have decided to go to college first and then come to the

United States later. Now he is 25 and still living undocumented in the United States. While he is making money, he does not see himself in a position for future advancement in the U.S., nor in Brazil, because he sees himself as being too old to enter the professional job market there. He feels stuck between the two worlds.

A unique motivating factor for those immigrants who decided to move to post-Katrina New Orleans was that friends and family members saw pioneer Brazilian immigrants to the post-Katrina disaster zone as being especially fearless and resourceful because they braved the unknown conditions of the destroyed city in order to make a better life for their families in Brazil. They were imagined as living in an unstable and inhospitable world in order to provide for family and friends back home. In describing the courage of his son in moving to New Orleans, one father in Brazil was moved to tears explaining the living and working conditions that his son had described to him. His son, however, described this same time period to me as being one of amazing adventure and camaraderie and a highlight of his time in the U.S.

Migration is, thus, a sort of storied rite of passage to adulthood. For many young adults who make this journey, this is the first time that they have lived independently from their family. They learn to cook, clean, settle their own problems with the support of a network that they themselves created, and share shopping responsibilities.[7] Through immigration, they earn a sense of independence. They learn to manage bills and make payments and at times even come to understand the ins and outs of legal systems in a language that is not their own. They learn to manage their finances and make investments for their futures, sometimes succeeding, sometimes failing, and sometimes making future migration trips in order to complete their projects. It is a chance for personal growth and development. Even in houses of mostly male Brazilian immigrants, immigrants who probably had done little cooking and cleaning before coming to the United States, lists of weekly chores divided among roommates are commonly seen posted on the

[7] When I visited Jackson in his hometown after he returned to Brazil, his mother told me that she felt Jackson had matured while he was in the U.S. (He lived two years in Boston and four years in New Orleans.) As an example, she mentioned that now, after she cooks lunch, he always washes his dishes because he learned in the U.S. that those who cook should not have to wash dishes. She was surprised by his actions, since he had grown up in a household where the mother was in charge of all chores dealing with the kitchen.

refrigerator door. Migration provides the space for maturation.

> Coming to the U.S. teaches us (Brazilians) to be more independent. In the U.S. you learn to be independent in order to survive. These skills help us when we return to Brazil (Edilson 30 December 2008).

Because cultures of migration in Brazil also value the hard work and sacrifice that Brazilians confront in the U.S., many immigrants who have returned to Brazil still think back on their time in the U.S. with fond memories because it was a time period when they worked hard, produced physical results of their labors, were able to give back to their families, and felt valued for their work. They themselves consider painting, roofing, and electrical wiring engaging and satisfying work. Construction skills are honorable and valuable forms of knowledge that many Brazilians learned only because they moved abroad— that can then be applied once they return home.

Return migrants put their skills learned in the U.S. to use to varying degrees. Many immigrants did the remodeling on their homes themselves after returning to Brazil. Others are now working in the construction industry and, because they often have specialized knowledge learned in the U.S. as well as specialized tools and equipment that they shipped home, they are often able to find themselves in a higher position within the industry than before they left. For example, a return immigrant from New Orleans has managed to change his standard of living in Brazil by opening a profitable sheet rock and roofing company in Goiânia. As a contractor in Goiânia, a sprawling metropolis in the state of Goiás, Reginaldo was able to take advantage of the skills that he learned in the United States and invest in the economic expansion there. He has even constructed a trailer to store his tools that is identical to the trailers that he used when he lived in New Orleans. His social connections made abroad also transferred over as construction contacts for him in Brazil. In March 2009, Reginaldo did the siding on an embroidery business building that had been opened by another recently-returned immigrant from New Orleans.

The satisfaction of manifesting oneself concretely to the world through manual competence is part of the appeal of the culture of migration. In 2006, *The Wall Street Journal* wondered whether "skilled [manual] labor is becoming one of the few sure paths to a good living"

(Crawford 3). We all, immigrants or not, can recognize the appeal of tangible work that is straightforwardly useful. It is common for Brazilians in the U.S. to pose for photographs with a wad of cash earned from their labors in the U.S., and a common complaint of those who have gone back to Brazil, or are contemplating going back, is missing the feeling of this wad of cash in their pocket each week and not working, producing, or consuming with the same intensity that they did when they were working abroad. Brazilians often comment that a wad of American dollars in the pants every week feels somehow different from receiving a salary in *reais* once a month in Brazil. The wad of cash signifies an economically viable way of life, for both themselves and their families. It ironically valorizes their local Brazilian community by earning dollars to maintain and improve it.

Brazilians at the Border

The border crossing experience itself has become mythical, especially as the underground economy of migration has grown. Immigration experts have said that the most common method of entry among the first Brazilian immigrants in the U.S., those who came in the 1990s and before, had been by overstaying a tourist visa. When talking about methods of immigration for the Brazilian community, one interviewee commented on the 1994 World Cup in the United States as being paramount in importance. "Many Brazilians obtained visas and then they never left. These people then established connections and helped other friends and families come over" (Fabio 25 Oct. 2006). But, with increased difficulty in obtaining a tourist visa, more and more Brazilians have been choosing to make the journey through Mexico. Since the early 2000s, it has been difficult for many Brazilians to convince U.S. officials that they have sufficient funds to vacation in the United States, thus tourist visas have been much harder to obtain. This has caused an increase in illegal immigration across the Mexican border as well as through islands in the Caribbean (Moeller).

The events of Sept. 11, 2001 also made it much harder for Brazilians to obtain tourist visas, causing more Brazilians to choose the route to the United States through Mexico and making it more difficult for them to move back and forth between countries (Margolis "September 11th …" 1) In *América*, the Brazilian *telenovela,* when protagonist Sol arrives in the United States by going illegally through Mexico, the first words of advice that her new friend Ju tells her is that life as an illegal immigrant in the United States after September 11th has become much harder.

Even though it has become more difficult and riskier to cross, the number of Brazilians detained on the Mexican border rose from 500 in 1999 to more than 8,616 in 2004 (Department of Homeland Security Yearbook of Immigration Statistics). In 2005, this number quadrupled, with the number of Brazilians trying to cross the border then estimated at around 30,000. (Margolis "September 11th..." 4, "Com América") Brazilians were recorded, except for Mexicans, as the largest and fastest-growing immigrant group detained at the Mexican-U.S. border in 2005 (Hay).

So even as the difficulty of immigration increased, so did the number of people who wanted to do it. And the stories that people continued to tell one another about crossing the border show how the migration corridor itself became reimagined as an adventurous rite of passage in certain communities. The myth-making and adrenaline involved in crossing the border and the ability to share those experiences with a *communitas* of other Brazilians who also went through this crossing instilled a further sense of group identity.

The 2004 and 2005 rise in Brazilian immigration to the U.S. is particularly important as part of the context for understanding how Brazilians in New Orleans imagine migration since a large majority of the pioneer Brazilian immigrants to New Orleans came to the U.S. during this time slot. They had come to meet other members of their communities already in the U.S. The increase in border detentions in 2004-2005 also illustrates, as Margolis has noted, a loophole in the U.S. immigration policy around 2004-2005 ("September 11th ..." 4). When "other than Mexicans" are caught at the border, under U.S. immigration policy, they are not supposed to be sent back to Mexico, but to their country of origin. However, since the United States was suffering severe shortages in space in detention centers during this time period, most of these immigrants who were caught at the border were processed, fingerprinted, given a court date and then released and asked to reappear for their court date. 98% of the people detained and released never showed up (Ibid). Edgar, an immigrant who spent three and a half of his four years in the United States in New Orleans, was one of the Brazilian immigrants who took advantage of this loophole:

Edgar: … We got out of the river and we were in the United States… then what happened was that during this time Immigration was accepting people to get past the immigration checkpoints. They had opened things up. I don't know what was happening, but they were letting people in. They gave us a letter. I have the letter. Here it is. I keep it as a souvenir… this is a letter that says that I was allowed to be in the United States for four months…

(Edgar shows Annie a letter issued by the U.S. Department of Immigration in which he is categorized as an alien who has not been admitted or paroled. The letter has a court date for him to return for a trial on Oct. 7, 2005. He was caught at the border in Rio Grande City, Texas, June 5, 2005. Edgar never returned for his court date.)

Annie: Did you want to be caught by Immigration?

Edgar: Before we crossed we were told that we would go through Immigration. The guy who took us across had already told us that he would take us, but that we would have to go to the immigration jail. He told us we would have to spend a few days in jail.

Annie: So explain to me what happened after you crossed the river.

Edgar: After we crossed the river we started walking until we found some immigration officers. The immigration officers filled out those papers for us that said we could stay in the United States for four months and then after those four months we had to go to court. The court would decide if we should go back or if they would give us more time. We didn't go back to find out… We filled out the form that asked us if we had any problem in Brazil. We didn't have any problems in Brazil, so the form was really quick, and then the immigration officers drove us to the bus station. One of the immigration officers even said, "Welcome to America."… The officers joked around with us. They knew that we were not coming back for the court date. (Edgar 29 December 2008)

A large number of immigrants living in New Orleans took advantage of this loophole in the U.S. immigration policy. This is because many of the immigrants who felt mobile enough to relocate to New Orleans after Katrina even in uncertain circumstances had come to the United States in 2004 and 2005, the years when this circumvention of immigration law at the Mexican border seemed to be most common. Using this loophole as part of the migration experience helped to instill the sense of adventure in the process. Edgar describes it almost as if it were a game to seek out the migration officials on the other side, for example. His account also imagines the border as being porous. There are times when the "openings" are larger than others. Migrants begin to conceptualize the border that way and learn to act quickly to take advantage of such openings.

Immigrants who have now returned to Brazil and who had previously been "caught" by immigration officials at the border during their entrance, however, find themselves with a greater obstacle to think about if they consider a return trip to the United States; this is true even if being "caught" had been part of the entrance package arranged by their *coyote*. The immigration circumstances of 2004-2005 make the possibility of a second trip riskier for immigrants. Rodolfo, who returned to Brazil but now misses his life in the U.S., commented to me that if he had not been caught by Immigration on his first entrance, he would try to come to the United States again. But since he had been caught, his name was in the immigration computers and he would face a more severe sentence if caught crossing the border a second time. He was not willing to risk it and thus does not plan to return.

The journey to the U.S. is also riskier right now because the job market for immigrants is less strong with the downturn in the economy (Bernstein and Dwoskin). The number of people planning to enter the United States through Mexico has, thus, slowed drastically with the economic crisis in the last three years (McLaughlin and Swift). In 2008, Potential Brazilian migrants to the U.S. told me that, while they still want to go to the United States, they were afraid to make the journey because they know many people currently unemployed. This speaks to the fact that transnational connections to friends still living in the U.S. influence their decision to stay or go, and also that the stories and narratives of the U.S. as the land of opportunity are starting to change with the American economic crisis.

It is a valid fear not to be able to pay off the $10,000 *coyote* fee from

Brazil in a timely fashion.[8] For many of the migrants, $10,000 is money that they do not have. They cross the border in debt. Usually the *coyote* will give them six months to a year to pay off this debt, but that is not always the case. The wife of a returned immigrant from New Orleans told me that, before leaving for the U.S., her husband, Vander, transferred the legal documents of their house in Mato Grosso to the *coyote* who was going to take him across the border. It was Vander's understanding that he would have six months to pay off the debt before the *coyote* would take the house. But, Vander left for the United States on a Friday and, on Monday morning, the *coyote* knocked on the door and told his wife that she and the couple's two-year-old son had 48 hours to get out of the house. She had to move all of the furnishings into a neighbor's house and she slept in the storage room that was still theirs until Vander was able to earn enough money in the U.S. for her to rent a new house. Telling these experiences of border crossings and the personal and financial investment that crossing undocumented into the U.S. entails is a way of perpetuating cultures of migration by sharing stories of people who persevered through difficult experiences—but is also a warning for future migrants of risks so that they may evaluate these risks in relation to the possible benefits for themselves and their communities.

The Work of an *Atravessador*

There are also myths and fantasies surrounding the *atravessadores* and *coyotes,* the people who directly link immigrants to destinations in the U.S. In Valadares, Minas Gerais, I interviewed Mauro, a native of Mantena, Minas Gerais, who had spent two years trafficking people illegally to the United States. Mauro was responsible for bringing at least two people into the United States who are presently living in New Orleans. According to Mauro, he was already living illegally in the United States when one of his friends from Mantena contacted

[8] A *coyote* fee refers to the fees that must be paid to the smuggler in exchange for his/her help navigating the border-crossing experience. Sometimes this fee is paid upfront and other times a deposit is made and the rest is paid once the person arrives in the US. The *coyote* fee from Brazil has gone up, according to the reports documented by Maxine Margolis in 1994. Then she documented that the fee was around $5,000 for airfare to Mexico City, transportation to the border, a *coyote* to help cross it, travel to a U.S border city, and a one-way plane ticket from the border city to a final destination (Margolis *Little Brazil* 48). Current fees tend to be between $10,000 and $12,000.

him to see if he would be interested in trafficking Brazilians to the United States by boat through the Bahamas. Motivated by the large amount of money that he would earn— amounts far exceeding what he could earn in his job as a house painter— Mauro began working as an *atravessador;* he picked up immigrants from the boat arrival spot in Deerfield Beach, Fla., and drove them to their final destinations, mostly in Boston. Once he learned how to manage a motorboat, he also began to drive the boat from the Bahamas to the United States.

Mauro says that he always made the crossing in a small tourist motorboat. All of the people he smuggled dressed in bathing suits and swimming trunks, and they made the trip from the Bahamas to the U.S. slowly so that it looked as if they were simply on vacation and enjoying the ocean. He did trips both day and night. Trips during the day were much easier because all his passengers could pretend that they were tourists. Trips at night were dangerous.

The normal fee for booking a trip to the United States through the Bahamas with Mauro was $14,000 and Mauro reported that he often made $22,000 in one day alone. He worked with one other person. When Mauro was driving the boat, the person that he worked with would then take the people by car to the cities of their final destination and collect the remainder of the money. With a laugh, Mauro remembers a trip from Boston when his associate came back with $42,000 in cash hidden in the sunroof of the car. They would split the money equally after the trips. In 2007 the Coast Guard caught Mauro and he received a sentence of one year and four months in jail. He was held in federal prison for one year and then in immigration jail for four months. Mauro commented that he didn't mind his time in jail because it gave him the opportunity to lose some weight; he was so rich that he was getting fat. "Jail helped me get trim and also taught me a lot of things." The week that he was caught, he was supposed to make $100,000 in smuggling fees.

When Mauro went to jail, the police did not confiscate any of the money that he had earned while smuggling people into the United States. His money is now located in two bank accounts: one in the United States and the other in Brazil. According to Mauro, he did lose about $200,000 from the last trips that he made because his partner stole it from him and then disappeared, never visiting him in jail and never answering phone calls after he was released. The Coast Guard never caught his partner because Mauro radioed him before the Coast Guard arrived at the boat to warn him of what had happened. Mauro has not yet tried to access his bank account in the United States. When I spoke with him, he had been out of jail and living in Governador Valadares for about six months.

Mauro also claims to have worked briefly in Mexico City smuggling people across the Mexican border, but he preferred smuggling people in from the Bahamas because he said that it was much more fun. When he was taking children across he would get double the price because he had to be with them the whole time. He says that if he ever decides to come back to the U.S. it would be easy and he wouldn't have to pay a penny because he has all of the contacts. He doesn't want to go back to the U.S. and stay illegally, however, because it is too uncomfortable to have to stay hidden. Also, if he were caught in the U.S. a second time his jail sentence would be quite hefty (Mauro 12 January 2008).

In my conversations with Mauro, two things struck me about his explanations about his life bringing immigrants to the United States: First, he was very nonchalant. He said nothing that suggested that he thought of the job as anything out of the ordinary. Mauro has grown up in a culture of migration and of trafficking people across the border; going to jail for an immigration issue was simply part of his job description. He had many friends and acquaintances who had experienced similar situations. Secondly, Mauro commented that he had loved his job because of the adventure and the fun that he had while working. He even took his American girlfriend with him on "vacation" during a few of his trips to the Bahamas. He would take her with him on the boat to the Bahamas and they would stay in a fancy resort for the weekend. Then she would get on a plane and fly home to the U.S. and he would return by boat with the immigrants. This sense of adventure was part of the satisfaction provided by his job.

While I cannot say whether or not Mauro was exaggerating his exploits in his stories, I imagine that there is almost always an element of mixing fictional images of Brazilian migration experience with real life. The representations of immigration in the media feed the popular imagination. I do know that Mauro was jailed for bringing people to the United States by boat from the Bahamas. And I can attest that those people around him seemed very impressed with the idea of what his life must have been like, at the same time that they considered it part of the migration culture in which they lived. His new girlfriend, who was sitting on his lap as he spoke with me (performing both her position of ownership over Mauro for me, a young single woman interviewer, as well as performing her privileged position as the beneficiary to Mauro's success), commented that when he first arrived in Valadares after being deported he did not have any clothes but he had lots of money. She said that when he needed a new shirt in the morning he would just go out and buy a new outfit! His girlfriend had been deported on her trip to the United States, so she was both interested in and proud of the work that Mauro had done. Those in search of the dream and helping others search for their dream are seen as heroic figures. The stories and the way in which Mauro told them tended to take on a Hollywood quality.

As Mauro talked to me about his work as an *atravessador* I could imagine his stories being part of the next *novela* with Mauro as the star actor. In fact, I would not be surprised if these stories, at least the way that they were told to me, were very much influenced by mass media representations of the migration experience, or by the ideas about the cultures of migration that surround Valadares and his neighboring city of Mantena. Though Mauro did not talk openly about his work to strangers, those around him seemed to respect him and have some idea of his previous job and seemed to consider it part of the culture of their community.

Minas as a Migration Hub

In March 2005, the Brazilian news magazine *Isto é* published an article about Brazilian immigration to the United States through Mexico. This was one of the first articles published in the Brazilian popular press about the border-crossing experience. The article opened by describing a grave located at Terrace Park Cemetery, in El Centro, Ca. The cemetery is a gravesite for unknown immigrants who have died during the crossing. Of the 500 bodies that are in the cemetery, about 100 are believed to be Brazilians. Nationalities are guessed at based on the brands of clothes that the people are wearing and on the basis of their physical appearance. Rarely are bodies discovered that have any sort of clear identification on them (Rodrigues 70). The week that *América* aired for the first time on TV Globo, Senator Marcelo

Crivella (PL) of Rio de Janeiro announced that he would be undertaking an investigation with the CPI (*Comissão Parlamentar de Inquérito*) regarding the trafficking of Brazilians to the United States.

As part of these investigations, detectives uncovered the complexity of a human trafficking ring in Minas Gerais. The death of an immigrant, Wendell Jonatas Pereira, 23, who died trying to cross the border, led investigators to discover that the leader of the operation that sent him was the mayor of São Félix de Minas, the hometown of Pereira. The operation was also linked to tourism agencies in Mantena and Valadares, Minas Gerais (Rodrigues and Filgueiras 56, Rodrigues 38). Allegedly, Mayor Wanderley Viera de Souza formed a campaign committee for his election in 2005 in which he promised to send the people working on the committee to the United States if he won the election (Rodrigues 39). The state of Minas Gerais is key to understanding how governments and institutions profit by making migration part of the local community economy.

An economic market has emerged in towns in Brazil with cultures of migration that encourages the continuation of transnational flows of people from (and to) their homeland. It is not surprising that we often discover that there are public officials and high-ranking members of the community involved in the migration process because it is both powerful and lucrative to be the person who enables migrant mobility. Nor is it surprising that in a city like Governador Valadares, the sending city of all sending cities in Brazil, there are organizations such as the "Center for Information, Help, and Shelter for the Family and the Worker Living Abroad." CIAAT (*Centro de Informação, Apoio e Amparo à Família e ao Trabalhador no Exterior*) was set in place specifically to aid Valadares citizens living in the U.S. through managing their remittances and helping with their reintegration once they return.

Governador Valadares

Interviewees living in New Orleans reinforced claims made by previous immigration researchers that Minas Gerais and Governador Valadares were especially important locations in the creation of the Brazilian migrant network to the United States. Governador Valadares has made a business out of trafficking a potential workforce to the United States. Even immigrants from other cities in Minas, such as Manhuaçu, Belo Horizonte, and Padre Paraíso, usually had some link to Governador Valadares in their border-crossing experience. Remittances from immigrants in the United States have become so important to the economy of Valadares that the mayor's office inserted a plaque honoring migrants in a major city plaza in town which reads: "This tribute to immigrants brings justice to the dignified work of these heroes for their contribution to the development of Governador Valadares."

Maxine Margolis refers to Minas as a red flag for immigration officials (Margolis *Little Brazil* 36). In Governador Valadares, the whole economy of the city is supported by money received through immigration chains connecting Valadares to the United States. Because of the large number of Valadarenses now living physically removed from their community as undocumented migrants abroad, it is virtually impossible for residents of Valadares to obtain tourist visas to the U.S. (Ibid). But, as I quickly discovered after spending time in Valadares, booking a trip through Mexico is quite easy. You will be hard pressed in Valadares to find someone who does not have a friend or a family member who has already made the journey through Mexico to the United States. The majority of the Brazilian immigrants from Minas Gerais with whom I spoke in New Orleans had not even attempted to go to the consulate, knowing that they would be denied. They booked their ticket to the U.S. directly through an *atravessador* instead of spending money to try to get a visa that they were sure not to receive.

A return Valadarense from New Orleans who arrived in December 2008 invested the money that he earned in the United States in a travel agency located in downtown Valadares. His travel agency books regular tour packages by plane and bus, but, according to José, most of his profits come from exchanging dollars on the black market and organizing trips to the United States through Mexico. The latter two activities are considered illegal and are not officially published as part of his travel agency agenda, but people interested in going to the United States or who have arrived from the United States with dollars to exchange, know that these services are provided. As is José, *atravessadores* are very accessible in Valadares, even making house calls when they learn of someone interested in going to the United States.

There have been several theories as to why Governador Valadares has created such extensive immigrant networks with the United States. The most probable scenarios have been outlined by Ana Cristina Braga Martes and were confirmed in my interviews: 1.) During World War II American mining companies were set up in Governador Valadares. After the war ended, American workers for the Morrison mining company returned to Boston and took their domestic servants with them. 2.) Students from Valadares went to Boston to study and decided to bring their families over, beginning the migration chain. 3.) After World War II, American companies began to come to Valadares buying and reselling semi-precious stones. Through these business operations, connections were made in the United States and Brazilians from Valadares became aware of the money that could be made in the United States. 4.) In the 1960s there were a group of adventurous Brazilians from Valadares who decided to make the journey through Mexico to Boston. Once they arrived and became settled, they began helping family and friends cross. (Martes 61-62)

Brazilian Enclaves in Other Areas of the Country

Massachusetts, in turn, became one of the principal destinations of Brazilians from Minas Gerais and is also one of the largest sending areas for Brazilian immigrants who relocated to New Orleans immediately after Hurricane Katrina. Most of the Brazilians from Boston did not come to New Orleans as part of a company contract as those from Florida and Atlanta often did, but came down on their own or with other groups of Brazilians in search of work. Perhaps they were more habituated in the culture of migration, either through their experience in migration hub cities in Minas or in the established Brazilian community of Massachusetts, to know that those who arrive first often profit the most. Now, in 2011, Brazilians are coming from many different destinations: Orlando, Pompano Beach, Newark, Boston, Atlanta, towns in Mississippi, and directly from Brazil.

Being part of a large immigrant enclave has both its benefits and limitations.

> I lived in Boston for 5 years and I did not know how to speak any English. I was only involved with the Brazilian community there. Here [in New Orleans], no. Here you are forced to learn English. If you don't learn, then you don't communicate. There is also an advantage here that there are more Americans that want to learn to speak Portuguese. Here it is much easier to integrate [into the New

Orleans community] than in Boston. There is no comparison. Here is like a little piece of Brazil (Luis 15 May 2009).

This interview expresses a positive aspect of moving to a city like New Orleans without an extensive Brazilian enclave. However, in early interviews with Brazilians in New Orleans in 2006, most interviewees expressed their satisfaction with New Orleans overall but often complained about lacking the social capital that they had experienced in more extensive Brazilian enclaves in other parts of the country.[9] In New Orleans, both work and social interactions, especially in the first two years following the storm, were more challenging for recent Brazilian immigrants because they were forced to make new contacts and social ties without the help of an enclave. In areas of the country with large Brazilian communities, it is relatively easy to find professionals like doctors, lawyers, dentists, and translators who speak Portuguese. And it is also much easier to come across restaurants and supermarkets that have Brazilian foodstuffs and a Portuguese-speaking staff. In cities with an extensive Brazilian enclave, Brazilians can go about their daily schedules without ever leaving the Brazilian community, creating a sense of security and mediating culture shock because nearly all daily interactions can be done in Portuguese. In New Orleans right after Hurricane Katrina, there were no services for the local New Orleanian

[9] One of the key characteristics of social capital is that it can be converted and transplanted into other forms of capital— most importantly, in the case of immigration, into financial capital (Bourdieu "The Forms of Capitol" 244). Bourdieu argues that it is impossible to account for the structure and functioning of the social world unless one reintroduces capital in all its forms and not solely in the one form recognized by economic theory. The world cannot be reduced to simple mercantile exchange that is always oriented toward the maximization of profit. Bourdieu sees all of these forms of capital as a source of power that is contested in social relationships and in the economic labor market. He describes social capital as the sum of the resources, actual or virtual, that accrue to an individual or a group by virtue of possessing a durable network of more or less institutionalized relationships of mutual recognition (Bourdieu and Waquant 119). Social capital, in the case of living within a Brazilian enclave, is made up of the networks between other migrants. These linkages between people create important socioeconomic consequences for migrants. According to this line of thinking, a sizeable and concentrated Brazilian population should create positive effects on the lives of individual immigrants.

community, much less for a community of immigrants.[10]

It is easy to imagine that the resources provided by an enclave would be beneficial and that lack of these resources because of a small or non-existent enclave would be negative. In the above interview, however, Luis highlighted the positive aspects of living in a city without an extensive Brazilian enclave. The Brazilian community in New Orleans is imagined as having more interaction and moments of cultural and financial exchange with New Orleanians than their previous cities of residency. For Luis, learning English has been an important skill learned in New Orleans as a result of the fact that there was not an extensive enclave network to mediate his interactions; he needed English skills to access work and social opportunities as a pioneer immigrant. Many Brazilians have commented to me in their interviews that if they had understood the employment system in the United States or if they had spoken English in those first months that they arrived in New Orleans, they would have "made a lot more money." Brazilians who have moved to New Orleans learned to become more self sufficient in navigating the local community because they do not have the large support of a Brazilian enclave. And because of this, Brazilians seem to be more personally attached and invested in New Orleans than they were in other cities in the U.S. where they have lived. In their prior cities, they were more likely to feel emotional attachment to their Brazilian enclaves rather than to the city itself.

English became necessary in New Orleans not only to gain autonomy in the job market, but also to be able to talk with women. Gender is a particularly complicated dimension of Brazilian integration into New Orleans. The fact that there are markedly unequal gender ratios within the Brazilian community in New Orleans has meant that Brazilians have been less willing to remain specifically within their Brazilian enclave setting socially. There are many Brazilians in New Orleans with American girlfriends. I taught a beginning Portuguese class at Tulane University in the fall of 2008. Of the ten students in the class, six of those students enrolled in the class because they had a Brazilian boyfriend with whom they wanted to be able to communicate better. I

---

[10] The Southern Poverty Law firm took on many cases of worker's justice abuses, opening the Worker's Justice Center after Hurricane Katrina. Loyola Law Clinic, which is run by prospective law students, has also played an important role in helping the immigrant community in New Orleans. However, these organizations mainly target the Hispanic community.

have not noted a similar phenomenon in the Spanish classes I teach at Tulane. So while early interviews with Brazilians expressed nostalgia for being able to meet women in Brazilian enclaves where they felt more comfortable, now it is clear that Brazilians are finding more ways to enter into American social circles in New Orleans.

Luis's interview also reveals that he felt as if there were more people in New Orleans interested in learning Portuguese than in Boston. That impression is probably erroneous. In a city the size of Boston with the large number of top-rate universities and a more established Brazilian community, I am sure that there are, in fact, more American Portuguese speakers than there are in New Orleans. Brazilians in Boston— because of the size of the city, the size of the Brazilian community, and the fact that there was no disaster moment that brought the Brazilian community in close proximity to Portuguese-speaking Americans— meant that Brazilians came into contact with American Portuguese speakers with less frequency. Brazilians in the first wave of immigration post-Katrina had a plentitude of opportunities for contact with members of recovery organizations and local universities because these were some of the first Americans back to the city. These people involved in reaching out to the immigrant community tended to have an invested interest in immigration, Latin America, and even Brazil, making it more likely that immigrants would meet a bilingual American.

In 1990 the magazine *Veja* published a report entitled "Brazukas de Boston" in which the typical Brazilian immigrant was described as male, young, single, and with family remaining in Brazil (Martes 40). In 1992, the *Boston Globe* reported that 90% of these immigrants in Boston until 1987 had come from Governador Valadares (Martes 53). This profile is also fitting in describing the Brazilian immigrants who would later relocate from Boston to New Orleans. While Minas natives lead in numbers, however, it should be noted that the first wave of Brazilian immigrants to New Orleans also showed a proportionately large number of immigrants from Rondônia and Southern Pará.

Weber and Marcus have explained how return immigrants from Boston are changing the urban landscape of Valadares. Marcus shows us stores such as the "Stop and Shop" Mercearia which recalls the Massachusetts-based "Stop and Shop" supermarket chain and the "Flowers and Love Store," both set up by returnees from Boston who have incorporated business and cultural practices learned in Boston to their new experiences at home in Brazil (Marcus *The Context...* 20). I witnessed a similar business endeavor in Valadares when visiting return migrants who had lived in New Orleans. In Metairie, La., a suburb of New Orleans, there is an apartment building complex that is famous for housing Brazilians. Daniel, a current resident of New Orleans from Valadares, liked the apartment building so much that he decided that he wanted to make a replica in Valadares to rent out as extra income for his family. Daniel has been in the United States for over 17 years (he immigrated and began working in the U.S. when he was 15). After Katrina, he made enough money to buy both a house in the New Orleans suburb of Kenner and to invest in the construction of the apartment building in Valadares. He sent pictures of the apartment complex in New Orleans to his mother in Valadares who then passed the pictures on to the architect so that he could replicate it in a lot for sale in his old neighborhood. The lot was not very wide, but it was deep, so Daniel also decided that he wanted the apartments to be modified version of the typical New Orleans shotgun style house with a long hallway running down the inside.

The shotgun-style apartment, so characteristic of New Orleanian architecture, is popularly thought to have gotten its name because the house is built with rooms that open into each other and with doors all on the same side.[11] It is said that if you shot a shotgun through the front door, then the bullet would go straight out the back door. Daniel designed his apartments with this idea in mind; however, instead of doors to each room, the architect designed a narrow hallway with doors to the side. So now in Valadares there is an apartment complex that is a replica of the apartment complex in Metairie, Louisiana on the outside and a modified shotgun house on the inside.

Recreating buildings, business styles, and lifestyles from experiences learned during time spent in the United States are examples of how geographical space, as Marcus notes, is created across national boundaries. Place is created that references multiple social worlds, as communities are becoming more and more translocal. These newly created places and cultural experiences that allow immigrants to remember

---

[11] For more on the history of the shotgun house, see John Micheal Vlach's chapter on the subject in *Common Places: Readings in American Vernacular Architecture.* He contends that the shotgun style is a West African architectural style reproduced in the Americas.

the missing country are very important to the identity-making process of migrants on both sides of the border. Physical places as well as tangible items are important emotional reminders of past experiences. While in the U.S., Daniel is reminded of the apartments that he owns in his hometown. And if he ever returns to Brazil, he will constantly be reminded of his Brazilian community in New Orleans. The fact that migrants are living such transnational lives opens up new ways to think about the complexity of local spaces and experiences.

Likewise, other return immigrants from New Orleans often brought work tools, t-shirts of New Orleans, and even Mardi Gras beads back with them to Brazil.

Figure 4: Picture 1: Apartments in Metairie, Lousiana

Picture 2: Apartments in Governador Valadares, Minas

One return immigrant from Belo Horizonte shipped back three garbage bags of Mardi Gras beads along with the furniture for his new house in a container from New Orleans to Brazil.[12] I asked what he planned to do with the Mardi Gras beads and he said that he planned to take them to Carnaval in 2009 and trade them for kisses just as he had done in New Orleans. He was finding ways of merging the cultural practices that he learned in New Orleans with his life in Brazil.

Working in One Place to Build a Life in Another

The return home is a constant point of fantasy for immigrants living in the U.S. As previously mentioned, it is common for immigrants to come to the United States as target earners, hoping to earn a set amount of money for a particular project so they can return home as quickly as possible. These migrants are living lives almost as if they are in suspension. Immigrants who come to the U.S. specifically as target earners accrue a large amount of money during their time in the U.S. in comparison to their lives in Brazil, mainly because they are often working 12-14 hour days (especially those immigrants who were lucky enough to take advantage of the construction opportunities available immediately following Hurricane Katrina). For those who arrived in New Orleans shortly after Hurricane Katrina when labor was in high

[12] The door-to-door container from New Orleans to Belo Horizonte costs $4,000.

demand and when payment for labor was also still high, the mere experience of living for a few months in the recovery zone was often lucrative enough for them to complete their projects at home in Brazil.

There are always moments when people live their lives in suspension, but immigrants often live with this feeling of life suspended for years. They are constantly imagining when their project will be complete so that they can live a life back home that they want to live. This life, of course, rarely happens the way it is imagined. The nostalgia for returning to Brazil is much based on fantasy. The migrant constructs a home in the U.S., trying to be as anonymous and transitory as possible, seeing the U.S. as a non-place that he works his way through to be able to more fully ground himself in the Brazilian home he imagines.

Edilson, for example, spent one year in New Orleans. He went directly to New Orleans (via Mexico) from Brazil in 2006 because he had friends there who could help him adjust when he first arrived. "It is important to have a support system that can help you when you arrive. Never go with a shot in the dark" (Edilson 30 December 2008). His goal was to be able to earn enough money to be able to buy an apartment in Brazil so that he could get married. He says he never fully adjusted to life in New Orleans because he never left the house except to work. He spent all his free time talking on the telephone with his girlfriend back in Brazil. In one year he was able to earn enough money to pay off the $12,000 *coyote* fee that took him across the border plus buy a small apartment in Belo Horizonte. His goal for his immigration experience was simply to buy this apartment and return as quickly as possible to marry his girlfriend. He had been in Brazil for four months when I visited him in January of 2009, but he had still not begun working again. His wife is a nurse, and so he was able to afford this sort of leisured lifestyle for a little while longer. Edilson was able to accomplish his goal, and there were many other skills that he thought that he learned, but he did not find himself integrating into New Orleans life in any way because that was not part of his goal. Being a target earner was all-encompassing for him. He, thus, had little contact with the social world outside of his work experience.

Similarly, João, a Brazilian immigrant who lived for two years and six months in New Orleans and three years in the United States said,

> Instead of taking the opportunity to learn English I preferred to work nights. I would work until 10 p.m. most nights, so I never

had the opportunity to learn. Working those late nights was also bad for me because I was usually alone. I would get really lonely. It probably made me want to go back to Brazil even more. Even on Sundays, rarely was I at home on Sundays. Usually I worked until 2 or 3 in the afternoon (João 30 December 2008).

Like Edilson's, João's heavy work schedule also meant that he had very limited contact with American culture outside of the work place. I went to visit João and his three brothers (who also lived for a time in New Orleans) in Belo Horizonte after they had returned to Brazil. Of the eleven children in the family, six of those children have lived or are still living in the United States. The six siblings who had migrated had all crossed the border in different trips. They did not travel together because it would have been too dangerous for all of them to get caught on the same trip, putting the family in too much financial debt to be able to recover. The oldest son went first and the rest followed, one by one, in a time span of approximately one year from one another. Although one would guess that the family would have had much contact with American culture and lifestyles since six of the children have lived in the United States, time spent abroad does not directly translate to cultural sensitivity and knowledge of the host country because, in these cases, their lived experiences in the U.S. revolved almost completely around work.

The first morning after I arrived at their house in Belo Horizonte they were happy to make me an American breakfast— a hamburger and a Coke. They said they knew that I would like it because all Americans eat lots of hamburgers and drink lots of Cokes. At least, that had been their experience eating frequently in fast food restaurants. They had even bought specially prepackaged patties for my arrival. I didn't have the heart to tell them that I wasn't a big hamburger fan and that it had been years since I had drunk a Coke. I spent a week drinking Coke for breakfast and eating hamburgers, until, thankfully, we ran out of patties. This experience marks the fact that, although the brothers had lived for years in the United States and one of their sisters is even a U.S. citizen (married to an American in Boston), the depth of their knowledge of American culture is entirely superficial. They know the ins and outs of the American immigrant cultural experience, but they had little contact with the daily lives and habits of Americans. What they observed, they observed simply from the outside as workers. Their imagining of their American Dream experience was inextricably linked to returning home in a timely fashion.

Edilson and João's stories are important. First, they illustrate how the imagination of migration experiences is often linked to a particular financial goal and how this goal influences a lack of interaction with the local community because their work schedule monopolizes their time. João's comment that working nights made him even lonelier in the U.S. shows how embracing the role of a target earner fully by not engaging in the local social world inevitably makes immigrants want to return to Brazil as quickly as possible. It is a double-edged sword. They want to return home because they don't adjust and they don't adjust because they want to return home. The U.S. is the place of work and returning to Brazil is the place of enjoying the fruits of their labors. What persons would not want to return to the community that represents a place to enjoy well-earned leisure? Though the dream at the beginning may be to be able to find a balance of leisure in the U.S. and be able to go back and forth between their homes in Brazil and the U.S., the reality is that this ping-pong migration is increasingly more difficult. The increased difficulty in going to the U.S. means that investments are happening in home communities in Brazil for a projected future when immigrants return permanently.

So as more cash is flowing into sending communities, one of my biggest questions when interviewing returned immigrants from New Orleans was whether or not all this work in the United States had actually helped them change their social or economic status back in Brazil in any significant ways— and whether this idealized vision of the return experience had played itself out in reality as they had imagined it would.

Many Brazilian immigrants in New Orleans began investing in building projects in the first two years following Hurricane Katrina when there was a lot of work and when construction labor was lucrative. As more people came down to work in construction, the cost of labor also dropped. Lower costs for labor plus the economic crisis in the U.S. caused a radical slow-down in construction projects back in Brazil because immigrants could no longer afford to send regular remittances back to their families. Cristiano began a construction project of an apartment building in Manhuaçu in 2006. He reported that in 2006, at the height of Katrina reconstruction, he earned $80,000, the majority of which was being sent home to build the apartment complex. He sent money to his brother who was administering his earnings for him. Cristiano had not actually seen the building yet because he is still in New Orleans earning the rest of the money necessary for him to finish the project and return home. Work has slowed in New Orleans, so in 2007 and 2008, he estimated that he sent about $20,000 a year to his brother for construction of the apartment. Given the new reality, it took him until 2011 to finish his construction project and return to Brazil.

I went to Manhuaçu to meet with his family and also to take pictures of the construction project that Cristiano had not yet seen. Only two apartments in the complex of eight had been finished and had people renting them. The rest were far from being completed. They were mere cement blocks with scaffolding holding the walls in place. When, after returning to New Orleans, I showed Cristiano the pictures of his construction project, he was thrilled with the location and the views of his construction, but disheartened with the progress. He had imagined that it was much farther along.

While the prospect of what this building could become was sold to me as an example of the progress brought to town due to immigration to the United States, I could not help but feel a bit saddened. In Cristiano's hometown of Manhuaçu, for example, it was hard to tell the difference between the middle class neighborhoods and the favelas; in both there seemed to be unfinished and poorly constructed houses with people living in them. And seeing Cristiano's reaction to the pictures of what he was investing in, it was obvious that there was disconnect between what he imagined was being created in Brazil and what actually existed.

He realized that he would either need to rethink the time frame for how long that he would have to stay in New Orleans or change his spending habits in the U.S. He decided to change his social life in New Orleans to become a target earner with little to no contact with the city outside of the work setting so that he could save almost all the money that he made. Although he loved New Orleans and the social life that he once enjoyed, his ultimate goal was to make his life in Brazil because that was the only way that he would be able to be with his family again.

Cristiano returned in April of 2011. His apartments are finished and his own apartment is fully furnished. He has managed to complete his goal, but in order to do it, he eliminated all but essential expenses in the United States for the last year and a half of his stay. He had no cell phone, did not go out on weekends, and did not eat out at restaurants. His entire paycheck, except money needed for rent and the most basic living expenses, was sent to Brazil as soon as he received it, thus eliminating any possibility that Cristiano would spend it frivolously. Before he left he was dealing with issues of depression and was counting down the days when he could return to Brazil, since he was neither living here nor there. Construction projects are both tangible markers of success, but are also tangible markers of disconnect between imagined migration experience and lived experience. Cristiano, for example, has had to sacrifice any vestige of social life in the U.S. in order to create a financial future in Brazil. And even with his sacrifices, his building projects took much longer than he would have expected.

As Jacaré's reaction to viewing the show *América* illustrated in the beginning of this chapter, there are many Brazilians who are seduced by the prospect of earning money quickly in the United States. But the reality of immigration is often quite different, both in terms of how much can be earned and what that money will buy in Brazil. In fact, some interviewees commented that if they had truly known what life would be like in the United States, they would never have decided to come. I have found that the economic goals of the return Brazilian immigrants that I visited rarely resulted in radical changes in the person's socioeconomic standing in Brazil. The money earned in the United States was enough to complete certain designated projects in Brazil—building houses, paying for the schooling of their children, buying land or cattle, paying off debt. But occupations before migrating to the United States and after migrating rarely changed dramatically. Return immigrants were able to enjoy economic stability (at least for the immediate months following their return), because most had a reserve of cash that they could invest into necessary projects, but life soon seemed to return to a standard much like that before their migration experience.

Successful return migrants seemed to be those who had figured out how to transition back into a lifestyle that was similar to that which they lived before going abroad. Although they now have the added bonus of a financial cushion for unforeseen expenses or for investments in business ventures, those who successfully transitioned back to their lives in Brazil often are the ones who continue to live their lives in the same ways that they did before immigration, not spending their money lavishly. The free time, the leisure, and the opportunity for fun imagined as finally attainable through returning to Brazil usually turned out to be myth.

How Cultures of Migration Affect an Entire Community: Colorado do Oeste, Rondônia

Figure 5: Main Street, Colorado do Oeste

Migration to and from Colorado do Oeste

Looking at Colorado do Oeste, Rondônia, we may begin to get a picture of how immigration affects local Brazilian town life in tangible ways. As the crow flies, Rondônia is about 3,000 miles from New Orleans. But it is about as easy (and as quick) to get to New Orleans as to the other side of the world. The bus schedules are sporadic and they also vary greatly with the rains. The roads are paved, sometimes, but the number of potholes still makes traveling slow and difficult. The trip from Cuiabá, Mato Grosso winds through rain forest and deforested plots of rain forest that are now used for raising cattle and soy.

Rondônia has the largest tract of tropical rain forest in the world with more than 3.8 million square kilometers of forest and a wealth of mineral resources (Browder 45). One of the most isolated regions of Brazil, Rondônia is also the state in Brazil that has experienced the most rapid rates of deforestation. So rapid is its deforestation that it came to the attention of international NGOs and the World Bank, who have lobbied for intervention in public policy and settlement operations that are environmentally and socially more sound. The early 1970s was a time of federal activity in economic development, occupation, and integration of the Amazon. The largest road in the network was the Transamazonian Highway, which was set up to link the Atlantic coast to the Peruvian border. In terms of colonization, the goal was to settle 100,000 families (around 500,000 people) in five years along the Transamazonian Highway (Stewart 13). In the beginning, however, this program was unsuccessful. The estimated number of immigrants had not yet moved to the region due to many factors, but mainly because of the federal government's failure to provide the proper titles for land, avenues to secure loans, or a proper road maintenance system (Stewart 14). Since these migrants were moving to previously unpopulated areas of the country, immigrants were relying heavily on governmental support to help create the necessary infrastructure to create towns and settlements. It took time, however, before the government could provide this.

But when the section of the highway linking Cuiabá, the capital of Mato Grosso, to Porto Velho was finally constructed, there was a major turning point in immigration to Rondônia because it allowed access to the state throughout the year (Mahar and Schneider 162). The number of farmers and the population in Rondônia overall, which had been the second lowest in the country only a few years earlier (FIBGE 1989),[13] suddenly rose from 69,792 in 1960 to 111,064 in 1970 (FIBGE 1991). But after creating the highway from Cuiabá to Porto Velho (the BR-364) the federal government no longer had the funds to maintain and pave it (Stewart 3). The paving of BR-364 highway had been initiated as early as the 1970s, but it was abandoned by the federal government after the completion of only a few miles due to a lack of funds (Rich 27).

The Brazilian government then entered into negotiations with the World Bank to finish the project and began debating issues of economic and environmental sustainability. In December 1980, the World Bank announced its decision to finance the Cuiabá-Porto Velho highway reconstruction program as part of a larger regional development package aimed at promoting the "orderly" socio-economic development of the region influenced by the road, together with the protection of the physical environment and local Amerindian communities. With the

[13] Fundação Instituto Brasileiro de Geografía e Estatística

road construction project, immigration to Rondônia began to happen at a rate that the Brazilian government was not prepared to handle. More people came than they were able to provide with land. The rhetoric surrounding migration to the area also changed. The government had once told migrants to clear land for agriculture, but the new policies told them that there was a percentage of their land that had to remain natural, undeveloped forest. Many people who had moved and bought land before the World Bank became involved were asked to replant trees. In my interviews in Colorado do Oeste, people expressed frustration with the current policy. Their parents had been given land and told that if they did not use the land to its fullest potential then it would be taken away from them; now they were being told that they would be fined if they used all of it. The effect of these decisions was to foster immigration to the United States because they were being told to replant trees or they would be fined. They no longer felt that being a rancher was a profitable job without some start-up funds. These start up funds, it was discovered, could be earned in the United States.

Migration studies have told us that migrants tend not to come from poor, isolated places that are disconnected from world markets, but from regions and nations that are undergoing rapid change and development as a result of their incorporation into global trade, information, and production networks (Massey "Why Does Immigration Occur?" 48). Massey contends that migration does not stem solely from a lack of development in a particular location, but from development itself (Ibid). So even though Rondônia would seem to be an isolated region for sending immigrants to the United States, in truth, policies of deforestation, which are linked to international markets and subsequent policies to save the rainforest, spurred contact with world economic and political systems, thus creating contact and motivation for immigration to the United States. As towns sprang up to work in the lumbering, ranching, and agricultural industries that the Transamazonian highway enabled, the policies around cutting the forests changed. There were more people than productive land available, causing high rates of unemployment in the region.

Colorado do Oeste is an example of such a town. Colorado do Oeste is in Southern Rondônia close to the Mato Grosso border. It is about one and a half hours by bus from Vilhena, the first major city entering Rondônia from Mato Grosso. Colorado itself is a town of migrants, most arriving after 1970 with the development of the road system between Cuiabá and Porto Velho. The majority of the population in Colorado comes from the South of Brazil. The municipality of Colorado do Oeste was only founded in 1973, and it wasn't recognized as an official city by law until 1981. Immigrants came seeking land which was promised to them by the government under the *Instituto de Colonização e Reforma Agrária* (INCRA), which developed a set of settlement projects to populate the Amazon region and prepare it for agricultural work. The returned immigrants whom I interviewed in Colorado are children of immigrants, that is, their parents had moved to Colorado from the South (Paraná, Rio Grande do Sul, and Santa Catarina) in search of agricultural land to start a new life in the 1970s or later.

Even though Colorado had only become an official municipality in 1981, by 1990, the children of residents of Colorado began looking to the United States as a possible place to begin a life because there wasn't sufficient industry and work in Colorado to support the number of people who had relocated there. At its height, Colorado had an estimated 53,000 people, but by 2006 the number of people in Colorado had decreased to 19,000.

Colorado is an agricultural city. Most of the industry comes from cattle farming and soy, coffee, and rice farms. In my interviews with residents of Colorado who had decided to move to the United States, I found that in Rondônia, the "fever of immigration," as it was referred to by immigrants themselves, was reported to be related to the policies put in place by the World Bank to protect the environment and stop deforestation. Many immigrants from Southern Brazil had come to Colorado when the timber industry was flourishing in Rondônia. The town was actually founded by timber farmers. When the trees had been cleared, the land became a center for cattle raising and agriculture. There were people who came to Colorado hoping to receive a plot of land for farming, but the allotted plots of land had already been given. Or, they had a plot of land, but were now being asked to reforest a portion of the land as part of environmental rehabilitation projects. Ibrahim said, "People who cut down trees here in Colorado were seen as heroes at one point. But now all the government talks about is reforestation" (Ibrahim 28 January 2009). In frustration, many children of these landowners decided to go to the United States. In fact, I was told that the *atravessador* who set up "packages" for illegal immigration through Mexico was the cousin of the governor of Colorado. There are economic benefits at the municipal level of having a percentage of the town living abroad.

Figure 6: Logging on the road from Vilhena to Colorado

Figure 7: Cattle farming in Colorado

How Immigration to New Orleans Influenced the Colorado Community

As you walk through downtown Colorado, it is easy to see the influence that money from the United States has had on the town. By looking at the immigrants who lived in New Orleans, you can get a picture of the importance of U.S. dollars to the local economy. Markinhos and his family own the largest general store in downtown Colorado. Markinhos spent three years in New Orleans and two years in Boston. The money that he earned in New Orleans allowed him to open a supermarket. He merged his supermarket with his father's smaller general store, so now the family has a larger market in a prime location, right at the central point for the bus and taxi stops on the main drag.

Figure 8: Markinho's Supermarket, Colorado do Oeste

Figure 9: Multi-Marcas Liquor Store, Colorado

Figure 10: Gabriel General Store and Ice Cream Parlor, Colorado do Oeste

Ibrahim, another immigrant who spent three years in New Orleans and six months in Boston, owns the largest event-planning business in Colorado, Depósito Multi-Marcas. He bought this company from a friend who decided to move his section of Multi-Marcas to Vilhena, Rondônia. Multi-Marcas is the largest liquor store in town. It is well organized, even importing some beers that had become favorites among Brazilian immigrants while in the United States such as Heineken and Bud Light. Ibrahim invested $150,000 in his store. He reports that $100,000 of that investment he earned through his time living in New Orleans. The remaining $50,000 he took out as a loan (Ibrahim 28 January 2009). Marcelene and Nego invested in a corner store and ice cream shop with the money that they earned in New Orleans. All of these new business owners expressed the conviction that, if they had not gone to the United States, it would have been impossible for them to get the necessary capital to open their businesses.

For many, the goal was to earn capital to invest in a particular project or simply to have a few years of work experience in the United States before beginning the next chapter in their lives. In addition to owning small businesses, return immigrants from New Orleans in Colorado work in both agriculture and the local government. Fernando invested money in a herd of cattle. Gabriel invested in milking cows. Reggi works as a private lender, using his money to provide loans with interest to other people in Colorado. These results confirm research done by Piore in *Birds of Passage*, documenting that large numbers of the new immigrants choose to migrate in order to achieve something in particular, the achievement of a target milestone. But often, target earnings and expected lifestyle improvements are never achieved, and migrants find themselves living lives quite different from what they would have imagined before immigrating. In fact, they return to find themselves living very much as they lived before (Piore 62-63).

Valdir works for the city electrical company and has a portion of his earnings saved in the bank as part of his retirement money. He says, "Life for me has not changed much since my time in the U.S. I just satisfied my curiosity of going there" (Valdir 4 February 2009). He has returned to work for the same electrical company that he worked for before he left Brazil. He also does construction jobs on the side, utilizing building skills he learned in New Orleans. He is still very frugal with money in the same way that he was before immigrating. He did not even buy a new car upon returning. He has extra money to invest in needed family expenses, but he says that he only spends money when it is absolutely necessary. His nest egg has helped his family become more secure financially, however. They no longer pass months in which they feel unsure about making all their monthly bill payments, for example, as they had before Valdir went to the U.S. In this sense, migration brought him a sense of security.

Orlis works as a public official in the sewage and water board for the government of Colorado, but he was able to pay off his mortgage on his house and fund his daughters' college expenses with the money earned in the U.S. Orlis's migration story is interesting because he is in his 60s and does not fit the profile of the average immigrant who is typically young and hoping to begin a new life. Orlis decided to move to New Orleans when he began to accrue a lot of personal debt after buying a house and sending his children through college. He realized that in his current job, there would have been no way to pay off this debt, so he asked for two years hiatus from his job, paid the $10,000 *coyote* fee, and went to the United States. Orlis's reasons for going were so that he could essentially "save" his old life that he could not support on the salary that he earned in Brazil. In fact, his daughter also immigrated to Italy, supported by her father, because they decided that

Colorado (and Brazil in general) did not provide a possible future for her. She took advantage of her Italian heritage and was able to get legal Italian resident documents.

The second reason why Orlis's story is unusual is that he went directly to New Orleans. He arrived in the United States on Sept. 14, 2005, only about 15 days after Hurricane Katrina. Friends told him that there was a lot of work to be done in New Orleans, so he went straight there, where he could be oriented to the United States by friends from Colorado who had already arrived in New Orleans. He first stayed in Motel Six, financed by an American construction company in charge of rebuilding Tulane University, while he and his friends worked on the repainting of college buildings. In the two years that he was in New Orleans, he earned enough to pay off his debts of about R$25,000 from Brazil as well as his U.S. $10,000 *coyote* fee.

The return migration experience can often be just as difficult an adjustment as the migration experience to the U.S. because the reality of the return experience rarely lives up to the dream of returning. (Just as going to America rarely lives up to the dream of going.) While there may be a time period of leisure and enjoyment with family and friends, this leisure experience is usually short-lived, as migrants soon fall into the humdrum rhythm of life in their community. For some, leisure time actually produces anxiety and unrest. Returned migrants must deal with the expectations of others who imagine them as rich because of their migration experience, often having to pay the way of friends and family who want to celebrate the return experience right along with them. Also, the transition from working 10-hour days to working every now and then is often quite difficult. Their time working in the U.S. engrained in them a feeling of never wanting to "estar parado" (be still, without work) and a need to enter into a steady routine of work to feel useful. Migrants often find themselves working hard in their new world post-migration, yet often without the monetary benefits that they had once received. They again find themselves battling the bureaucracies, the practices of corruption and the favor system, and the difficult job market that had made them dream of migration in the first place. Their time abroad, then, becomes idealized in ways that it was not while they lived the reality of immigration.

When I left Colorado do Oeste, a group of return immigrants from the United States was in the process of organizing a party in Colorado, a party at which you had to present some sort of identification from the United States for admittance. This is an ironic phenomenon because these same sorts of insider parties had happened in the U.S., except in the U.S. you had to be from Colorado do Oeste in order to attend. I am told that the 2008 party for people from Colorado do Oeste living in Boston had over 500 people on the invitation list.

Organizing a party for people with documents from the U.S. reveals the pride and prestige involved in the migration experience and in the sacrifices made in order to obtain these documents. It also speaks to the fact that the experience of migration itself is community forming. Immigrants create close relationships with other immigrants out of both necessity and longing for the place not present. These relationships continue upon returning to Brazil, though the closeness of members often wavers with the new life situation back home. Documents from the United States represent the earning of a certain amount of social status and a bond with the community of people who went through the migration experience and worked hard in order to improve their living situation back in Brazil. Those who hold documents from the United States unite behind the hard work and sacrifice needed to obtain those documents, the symbolic representations of their migratory accomplishment.

The Brazilian migrant chain to New Orleans begins in Brazil. Migrants go to the U.S. in search of their fortunes, but they are not content to leave their home communities behind when they go. The constructions of communities in Brazil, financed with money from abroad, become markers that perpetuate the myth of migration wealth and ironically root migrants closer to their hometowns through the act of leaving it. Becoming an immigrant is actually a way to invest in their futures and become part of the culture of migration in their home towns.

Brazilian Pioneers: Hurricane Katrina Marks the Brazilian Enclave in New Orleans

I ask Gardeão how he arrived in New Orleans, and he says,

> I was watching the images of Hurricane Katrina on TV. I saw the craziness that was going on there. I said to myself, "You know what, I am going to go there. I am going to help people out and make a small fortune for myself." So I got my things together, sold everything that I could sell and caught the first flight out to Mexico. (Gardeão 4 June 2009)

Gardeão began his life in the United States in New Orleans since he already had an uncle working in construction there who gave him a place to stay and a job upon arrival. He crossed the border in October of 2005. Watching the devastation of New Orleans caused by Hurricane Katrina (and perhaps even being reminded through the novela *América* of the size of the Brazilian immigrant community working in the U.S.), Gardeão felt confident that he would find work upon arrival. New Orleans was imagined as place of financial opportunity where he could help others heroically and in meaningful ways through his work.

In the saga of Katrina, at least by October, the media had begun to describe New Orleans' dire need for workers, the signing bonuses for those who were willing to move to New Orleans, and the lucrative clean-up grants in rebuilding that would become available. New Orleans policy-makers and the media imported labor and got immigrants. Contractors from all over the country came to put tarps on houses and work in demolition. And while the state may not have had the power to fully control the powerful forces (media being a major one) that support and sustain migration, state policies directly affected the size and flows of immigrant communities to New Orleans following Hurricane Katrina. Brazilians arrived in New Orleans encouraged by a desperate region-wide need for labor and a promise that scrutiny over legal documentation would be waived in the Katrina recovery zone.

The Media Lays the Foundations for the Myth

Hurricane Katrina was the first hurricane to hit the U.S. that ever received continuous 24/7 television news coverage. The images, many broadcast live, came to define what Hurricane Katrina, and inextricably New Orleans, meant for both audience members and policymakers (Dynes and Rodríguez 24). Watching the sensationalism of those images moved all of us. I remember sitting at my parents' house in North Carolina a week after the storm, sobbing uncontrollably at the images that I saw on the screen, representations of the crime committed against a city I had already come to think of as my own adopted city. Katrina, and New Orleans in particular (since the damage to New Orleans received more coverage that the rest of the Gulf South), was a prime-time feature presentation filled with the riveting images of any effective television show. There was disaster, drama, death, the criminals, the bad guys (the government), and the heroes (the workers). Usually exaggerated and often biased, these images, nonetheless, came to be part of the way that New Orleans is conceptualized now and will be known into the future.

For Brazilian immigrants, those images meant something more. For Brazilians watching from their cities, mostly cities in the U.S. such as Boston and Atlanta, those images seemed out of context for what they knew and imagined of the U.S. These immigrants had little understanding of the geographical location of New Orleans nor the social context that they were viewing; New Orleans had not yet become "their city." In the images of destruction and death, however, the media emphasized the extensive physical damage caused by Hurricane Katrina. Houses were obliterated, office buildings were destroyed, and cars and boats were swept away.

Through the media images projected in the aftermath of the storm, Brazilians saw the desperate need for help in cleanup and rebuilding and the absence of any sort of control in mediating these jobs. They saw the social chaos and a lack of authority in the face of the disaster. The images emphasized how the real first responders to the hurricane were people themselves helping one another. Brazilians began to imagine their own possibilities in this environment of reconstruction.

Along with the destruction, the media coverage focused on the fact that the government had not been present to help the people of New Orleans. FEMA, Homeland Security, and President Bush were criticized heavily for their inadequate response. The Katrina disaster was defined as a manmade disaster because of the anarchy and lack of order caused by the failure of government. There seemed to be no one in charge, no one making decisions. President Bush suspended the Helms Burton Act and, along with it, the need for employers and police officers to check personal documents, since many New Orleanians had lost papers in the flood. Moreover, the OSHA regulations that should have guaranteed baseline safety procedures in the workplace were nixed. These measures were taken in the hopes of getting the rebuilding process started quicker, yet it also became a way in which immigrants imagined that New Orleans provided more opportunity for their success through the lack of order and regulation present in the disaster zone. FEMA t-shirts began to go on sale downtown that said, "FEMA: Find Every Mexican Available." Brazilians, the invisible minority, moved down silently to try their luck as well.

The city seemed (and for a window of time was) unregulated. People made their own rules. For Brazilians watching, New Orleans seemed to be a place where self-starters, those not afraid to brave the chaos, had an opportunity to find never-ending possibilities of work. After all, it was estimated that close to 80% of New Orleans was flooded. Television helped create important myths about New Orleans that motivated pioneer Brazilians to move down, and television also shaped how immigrants interpreted New Orleans as a place unlike other places in the U.S. They began to imagine that perhaps New Orleans was "their city" in the sense that perhaps this could be where they would accomplish their financial dream and find their place in the U.S.

Pioneers: Stages of Post-Katrina Reconstruction

Before describing the pioneer Brazilian immigrant's arrival in New Orleans at length, I would like to outline, briefly, the phases of post-Katrina recovery that have been laid out by Katherine Donato (227-

232):

Phase 1: Immediately post-Katrina, lasting until November 2005. This was the phase that required the most limited amount of skill, when health risks were high, and when key tasks were cleanup, initial removal of debris, and demolition. Along with spontaneous migration, there was recruited labor that came from other states. In terms of recruited Brazilians, many of these workers came from Kansas, Florida, and Georgia. This was the time period in which ideas about the prospects for life as an immigrant in New Orleans were first established. In my research with Brazilians, I heard the first phase described as the "moneymaking" phase. Though the labor market was volatile since it was relatively unstructured, those immigrants who made enough money in New Orleans to return quickly to Brazil usually worked in New Orleans during this initial catastrophic time period.

During **Phase 2, from November 2005 until March 2006,** there was a diversification in the employers and contractors working in New Orleans. Many of the same activities of debris removal and demolition were still present, but this phase became unique because the subcontracting agreements for completing these jobs became less and less formal. Contractors would sometimes subcontract out to other workers who would then subcontract out other workers. Those workers at the end of the chain often did not even know who the employer was that they were actually working for, only having contact with their immediate subcontractor, often a migrant worker himself. During this time period, there was an emergence of migrant-owned subcontracting businesses. These informal contracts, with little regulation, resulted in an increase of worker abuses because there were no legal documents signed to regulate workers' rights.

Phase 3, from March 2006 until 2009, is when New Orleans emerged from being a recovery zone into a reconstruction zone. Recovery activities of Phase 1 and Phase 2 were still present, yet there was slightly more attempt to regulate and prevent exploitation of workers as the urgency of rebuilding slowed.

I would add that there is another phase in post-Katrina recovery construction beginning in 2009 and influenced by the current economic recession. Brazilians often comment that 2009 was their most difficult year financially. While in all phases there have been inconsistencies in labor demand in an often chaotic labor market, 2009 was the year in which it was markedly more difficult for all to find steady construction work in New Orleans. In 2010, job prospects increased slightly, but migrant workers still found themselves dealing with a conspicuous slow-down in the New Orleans construction market.

Brazilians in New Orleans Pre-Katrina

When Brazilians first began moving to New Orleans in large numbers in 2005 after Katrina, there was not a Brazilian enclave present in the city. According to the 2000 U.S. census, the entire Brazilian population of the state of Louisiana was then only 689. This figure may be slightly higher if we include undocumented immigrants and also acknowledge that many Brazilians' identities may have been subsumed by the awkwardness of the U.S. Census when enumerating Brazilians. Brazilians are often hesitant to check Hispanic on the census forms because they are not Spanish speakers. For example, the 2000 U.S. Census estimated that there were 212,428 Brazilians living in the entire United States, although Fausto Mendes da Rocha of the Brazilian Immigrant Center in Boston estimates that there were 231,000 Brazilians living in Massachusetts alone in 2003 and something like 1.2 million Brazilians living in the United States. In any case, the number of Brazilians in Louisiana prior to Katrina was extremely low. The majority of these Brazilians in New Orleans pre-Katrina were professionals and did not make up a significant part of the manual labor workforce.

Riba, one of the few pre-Katrina Brazilian immigrants who has lived and worked in the bricking industry in New Orleans since 1998, confirms that there were very few Brazilians living in New Orleans and working with him in construction before Katrina. Riba had been hired by a construction company in Florida in 1998 to build Harrah's Casino, the Riverwalk, and the Convention Center. The first Brazilians living in New Orleans who were working in construction (probably fewer than 100) all seem to be connected to these late 1990s building projects. Riba says, "There were about 70 Brazilians living in New Orleans before Katrina. Of the 70, I knew about 65 of them. I could show up at their houses without calling first. All of them. Even the university students" (3 April 2009). Riba's numbers probably do not account for the total number of Brazilians in the area, but it does give an idea of the small size of the pre-Katrina Brazilian enclave community in comparison to the Brazilian community post-Katrina.

These pre-Katrina Brazilians rarely became migrant hubs of the community after Katrina because they did not actively call Brazilians to New Orleans from other cities. They did not have the contacts in these cities and they also did not have the social or economic capital to be of much use in financially assisting recent immigrants. Also, the bricking industry was relatively superfluous immediately following the storm when demolition crews, roofers, and painters were most necessary. Many of those pre-Katrina Brazilian workers who had been working in the bricking industry found themselves not working in their normal field of expertise for the first few months after the hurricane. They worked in demolition, sheet rocking, and painting until the bricking industry returned again to the city.

Those few pre-Katrina residents who did have economic capital, however, were able to invest in houses in flooded zones of the city, buying and then employing other Brazilians in property renovation. They were able to buy houses at bargain prices in parts of the city that had flooded. Those who planned on staying in New Orleans long-term saw this as a great investment since they could do much of the reconstruction themselves and then resell properties for a higher price to make a profit. Many Brazilians, both pre-Katrina residents and post-Katrina pioneers, invested in the Chalmette, Arabi and Gentilly neighborhoods, areas that had experienced flooding but that were rebuilding at a steady pace. These areas have also attracted Brazilians to live because of steady work in construction jobs in these areas and because these neighborhoods provide a calmer and safer environment for families with children than downtown New Orleans. Joana commented to me that she and her husband were eager to buy a house in Chalmette for two reasons: First, they could buy a house for a lot less money than if they were to buy a house in the city of New Orleans. Second, because she has a young son, she likes having a large backyard in a neighborhood where she feels it is safe for her son to play outside without worries of violence or heavy traffic.

Pre-Katrina immigrants who had an understanding about life in New Orleans did become important contacts for everything from figuring out the hospital system to learning about Brazilian cultural events in the city. Some pre-Katrina immigrants were able to take advantage of this position in order to work as cultural ambassadors or as unofficial employment agencies for recently arrived Brazilians. The Hurricane opened up new possibilities for them.

Gege, for example, from Rio de Janeiro, had lived in New Orleans since 2001. She arrived following the father of her child, a New Orleanian whom she had met and fallen in love with during his vacation in Rio. They were no longer romantically involved, but she felt that living in the U.S. could offer more opportunities for her daughter. After Hurricane Katrina, she began using both her language skills and her knowledge of New Orleans to work as a subcontractor for Brazilians who were arriving to work in construction. She herself had never worked in construction, but because she spoke English and because of her connections to the New Orleans social networks, she was able to find jobs for others and receive a commission on those jobs.

> I started working in construction because I started translating for Brazilians on the job sites. Then they said to me, "Wow, you could make a lot of money doing this because we don't have anyone to translate for us. We will give you a commission if you will find us jobs." Through helping to translate, I also met and started dating an American contractor. So, I started to get people to work on houses for him. Later he left New Orleans and asked me if I wanted to take his job. I didn't know anything about construction but he said that he would teach me. He taught me how to measure square feet and all of that. Of course I could do it in theory, but it was much different in practice. I had to fall down many times to be able to learn. Also, I would contract Brazilians. Since people were desperate to earn money, they would tell me that they knew how to do everything when really they didn't. They would do the job, but they would do it all wrong. It was a lot of pressure, so I stopped being a contractor (Gege 8 July 2009).

Although Gege has stopped her work as a contractor, she still uses her language skills to work as a subcontractor with the contacts that she has already made. She adds a small commission fee on top of the construction estimates that the Brazilian workers give to her when she receives a job. She also continues to help Brazilians access needed resources around the city. Brazilian immigration to post-Katrina New Orleans has completely changed both her social and financial life.

Brazilians' Arrival in Post-Katrina New Orleans

So who were the pioneer Brazilians who arrived post-Katrina since there was not a substantial community of Brazilians pre-Katrina? Estimates of the number of undocumented post-Katrina Brazilians who had arrived in New Orleans by the fall of 2006, according to Brazilians themselves, range from 1,500 to 10,000. The honorary New Orleans Brazilian consulate established after the storm estimated the number at several thousand during the summer of 2006. As I mentioned in the introduction, from my own estimates based on Brazilian immigrant surveys, the number of Brazilian satellite dishes installed in New Orleans after Katrina, and my own personal experience with the community, I would put the number at about 5,000-8,000 during the height of Brazilian immigration in 2006 and 2007.

The majority of the Brazilian immigrants who arrived to work in reconstruction in New Orleans did not come to New Orleans directly from Brazil, but from another city in the United States. As we have already seen in Chapter 1, a large portion of the first wave of immigrants to New Orleans arrived from Boston, Atlanta and Pompano Beach, Fla. Although some did arrive in the U.S. by overstaying a tourist visa, the majority of Brazilians who relocated to New Orleans had recently come (within the last three years) to the United States, undocumented, and through Mexico. The first wave of immigrants to New Orleans was not as fully established in previous immigrant communities as those who had been in the U.S. for longer periods of time. Many of the first-responding Brazilian immigrants were less skilled in construction than their compatriots in established communities in other parts of the country who had been in the U.S., and in the construction industry, for a longer time.

This is not to say that all pioneer Brazilian immigrants to New Orleans were untrained construction workers. Especially those migrants who came to New Orleans from Florida often came with contracts from the construction company that they had worked for in Florida, companies that had been recruited by both the state and federal governments to help in New Orleans. These large companies that were hired from Florida and Atlanta to do demolition and cleaning work were themselves unknowing hubs in Brazilian migration as well, since many of the workers decided to stay after their contract ended because they saw the possibilities for employment as independent workers or subcontractors in the Gulf South. In general, Brazilian pioneers to New Orleans were not established in construction in other areas of the country. If they had been, they would have been comfortable enough financially in their previous cities not to pull up stakes and move to a chaotic place with uncertain work opportunities. Many pioneers came to New Orleans because they had found it difficult to find a job in the U.S. city where they had first located, so moving to the unknown situation of New Orleans with no previous contact was a risk that they were more likely to make than those immigrants who were more established with a regular job in another city.

The Brazilian Pioneer Stories of Post-Katrina Call More Down

A Brazilian worker who arrived in New Orleans in December 2005 came down after hearing from other Brazilians that New Orleans was a friendly place for immigrants and offered many opportunities to work.

> I was living in Orlando. All the Brazilians there were coming here [New Orleans] because there were a lot of opportunities to work. The pay right after the city closed was good… in September (2005) people were earning a lot of money because the government was paying the insurance companies and the insurance companies were paying to rebuild the city. The pay was much more than we were receiving in Orlando or in Miami (Rosa 8 July 2009).

Many Brazilians moved down to New Orleans and moved onto the couches and even onto the kitchen floors of the houses of other Brazilian immigrants who had made the journey first. Since housing was scarce, living arrangements were often in tight quarters. I remember visiting a house in 2006 in which a Brazilian immigrant was even sleeping in the bathtub. Other Brazilians who came down to New Orleans did not stay in houses at all, but stayed in the many tent communities for recovery workers throughout the city.

Frank, a Brazilian immigrant who lived for a year in New Orleans, but then returned to Somerville and Newark before returning to Brazil, said,

> I arrived in New Orleans about three months after the water went

> down. There were lots of houses to rebuild and I lived in a tent near the Wal-Mart on Tchoupitoulas... There were about 15 of us who came down. Each in their own car because you need a car to work. Some people I knew had already come down. They called and told me that things are not pretty down here, but there is a lot of work... We went down to New Orleans out of curiosity, not to move there. We went to pass the winter. We left Boston and bought some tents on the way down. One to sleep in and the other to take showers and change in. Living in the tents was a party. People would come around every day and give us a food box (Frank 3 January 2009).

Frank's story is a common one among the many Brazilian immigrants to New Orleans in the months following Katrina. They often came down in groups after seeing images on television or hearing from a friend or work acquaintance that there were opportunities for work in New Orleans. They came down not knowing where they were going or exactly what to expect. They simply followed a GPS, such as Frank did, or were led by someone who already knew the route. New Orleans was imagined as a place of adventure and camaraderie.

The importance of the GPS system in these founding days of the Brazilian immigrant community in New Orleans should not be underestimated. The GPS system was an important technological advantage for Brazilian pioneers to New Orleans, reconfiguring how immigrant relationships functioned. GPS systems allowed immigrants to gain much more autonomy. With a GPS system, Brazilians, who often had little spatial understanding of the city, could simply type in an address to get around to job sites, to visit friends, to explore areas of the city, or to go to important legal meetings.

Also, it is of significance that Frank mentions that he went down "out of curiosity," highlighting the fact that the New Orleans experience was imagined as unique from his normal immigrant routine in Boston. The fact that he wanted to go to New Orleans as a place to "spend the winter," makes it sound as though he were going on a work-vacation. Although motivated by work and the fact that the construction market slows down in Boston during the winter, New Orleans was an opportunity to see and explore new sights. Boston was imagined as the serious Brazilian enclave space and New Orleans post-Katrina as the exotic and adventurous other place. Even in the difficulties of living there, the surreal quality of the whole experience felt festive to him.

The fact that many immigrants to New Orleans had lived in an extensive Brazilian community such as Boston influenced their perceptions of New Orleans. Boston, for example, is home to a Brazilian Immigrant Center, one of over a dozen associations specifically targeted to bringing services to the Brazilian community there (Martes 7). Boston also has many established entrepreneurial ventures such as *lanchonetes* (sandwich shops) and *padarias* (bakeries) run by Brazilians. New Orleans had no such Brazilian immigrant-generated infrastructure set up when pioneer Brazilians moved down to work in reconstruction. These differences in social capital created by an established Brazilian community in a place like Boston were important points of comparison that helped to make New Orleans feel as if it was a unique and adventurous destination.

Joaquim: A Vignette of a Pioneer

Overall, the pioneer Brazilians to New Orleans post-Katrina revealed that they moved down because the imagined idea of the success attainable through immigration did not materialize into reality for them in their previous cities of residency. Either they were having a hard time finding regular employment or winter in the Northeast meant a slowdown in their earning potential. New Orleans was seen as a new dreamland of employment possibilities, an untapped informal construction market for those willing to take the risk.

Joaquim (who was 19 years old at the time) was one of the pioneer Brazilian immigrants to come to New Orleans, arriving in September of 2005. He says that he crossed the border from Mexico and first went to Boston because two friends who once lived on his same street in Manhuaçu, Minas Gerais now lived in Boston and could help him adjust. Joaquim comes from a middle-class family. His father earns R$1,200 a month working for the Rio Doce bus company, and his stepmother is the manager of a furniture store in Manhuaçu. When I asked him why he had decided to go to the United States he said that he didn't like to work for other people. He would never be able to own the car that he now owns in Brazil (he returned to Brazil in 2008) if he was only earning his father's salary.

Joaquim arrived in Boston in the summer of 2005. But when he got there, he found that his friend Cristiano had been injured on the job and had not been able to work for six months. Meanwhile, his friend Jacson had just lost his job with a construction company. Finding work in Boston was more difficult than Joaquim had imagined. In August 2005, frustrated with his situation, Joaquim called his father and asked him if he could buy a plane ticket so Joaquim could return to Brazil. Joaquim had not earned enough money working in the U.S. to even afford a plane ticket home at the time. All was set for him to return to Brazil when Hurricane Katrina suddenly hit New Orleans.

Joaquim decided that he would drive down to evaluate the work opportunities there as a last resort before returning to Brazil. He hoped to be able to make enough money to at least pay off his *coyote* fee. His friends Jacson and Cristiano did not want to go down to New Orleans at first (even though they were still unemployed in Boston) because they thought it was too risky. The footage they saw on the television showed New Orleans as a disaster zone. They were renting a house in Allston, Mass. and they did not want to move and leave all of their contacts behind with no way of knowing if things would work out in New Orleans.

So Joaquim went down with a group of five other Brazilian acquaintances he had encountered in Boston. They found a house to rent in Uptown New Orleans. When he arrived, the house had no electricity. He spent over a month taking cold showers and being unable to cook his own food. But soon after arriving in New Orleans, he started working every day, even though he had no previous experience working in construction. Joaquim is very personable, even with limited English skills, so he began getting jobs and then contracting them out to other Brazilians. He called his friends back in Boston and told them that there were many opportunities for work and they soon followed him down. In New Orleans, Joaquim was able to satisfy his wish of "not working for others" by becoming a subcontractor. The money he earned allowed him to continue to be independently employed now that he has returned to Brazil, after only three years in the U.S. He has invested his money earned in New Orleans into opening a *jogo do bicho* operation in his hometown. (*Jogo do bicho* is an illegal, though highly popular, lottery game in Brazil that can be very profitable.) He now has his own family and does not think of returning to the U.S.

Immigrant Subcontractors

In the chaos of the construction market post-Katrina, many undocumented immigrants found themselves working as subcontractors as Joaquim did. This meant that there were not always written contracts signed between contractors, subcontractors, and workers. Some of the immigrants did not sign for fear of deportation or because they did not hold the proper legal documents. Others simply did not sign because, in the aftermath of the storm, construction needed to happen so quickly that there was no time to put the proper paperwork together. Many simply didn't know how to ask for one. Contracts were confirmed between contractor and subcontractor simply through word of mouth or a handshake. With no written and legal binds to the job, undocumented subcontractors were at the whim of the contractors. Those who did not take on the legal position of a subcontractor (signing documents, getting licensed) were in a position where they simply appeared to attain social mobility without really moving up. They remained completely dependant on how and when the general contractor would pay them, and they became very vulnerable because they assumed the risk of paying their workers regardless of whether or not they themselves had been paid. The workers under these subcontractors were then doubly vulnerable, dependent on both the honesty of the general contractor and the honesty of the subcontractor who employed them.

The logic behind becoming a subcontractor is that it is a position by which one could presumably make a profit from simply "signing the deal." Thus, it is considered a position of privilege and freedom, allowing subcontractors to work more than one job simultaneously. Yet many— in fact, most— undocumented subcontractors do not actually sign anything. The fact that many do not sign legal contracts for work means that there is the potential to find themselves in great debt if the general contractor does not follow through with his word, since the subcontractor should take on the responsibility of paying his workers whether he, himself, is paid or not. (His workers have made a pact with him and not with the general contractor.) There are also many cases where immigrant subcontractors (and workers) have been paid with the barter system instead of in cash, receiving a car or tools in compensation for the completion of the job because the contractor could not pay. Because the immigrant is in a position of favor rather than a legal position (no documents were signed), there is little that can be done.

In a description of how he ended up coming to Uptown New Orleans, one Brazilian interviewee describes his relationship with a Brazilian subcontractor:

> Right after the hurricane, Jorge's wife brought about 100 or more people down from Boston. Jorge had come down right after Katrina to put tarps on roofs. He speaks English OK, so he knew that there was a lot of work to do. So Jorge's wife put an announcement in the Brazilian stores in Boston saying that her husband needed workers down in New Orleans. She charged $500 a person to come down in the car. She had places set up for us to stay. The house was $1,600 and the other $1,200 to split between those who came down. There were eight of us when I first arrived so it was really cheap. Once you were organized in New Orleans you were expected to find your own place so that new people could come, but there was no pressure to leave. I wanted to get out soon because no one else in the house knew how to find banks, stores, and things, so I ended up having to do everything. I called up my brother who was still in Boston and told him to come down. He came down with a car full of people that he charged $500 a person as well and we got a house together on Broadway [a few blocks away, still in Uptown] with some other friends (Glauber 13 November 2006).

The very first Brazilians to arrive in the arrangement described above came down in October 2005. Jorge had come down, only days after the storm, to begin looking for construction jobs. The immigrants who moved down to New Orleans following this subcontractor describe the conditions of this arrangement as being mildly exploitative. The $500 fee, for example, bought nothing more than a live GPS system and a guarantee that they would have a place to stay upon arrival in New Orleans. Their housing conditions, however, were far from adequate. There was no working electricity for the first month that they lived in the house. They could not take hot showers, they could not heat their food, nor did they have lights.

The second reason for paying the $500 fee to be driven down to New Orleans was the promise of a job with Jorge's construction company once arriving. Jorge, however, did not own a construction company since he was undocumented himself and did not hold a social security number. He worked independently as a subcontractor to get jobs and then subcontracted out to the Brazilians whom he had brought down. At times, he was not able to receive enough contracts to be able to provide work for all of the men. He had no prior experience as an employer of other workers in Boston, since his possibility of working as a subcontractor presented itself only after moving to New Orleans (Jorge 20 June 2009). Those workers that had come down with him often felt exploited. "He blew us off. He didn't pay us, or paid us late" (Fabio December 13 2007).

Stories such as these are common. For example, Jaca commented that he came down to New Orleans from Boston with a group of twenty-four workers about twenty days after Hurricane Katrina. A Brazilian subcontractor with a false work visa had recruited them. This subcontractor rented a house for them near Esplanade and Claiborne, an area heavily affected by flooding and close to the French Quarter. Jaca spent his first months in New Orleans working in the French Quarter and the Central Business District. The subcontractor paid the first two months rent and the workers were to pay him back through the work that they provided for his company. Jaca reported that there were many times when he was not paid for his work, even after paying off his housing fee. Jaca constantly had to go to the home of the subcontractor and demand that he receive his payment, often to be told that there was not any money (Jaca 13 May 2009).

The work environment in post-Katrina reconstruction was unique in that it provided an opportunity for undocumented immigrants to take on a subcontracting role. This situation, however, also provided opportunity for exploitation because of the informality of the social and financial contracts. Many of the work-related financial problems between Brazilian subcontractors and Brazilian workers were caused largely because these subcontractors were simply not equipped with the financial or the social skills necessary to undertake the role that they had assumed in the reconstruction market.

In the interview about working for Jorge, for example, the interviewee comments that he came down to work for Jorge because Jorge spoke English and could get jobs. Jorge's English, however, is very minimal. Especially when he first moved down to New Orleans, Jorge hardly spoke more than the basics of construction terms. To this day, he still does not read or write in English, necessary skills if one hopes to be the head contractor for a construction company as Jorge not only hoped to be, but also marketed himself as, to the workers that followed him down to New Orleans. There was also mismanagement of money among subcontractors, who sometimes invested in their building projects in Brazil before paying their workers or kept poor records of overtime hours and the prices of materials. At times, this was because they were unscrupulous, but often it was only because they had no experience in keeping records and there was no official system that had been set in place to enforce good business practices.

What this means is that, overwhelmingly, work conflicts were linked with the volatility of the construction market in New Orleans. While there was a lot of work to be done in the city, who received the contract and who would pay workers for the labor became points of dispute because they were often two different people. For example, Brazilians who received subcontracting work and contracted other workers often found themselves mired in a situation where they couldn't pay their workers because the contractor who had given them the initial job was not able to pay because the money was held up in insurance or in governmental disputes. Sometimes corrupt contractors simply took advantage of the unregulated labor market, neglecting to pay undocumented workers who would be less likely to complain. It became difficult to decide the source of the workers' rights violation. So, while for some immigrants, New Orleans became a place where Brazilians earned more than they had ever earned in construction, it also became a place where many suffered serious wage abuses and had little to no public health and safety regulations. Most Brazilians can recount at least one story about when they worked a job for which they did not receive payment, though the frequency of these occurrences varies from person to person. These stories all became part of the myth of New Orleans. The city signified the possibilities of transformation in their social and economic status, but this transformation was often marked by greed and even trickery as well as by idealism.

Hubs and Spokes

The way that transnational (and even transregional) immigration networks influence patterns of migration has been illustrated by Vilna Bashi's "hub and spoke model," which develops out of the new economics model of immigration.[14] The "hub and spoke" model explains how select veteran migrants (hubs) act as migration experts and send repeatedly for newcomers (spokes) to come join them in their new location. The hub that migrates first is usually at a more advanced financial and educational level than the later spokes. The hubs, because of having social and education skills to make the transition to the new environment smoother, are able to collect information on how to migrate and use this knowledge and their reputation to help newcomers (Bashi 77). Bashi focuses her study on West Indian social networks in New York, London, and the West Indies and notes that, in the case of West Indians, hubs are of a higher educational and social status than the general population of migrants. Bashi comments on how education is seen as paramount to being considered a successful hub among West Indian migrants (Bashi 94).[15] In Bashi's study, West Indian hubs also kept ties with those they helped, making sure that the network remained a community long after the initial migration experience. West Indian hubs took on the role of the sponsor, a role that requires much effort and commitment and is costly in both time and money. The later migrants, "the spokes," often lived cost-free with their hubs until they could become established.

Hub and spoke relationships were formed under much different circumstances for Brazilians post-Katrina. The hubs of the Brazilian community in New Orleans were, by and large, those resourceful immigrants who took a chance and came down from other areas of the country right after the storm, realized that there was an opportunity

[14] Under normal circumstances following the new economics migration model, the first people to migrate as immigrant pioneers to a new location tend to be in the upper to middle ranges of the income hierarchy in a given location. According to Massey, an enclave community usually emerges when this initial wave of elite immigrants who possess a significant amount of financial, human, social, and cultural capital concentrate disproportionately in one urban area. As this happens, they then establish new business enterprises and support the migration of successive waves of lower-status but aspiring immigrants from the same country. The prospects for enclave formation are especially enhanced if these initial immigrants are well educated and possess organizational or business skills (human capital), or if they have access to savings, credit, or government assistance (financial capital) (Massey "Why Does Immigration Occur?" 39).

[15] Brazilian hubs in New Orleans did not seem to imagine formal education as a particular priority of their immigrant experience as hubs. There were some immigrants whose motivation for coming was to help send a child or a family member to college in Brazil, but rarely did Brazilians see their own time in the U.S. as an opportunity for intellectual enrichment.

to make money out of the labor demand in New Orleans, and began recruiting other Brazilians to come down and join them through their contacts in previous cities in the U.S. Although these immigrants played the role of the hub, they did not have the same social capital detailed in descriptions of hubs in Bashi's account of the hub-spoke relationships in the West Indian communities. Acting as a hub was more economic opportunity than an exercise in bringing friends and family members together in the immediate months following the hurricane.

Following these initial pioneers, Brazilians with more stable construction jobs in other areas of the city arrived in New Orleans a few months later once they saw the potential for their business to grow in New Orleans. The second wave of Brazilian immigrants, especially if they held legal work documents, spoke English, and had experience in construction, also became new "hubs" of the Brazilian community in New Orleans. Because there was not a significant network of Brazilian community centers, stores, or churches to perform the work of a support group in the first year after the storm, these migrants with some knowledge of U.S. social and legal culture found themselves quickly serving an important role as contacts for the Brazilian community for employment and for social life.

Characteristic "Men's Work" in Post-Katrina New Orleans

The fact that there was not a previous community of Brazilians in New Orleans to provide much economic or social security meant that Brazilian immigrants often decided to branch out on their own. The recovery zone provided the space for all workers to take on a leadership role in construction if they took the initiative. Brazilians, who were new in the U.S. and had never been in a position to get construction jobs directly, had the opportunity to become self-starters in New Orleans. They went house to house, asking people who they saw rebuilding and cleaning up their houses if they needed any construction work done. Those who were organized and professional and who also had the good fortune to meet someone who needed work done on his or her house (and had the money to pay for it) were able to set up a small independent business. Through word of mouth between clients, these individual workers were able to keep themselves relatively busy working from job to job in the months immediately following the storm. They worked gutting houses, putting tarps on roofs, helping

New Orleanians move into and out of houses, and rebuilding.

The most successful Brazilians in the construction industry in New Orleans today are those people who were most successful at networking with Americans, better at using the computer, putting out a website (or at least publishing their telephone number and the services that they could provide over the Internet), searching for jobs over the Internet, and creating fliers and business cards. They were able to accrue larger numbers of contracts and, thus, were able to subcontract out to other Brazilians.

Brazilians Network for Work through Their Community

In general, Brazilians did not (and to this day, do not) go to day labor pick-up sites to look for jobs in New Orleans. Many Hispanics in New Orleans station themselves at busy traffic intersections in Orleans Parish, waiting to be picked up for day labor, in numbers that can amount to several dozen at any given time. This is a highly conspicuous form of self-advertising and can at times be problematic— as illustrated by the Lee Circle raid in New Orleans that took place on March 18, 2006. Some forty immigrants were caught and jailed by federal agents in a raid on what was one of the most popular and public spots in New Orleans for Spanish-speaking Latinos to find employment. While other immigration raids have followed, this was the first and perhaps the most conspicuous, given that it took place in a central location known to locals and tourists alike.

However, such "raids" more closely resemble a PR campaign to combat anti-immigrant sentiment. Indeed, officials with Immigration and Customs Enforcement stated that the events of March 18 occurred because of complaints from local businesses around Lee Circle that those people waiting for jobs seemed as if they were mere loiterers and were distracting to their businesses. One official was quoted as saying that concern was about the loitering "bad guy" rather than the "sheetrocker" (Varney). A federal spokesperson for another raid stated, "This is for people who actually are ordered to leave the country but have melted back into society" (Rainey). But raids on day labor sites hardly apply to Brazilians, since their strategies of gaining employment differ from those of many other Latino groups. In the months following Katrina, Brazilians tended to find work within their own enclave or by proactively networking house-to-house rather than waiting at day labor sites. This may be one of the reasons why Brazilians seem to express less fear of immigration raids than their Hispanic counterparts in New Orleans. They were less conspicuous targets of anti-immigration sentiment. Brazilians remained relatively invisible, not self-identifying as Hispanic.

Brazilians also reported that they earn more than their Hispanic counterparts, and, in surveys conducted at the Brazilian Consulate in New Orleans, Beth Fussell confirms Brazilians reported higher pay than their Hispanic coworkers (Fussell "Hurricane Chasers" 3). When asked why Brazilians thought that they received higher wages than Hispanic workers, Brazilians often replied that, as a group, they were more hardworking than both the Hispanics and the Americans that they worked with.

It is problematic to claim that working hard and being honest are ideals that are characteristic of Brazilian immigrants, (or indeed of any ethnic or national group), but this comment reveals a truth about how Brazilians actively constructed an image of their ethnic enclave in post-Katrina New Orleans in ways that separated themselves from Hispanics. One of the most highly-regarded compliments within the Brazilian community in New Orleans is to be regarded as a hard worker. The act of work itself is valued, even if it means using informal Brazilian labor market chains and subcontracting to find it. This claim is a tactic used to carve a niche within a competitive immigrant marketplace and becomes empowering as an imagined idea of Brazilian workers' own lives and circumstances as being unique from other immigrant groups, even if the claim is embellished or unfaithful to reality.

Post-Katrina Construction Market Employs Workers Regardless of Skill

Brazilians imagined New Orleans after Katrina as a place where this hard work was particularly valued because of the overwhelming urgency of rebuilding. It was a place for those starting out in the U.S. to have an opportunity to "make it" in America. In 2005-2006, Brazilian pioneers reported that anyone who was willing to work was able to find a job working in construction, regardless of skill or experience. I asked a Brazilian who had been working in construction in New Orleans for four years if he had learned the trade in Brazil. His response was, "In Brazil I only knew about cows!" There were many interviews in which Brazilians reported that they learned how to work in construction in New Orleans. Brazilians reported that they felt that, in the recovery zone, the quality of painting and refinishing was not as important as it had been in other areas of the country because homeowners in New Orleans were more preoccupied with getting the job done quickly so that they could move back home or so that they could rent out their house for extra income.

Among those Brazilians who had considered themselves "professionals" in the construction industry in other parts of the country, this situation was a point of irritation. They saw men who had never worked in construction earning the same for their labor as they did. One Brazilian said, "Painting in Boston is much more refined, much more correct. For those Brazilians who need to learn a trade, New Orleans is better. There is more opportunity. Painting in Boston is more professional" (Gol 30 December 2008).

Another Brazilian commented,

> The first couple of months right after the hurricane, the work was really good in New Orleans. But then things fell out. There was a lot less work and the price that people got paid for their work fell. In Boston, no. In Boston you are paid for your professionalism. If you are good at doing your job, then you have a certain price. If you are just beginning or if you aren't good at doing your job, then you have another price. In New Orleans, this isn't the case. In New Orleans, everyone gets paid the same amount. This doesn't work. I would never accept the amount of pay that I earned per hour in New Orleans in Boston. I worked in a hotel in New Orleans when I first arrived. Only my boss and me were professionals, so the two of us went to work on the bathroom because that is the most difficult room to paint. Someone who had never picked up a paintbrush before got paid the same amount of money that we did. It made us angry. We thought to ourselves, man, we are professionals. How can all of these people be getting paid the same amount of money as us?... Most of the painters in New Orleans would not pass in a professionalism test in my company in Boston. They say that they are painters, but they really aren't" (Frank 3 January 2009).

But those Brazilians who had recently arrived in the U.S. had a different perspective than Frank about the opportunities granted in New Orleans.

> In Boston, when you first arrive there, they [other Brazilians] think that because you are new that you don't know how to do a good job. Really they know that you are doing a good job but they don't want to admit it because that means that they will have to pay you more and they don't want to have to pay you more (Alberto 30 December 2008).

While Frank seemed to think that he was under-recognized because he was paid the same as a "non-skilled laborer," those Brazilians who had less experience working in construction such as Alberto felt as though they were given the chance to work and earn a fair wage in New Orleans in the first months after Hurricane Katrina.

Business Opportunities to Meet Brazilian Needs in New Orleans

As the Brazilian community became more extensive, Brazilian men also began working in jobs to meet the needs of the emerging Brazilian enclave in New Orleans. Brazilians are working as car salesmen, as mechanics and in body shops, and as computer repairmen exclusively for other Brazilians. There is now even a Brazilian dentist in New Orleans. (Though this practice is a clandestine operation because he is not officially licensed in the U.S., or in Brazil for that matter. He was a dentist assistant in Brazil. Construction is his official job, but, if you need a tooth pulled, he will do it for you from his home office.)

The story of Edmilson Navalha poignantly illustrates how Katrina offered a space for immigrants with little social capital and little experience in the U.S. to become small business owners in Louisiana by opening businesses marketed specifically for the Brazilian community. Navalha arrived in the United States in 2004. He came to New Orleans from Georgia in December 2006 to work in the construction industry. Upon arrival, he noticed that there were very few open restaurants and no restaurants that catered to the Brazilian workers in the city. His wife had come down with him to New Orleans, so she began cooking and making to-go boxes for Brazilian workers. First, she began selling lunch to the men working with her husband. But the business quickly began to expand. In fact, these lunch boxes became famous among the Brazilian community. So many people were interested in buying lunches that Edmilson stopped working in construction to be able to help his wife make food. As more people discovered their service, not only were the Navalhas taking food to job sites, but Brazilians would also come to their house at all hours of the day to pick up food. The quantity of people coming in and out of the house brought attention from the neighbors. The local police even came to investigate them under suspicion of dealing drugs since so many people were coming in and out of the house. On this occasion, the Navalhas were told that they were not allowed to sell from their residence; they would have to open a commercial business if they wanted to continue selling food.

Navalha had no prior experience opening a business in the United States, but he rented an office space for one year, hoping to convert it into a kitchen and open a restaurant. He claims that he invested $50,000 into the renting and renovations of the office space, but he only lost money in this business venture because the construction codes for restaurant use in the U.S. meant extensive remodeling of the space and he was unable to secure the necessary permits. His year contract ended, he was never able to open his restaurant, and he almost went bankrupt. All the money that he had earned the first two years in New Orleans had been invested into this failed business attempt.

Before Navalha had left Georgia, however, he was in a job site accident. A cement block fell on his thumb, crushing the bones beyond repair. At the end of his first unsuccessful year at opening a small business in New Orleans, he finally received $52,000 in worker's compensation for the accident in Georgia. That money gave him the capital to invest in a second attempt at opening a restaurant. He had learned a lot about the type of building that he should rent to lower his costs and he decided to purchase a space in Kenner, La. that had once been a Honduran *pupuseria* because the building already had the proper restaurant permits. He had to buy kitchen equipment such as refrigerators, a stove, and a dishwasher, but the main infrastructure (proper drainage and ventilation) was already in place. Navalha did not have a social security number or a Louisiana driver's license, both necessary documents to open a business in Kenner, so he arranged for an American friend whom he had met through his construction work to register the business in his name and the restaurant opened in February of 2007.

The business is going well today. In 2009, Navalha expanded the restaurant to make room for more seating. In 2010, he bought a second building to open an even larger restaurant that was a Brazilian *churrascaria* (outlet for Brazilian barbecue served on skewers) by day and a Brazilian nightclub by night. "Navalha's Brazilian Restaurant" is an illustration of the entrepreneurial ventures of Brazilians after Hurricane Katrina. What started as a supplementary side business for his wife while he worked in reconstruction turned into the main source of income for the family because of the needs of the emerging Brazilian community.

Today, there are still a few people who sell Brazilian meals at jobsites, but nothing like the number there were in 2005-2006. It is not as profitable anymore because workers have more options for eating, job sites are less concentrated than they had been right after the storm, and American restaurants and the Brazilian stores (which also sell meals and snacks) have taken over the role of selling Brazilian lunch food. Brazilian entrepreneurs do continue to provide specialty foods and catered events. For example, Ademir, 70, sells *pamonha,* a Brazilian *tamale* made of corn and stuffed meat, every Saturday. The local police also told Ademir that he cannot sell from his house, so his clients now order by telephone call and he makes home deliveries by putting the address into the GPS system of his car and delivering hot, fresh *pamonha* to just about any location in the greater New Orleans area.

Characteristic "Women's Work" in Post-Katrina New Orleans

There were few immigrant women in comparison to men in New Orleans in the months following Hurricane Katrina. A small number of Brazilian women moved to New Orleans on their own, most often coming with a work contract from their previous city of residence. These women found themselves working alongside men in demolition and city cleaning. The majority of Brazilian women, however, began to come a few months after the storm, either to accompany a partner or to join partners already in New Orleans. Some of the women who accompanied spouses or boyfriends either did not work or did food catering as Navalha's wife did. Often they were in charge of taking care of children at home.

Chiquena, for example, moved to New Orleans from Georgia to

be with her boyfriend, who had gotten a job working for the American construction company that sent reinforcement workers to New Orleans. She lived in New Orleans for two years without working because she was pregnant when she arrived. She bore her son in New Orleans and then waited until he was a year old before she started working (Chiquena 24 February 2009). Indeed, the number of immigrant women who came down to accompany their spouses is notable. According to the Louisiana Department of Health, from January to mid-November of 2006, virtually all of the 1,200 pregnant women reporting for prenatal care in New Orleans were Latina. *The New York Times* reported that in a study conducted by the Louisiana Department of Health, Beth Perriloux, the head nurse in the department's health unit in Metairie, said, "Before the storm, only 2 percent [of the women in the prenatal unit] were Hispanic; now about 96 percent are Hispanic.'" There were so many pregnant women, in fact, that the clinics, understaffed at the time, had reached capacity. Dr. Erin Brewer, the department's medical director, said, "We've gone from having a maternity clinic two to three days a week to five days a week" (Porter "Katrina Begets a Baby Boom by Immigrants" A20).

While this report by the Louisiana Department of Health does not mention Brazilians, according to my interviews and considering the number of Brazilian babies under the age of four that I have met in New Orleans after Hurricane Katrina (and because of the difficulty in identifying Brazilians as distinct from Latinos in surveys), it is clear to me that Brazilian women are included in these "Latina" statistics. Childcare was an important role for many of the women who accompanied men to New Orleans post-Katrina. Their role as care givers in post-Katrina New Orleans should not be overlooked.

Brazilian women who arrived in New Orleans without children and even those with children found a difficult labor market for women in the recovery zone of New Orleans. First, many of these women were coming from areas of the country that had a more extensive Brazilian labor network for women, making it easier to find a job in "women's work" through a friend. In the months immediately after Hurricane Katrina, the women who moved to New Orleans found that, except for the niche of cooking food for workers, there were not a lot of options for what had been considered "women's work."

In New Orleans, breaking into the restaurant business, for example, usually required some English, and there was not an already established network of known restaurants that would hire people who did not have the proper work documentation. Also, there were a limited number of restaurants open in New Orleans right after Hurricane Katrina. Those women who did have some English skills managed to break into the restaurant market and then began to help those who had more recently arrived, but this was a slow process (Roberta 20 Oct. 2006). The most common job description for Brazilian women in the U.S. overall is housekeeping, but not enough people in New Orleans had returned to a normal life routine in the first months after the storm to even consider hiring a housekeeper. Though a few Brazilian women were able to find a housekeeping position in one of the hotels providing lodging for recovery workers, the housekeeping niche for Brazilians in New Orleans really did not start to be a significant employment option until well into 2007.

Freelancing as Cooks

So it was that, in the months after the hurricane, many Brazilian women began freelancing as cooks within the enclave community of Brazilians and Hispanics working in reconstruction in the city. The women knew where to locate job sites from their husbands, boyfriends, and friends and they would bring box lunches of rice, beans, and cooked meat to sell to the workers. This was a needed and profitable service. The market for boxed lunches at construction sites lasted for almost a year. Over time more restaurants opened in New Orleans and Brazilians became more familiar with the city and restaurants, so the business of making Brazilian food to sell at job sites was transferred to the Brazilian stores that later opened to meet the needs of the Brazilian enclave.

> My husband worked in demolition and construction. He decided to go there [New Orleans] because he saw Katrina on TV. He decided to go there to see how it was for work. He went down first and then I came a few months later. I didn't work at first because I had just had a baby. When he [the baby] was about seven months old, I started working as a cook for the men. I made boxed lunches for all the men working with my husband (Magda 19 February 2009).

> I spent about four or five months selling lunches. I sold them for $7-8 a plate. Rice, beans, and meat. I also sold breakfast. Grits and eggs. This was what people needed because there was not anything open…there were times when I would get up at 5 am and then go to bed at 10 pm, working non-stop (Carol 8 April 2008).

Women in the first two years after Katrina often reported that work was better for them in other areas of the country, but the money that their husbands were making in construction made up for their own pay cut. These comments reveal that the decision to move had often been a joint family decision rather than a decision made about women's wage earning.

But even women who expressed that they had preferred their work situation in other areas of the country noted that they preferred their lives in the U.S. to their lives in Brazil. They liked the independence that being a working woman provided them. Carla, a Brazilian immigrant in her early fifties, says that she has no desire to ever return to Brazil because the labor market in Brazil offers no place for an older woman in an entry-level job. She hopes to create a permanent life for herself in New Orleans. In 2010, she paid a *coyote* to bring her son to New Orleans to join her. Magda returned to Brazil with her husband to be reunited with her children at the end of 2007. She comments that she misses her lifestyle in the U.S. and that it was hard for her to become reaccustomed to life as a housewife in Brazil after earning her own money in the U.S.

Women Workers Doing "Men's Work" in Post-Katrina New Orleans

Interestingly, in the immediate months after the storm, it was common to find women employed in what is usually considered to be men's work: demolition and reconstruction. Below are some extracts from interviews in which women described their time in New Orleans' recovery zone.

> Work was better for me in Boston. I had more opportunities to work... [In New Orleans] I worked in demolition and in street cleaning in the beginning. Later I worked in housecleaning in a hotel [specific name is omitted]. For women, I think living in Boston is better. For men, New Orleans. Demolition and street cleaning

are both jobs that require a lot of strength. It is difficult for women (Marcilene 4 February 2008).

New Orleans was better for work than Boston for my husband and me. We earned more there. In Boston, I worked in a doughnut chain restaurant [specific name is omitted]. In New Orleans, I worked in construction with my husband. Construction work was difficult. Because there weren't many Brazilians in New Orleans when I arrived, it was harder for me to get a job in a restaurant. It was hard to get into the service industry in general in New Orleans because I didn't know anybody and there was not a network of Brazilian women to help get these service jobs. I didn't have any other option. I needed to make money so that I could get home to my children in Brazil as soon as possible, so I worked construction. I would do the molding and the grounding. I would paint as well. I did the easier work and my husband did the harder part like the sanding… I learned to do all this kind of work in New Orleans. When I lived in Brazil I never worked. My children were young, so I was always a housewife. I would take the kids to and from school and I would cook. I liked working in New Orleans (Sandra 18 February 2009).

I did just about everything to be able to earn money. I painted, I put in floors, let me try to remember in sequence: Because when I first arrived I was living with a lot of people [15 people in a one bedroom], this was uncomfortable for me. Then this job came up working for [X] Construction Company. They paid us a salary and also paid for us to stay in a Motel 6 in Kenner. We planted the grass at Tulane. We are the ones that put that park [Audubon] and Tulane University back together. All the grass that you see planted, I did it. I cleaned the street, put in grass, planted trees, pulled up trees and bushes that had been damaged by the hurricane, I had to learn to do everything. Any job that came up, I was willing to do it.

Then I worked painting the doors of a hotel. I demolished houses, tore them all the way down. I put up sheet rock. I worked in painting just like the men. Work started to go down with the company I worked for because the city was practically rebuilt. I didn't have any other choice, I took a job in Slidell [30 miles from New Orleans]

> mixing cement. I would never have imagined in all my life that I would mix cement. They said they would pay me $150, so I said, "Yes, I know how to mix cement." The first day of work was horrible for me. I went to mix, and it was almost like I was mixing a cake, but what I was really mixing was cement. It was really hard. I suffered a lot in that job. It was one of the worst jobs of my life. I cried out of tiredness. Sometimes I thought that I was going to die, I was so tired. I only managed to stay in that job for a month. That is hard work for a man, imagine for a woman. I returned to New Orleans and started working for the same company again. That job was not as hard as mixing cement, but we still had those heavy mops to carry around. We suffered. But thank God, everything got better. Now I work for myself [in housecleaning] (Rosa 8 July 2009).

The possibilities of women working alongside men in construction and demolition work lasted for about two years after Katrina. This was the amount of time that it took for New Orleans' service industry to get back into working order, and it is also the amount of time that it took for Brazilian women to become sufficiently familiar with the city to find service industry jobs on their own. The hotels in New Orleans became a site where many Brazilian women found work. In the post-Katrina environment, they were able to make money as housekeepers for the hotel chains even before the tourist industry really picked up again because many people came from out of town to New Orleans to work in the rebuilding and stayed in these hotels.

Dewey Weaver, president of Monroe, Louisiana-based Intermountain Management, the owner and operator of Marriott hotels, has said, "The reality is, without the neighbors to the south, we wouldn't be able to operate hotels" (Walsh). Immigrants, both legal and illegal, fill a large number of bottom-end service jobs in the hotel business throughout the country, largely because American-born workers do not want to work those jobs or because they expect to earn more money than these jobs pay.

The economic crisis that began to hit New Orleans in 2008, however, affected the number of people vacationing in New Orleans, and this paralleled the slowdown in reconstruction, thus also affecting the number of rooms that Brazilian women cleaned per day and, subsequently, their paycheck. "Things have gotten slower. I used to make $700 every two weeks. Now I get $300 every two weeks. There are few guests. The hotel industry is affected by the economy" (Francielly 6 January 2009).

Opening Small Businesses: The Housecleaning Niche Shines

As the community grew, Brazilian women in New Orleans also began opening their own businesses; beauty salons and catering businesses are the most common examples of the entrepreneurial services provided by Brazilian women marketed for the Brazilian community. But as New Orleanians moved back to New Orleans and began to fall back into the normal rhythm of life, Brazilian women found that the most profitable and secure work industry for them became the private housecleaning business. There was not a network of Brazilian housecleaners already in place, so Brazilian women had to find houses and set up contracts independently. Lívia, for example, lived for five years and ten months in the U.S. She lived for about two months in Florida; two months in Brighton, Mass.; one year in Atlanta, Ga.; and four years in New Orleans. She met her husband in Atlanta and moved to New Orleans with him, arriving in October of 2005. When her baby was a year old, she decided to begin a housecleaning business.

> Everything that I achieved in the United States I achieved in New Orleans… My husband helped me make fliers and did the interviews with me. He helped me get my schedule together… New Orleans is a state [she means city] that does not have a custom of housecleaning. New Orleanians are not used to having people come into their houses to clean. There was not an established network of housecleaners already. The hardest thing was getting things started because people in New Orleans were not used to that kind of work. Few people were familiar with Brazilian cleaning (Lívia 24 February 2009).

Creating "Schedules"

There were no previous "schedules" to be bought, so Brazilian women made up business cards and went door to door to find clients who were interested in using their services. A "schedule" is what results when Brazilian women accrue a list of clients who are currently using their housecleaning services. If women are able to accrue more clients' houses than they can handle during a week themselves or if they decide that they are leaving the area for whatever reason, they can sell that list of houses as a commodity, "a schedule."

Buying housecleaning schedules is common in areas of the country where Brazilians already have a hold on the housecleaning industry. Buying a schedule usually represents the equivalent of three months' salary (Martes 106). Many of these women had limited English skills, so creating their schedules was a huge learning experience for them. They had to learn enough English to be able to communicate the basics of timetables and cleaning methods with the heads of households. Having their own housecleaning schedule also meant that Brazilian women needed access to a car. Thais, however, says that when she first decided to get a housecleaning business started in New Orleans she did not have money to buy a car. She walked door to door to deliver fliers and she traveled by taxi to clean her first houses (Thais 8 July 2009).

Lívia had the advantage that her husband spoke English relatively well. Many Brazilian women in New Orleans post-Katrina set out to make a housecleaning schedule with very limited English skills. Ana Carolina, for example, had previously lived for six months in Tampa, Fla., where she had worked in the restaurant industry and in housecleaning. In Florida, she did not have her own "schedule" of houses, but she worked as a "help"[16] with one of her friends. She came to New Orleans following a boyfriend who moved to New Orleans with the construction company from Florida in 2006.

In the area of Tampa where she had previously lived, the Brazilian network was extensive enough that she could get by without knowledge of English. When she arrived in New Orleans, she spoke almost no English, but she began to put together her own housecleaning schedule. Her boyfriend supported her for the few months that it took her to get her business running. She went door to door and dropped off fliers with the help of a friend who spoke English. Slowly, she began to build up a clientele. By 2009, when she decided to return to Brazil, she claims that she had made a great schedule and worked for very friendly clients.

Housekeeping is such a profitable and stable industry that, with the slowdown in the construction industry, it is not uncommon for Brazilian men to accompany Brazilian women on their schedules when they

[16] Slang for assistant.

are unable to find a job in the construction industry. Having a good housecleaning schedule is considered to be a secure job. It is much more secure than the construction industry, for example, because in construction immigrants have to find a new job each time their current contract ends. Once a woman has secured a house for her cleaning service, however, she is usually able to maintain that house for many years if she chooses. That one house can also generate more houses as children move out and get married or as family members or friends become interested in her service. Some Brazilian men in New Orleans have left the construction industry altogether because of its volatility and are now accompanying their wives on housecleaning schedules.

Personalizing Housecleaning

Brazilians see themselves as having a superior cleaning style to Americans because they say they personalize their housecleaning services. Sonia Melo de Jesus' research explores this attitude with Brazilian housekeepers in Boston. Jesus notes that interviewees in Boston explain that Brazilian housecleaners clean the whole house, removing books and objects to clean all the dust and cleaning the floor with soap and water (106). Clients of Brazilian housecleaners commented to me on the thoroughness of the cleaning style of their housecleaner, often referring to it as a service fit for the hotel business because, as in the case of my neighbor's house, the Brazilian housecleaner folded the ends of the toilet paper rolls into little swans and does the same to her washcloths in the bathroom. Many Brazilian housecleaners have learned some of these skills by previously working in hotels, though it should also be noted that cleaning a home, with years of clutter and personal objects to care for, is actually much more difficult than cleaning an empty, standardized hotel room.

These artful folding details are examples of the personal attention that Brazilian housecleaners dedicate to each house. It is this commitment to detail that is later sold as a commodity within the Brazilian network when Brazilian cleaners leave the market.

Roger Waldinger and Michael Lichter in *How the Other Half Works* explain how employers in certain workplaces lose control over hiring practices, ceding control to immigrant networks. Immigrants themselves will know about job openings even before the employer does, and they are able to find replacements the moment they hear that someone is about to leave their position. Waldinger and Lichter found that crucial performance-enhancing and on-the-job training occurs among co-ethnics in order to facilitate personnel changes. It is often easier for the employer to allow a recommendation of the network to fill an open position rather than to ignore the recommendation and begin a whole new hiring process. The buying and selling of schedules among the Brazilian community is an example of this community practice. Obviously, Brazilians themselves are aware when a vacancy arises in the housecleaning industry before the employer. They are able to take advantage of this opportunity to train another Brazilian to take over the job. From the perspective of the employers, if they had previously had outstanding results from working with a Brazilian, it is more likely that they will continue with the same service.

Buying and Selling Schedules

To my knowledge, the buying and selling of housecleaning schedules as a commodity is not practiced in Brazil, yet it is standard operating procedure among Brazilian housecleaners in the U.S. Housecleaners in Brazil may recommend a friend to an employer if they leave, but I have read no report of selling the job as a commodity on an informal market, which is actually quite surprising given Brazil's large informal economy. Among Brazilians in the U.S., however, the practice is widespread. In personal ads in Brazilian-American newspapers such as the *Brazilian Times* and on websites such as Orkut or Brazilian Space, it is common to see advertisements such as "Vende-se Schedule de Casas" (House Schedule for Sale) or "Vende-se Schedule de Limpeza" (Cleaning Schedule for Sale). This is a tactic employed by immigrants to exploit capitalism through capitalism itself. By making a franchise out of what is usually considered a job for a second-class citizen in the U.S., Brazilians are able to maintain secure, autonomously managed employment that is an investment in providing them both their sense of livelihood and a commodity that can later be sold.

Ana Carolina decided that she would return to Brazil after living in New Orleans for three years. She sold her schedule to a friend for $4,000. The price of a schedule varies on the quality of that schedule. The women defined the quality of a schedule as being the number of houses that were to be cleaned per day, their location (meaning how much gas one would have to use in order to get from one house to the next) and also the size of the houses, since larger houses mean more money. The selling of schedules is very common in the Brazilian community, though it is a practice that did not exist in New Orleans prior to Hurricane Katrina. I spoke to another woman who has put together her own schedule here in New Orleans, but she had bought her first schedule in Boston for $6,000. She said that she was glad that she bought the schedule because she was quickly able to begin earning a profit and pay off her debts, and now she has a commodity which she can sell for extra cash when she decides to return to Brazil. Housecleaners justify their right to sell a schedule because they are not selling simply the cleaning job, but the information about *how* to clean each particular house. They are selling the labor that they put into handing out fliers, the contacts that they worked to make, the training involved in teaching new housecleaners, and the knowledge of the personal habits and cleaning expectations of each individual family. Selling a schedule takes all of the worry of training a new housecleaner from the hands of the homeowner, thus justifying how a schedule can be sold without the homeowner's knowledge.

But buying a schedule can be risky business because there is no guarantee that the owners of the house will want to continue the service with the change of personnel. The homeowners are mostly unaware that their houses are being sold as part of a housecleaning schedule. Especially in times of economic crisis, a change in a housecleaner could be the opportunity for a household to decide that they no longer need a cleaning service. But in general, Brazilians claim that the people whom they work for continue with their recommendations.

To try to insure that the homeowners would feel comfortable with the change of housekeepers, Ana Carolina sold her schedule almost two months before she was actually returning to Brazil. The woman who bought her schedule then began to work with Ana Carolina for those two months as her "assistant" so that the people at the various houses where Ana Carolina cleaned could meet the new housecleaner. Ana Carolina explained that it was important to have this transition time so that the clients could come to trust the new housecleaner and also see that she did competent work and was reliable. During the training period, the understudy learns what cleaning products each family likes to use, how the family likes to have their sheets folded, or in which direction the rug should be placed. Learning these personal details of each house are important because they ensure that, during the transition, the new housekeeper will also continue to attend to these details. This makes it less likely that the client will decide to discontinue with the housecleaning service or switch to another. Ana Carolina finally told her clients that she would be going home to Brazil two weeks before she was to travel. All of the houses she cleaned decided to continue with the "assistant" that Ana Carolina had trained. This time period of transition has become standard and can be noted in the Brazilian cleaning enclave in other parts of the country as well (Martes 106-107).

Ana Carolina's assistant reports that she is happy that she purchased the schedule. Ana Carolina also reports that she is happy that she sold her schedule. She is living in Goiânia with her two teenage children and working with her brother in a family-owned business. When asked if she wants to return to New Orleans, she responded with a laugh, "I miss it there, but not to live, only to visit and to spend money!"

The Gender Dimension to the Brazilian Experience in New Orleans

As Maxine Margolis has noted, Brazilian women decide to immigrate to the U.S. for the same reasons that Brazilian men do— for jobs that pay more than what they could hope to make back home (*Little Brazil* 237). The decision for the pioneer women to move to New Orleans during the aftermath of Katrina, however, tended to be linked to a male companion or spouse since, as we have seen, the "female" service industry was not yet functioning in the immediate aftermath of the storm. The unequal gender ratios among Brazilians in New Orleans have dictated the development of group dynamics not only between men and women, but also between men. In all-male immigrant households, for example, men systematically divided the household chores of cooking and cleaning, often placing a written schedule on the refrigerator to remind each other of their duties. Male workers are thus breaking gender norms by engaging in activities traditionally considered women's work. The homosocial friendships between Brazilian men, especially among the pioneer immigrants, were particularly significant in marking community identity.

Men and women in the post-Katrina recovery zone found themselves in a context where new gender roles were constantly being established to navigate their surreal environment. The argument that Brazilians in New Orleans during the post-Katrina months integrated more with New Orleanians than Brazilians in other enclaves have with their local communities is partly related to the fact of unequal gender ratios among Brazilians in New Orleans. To create relationships with people of the opposite sex, Brazilian men had to leave their enclave. But in branching out to these places where they could encounter women, Brazilians always went in numbers. Groups of male friendships are of paramount importance to group success not only in their working environment, but also in their social lives.

A group of Tulane University students in my "Ethnographies of Brazilian Immigration to the United States" class commented that they could always point out who the Brazilians were at the Boot, a local bar hangout for both college students and Brazilian immigrants (since Brazilians search for spaces where they can encounter women), because the Brazilian men will dance together in a group by themselves, an action highly uncommon among the American men present. (It should be noted that my students were being "trained" to be conscious of Brazilian immigrants in their community as prospective ethnographers. I find it doubtful that the average college student would have distinguished Brazilians from another Latino group, or even from other college students for that matter. But their comment does reveal the importance of male Brazilian friendship bonds in the social scene of New Orleans.)

We have already seen evidence that the post-Katrina environment diversified "women's work." The necessity of working in demolition and reconstruction in the first stages of rebuilding meant that some immigrant women found themselves breaking gender norms in the workplace. As mentioned earlier, for a short time period immediately following the storm, work identities of both men and women were often very similar. But the speed in which a female-run service industry was, essentially, generated by entrepreneurial Brazilian women is a testament to the fact that immigrant roles still remain strongly gendered. Women entrepreneurialized their skills of cooking and cleaning while men entrepreneurialized through construction subcontracting. Both paths are seen as ways to gain independence in the labor market, yet expectations and attitudes differ between the sexes.

Yet, immigration in general often reconfigures normal gender roles. In an interview in Brazil with a return (male) migrant, I asked why he had decided to return to Brazil and he answered, "Because I love my wife too much." I asked him what he meant by that and he responded that he did not want to bring his wife to the U.S. because he was afraid that she would like the U.S. too much and she "would change her way of thinking," forcing them to separate. In his mind, the only way for them to be together in their established gender norms was for him to return to Brazil. The fact that it is common for women to enter the workforce and earn significant financial autonomy by doing so often marks a difference in the way premigration gender roles were established between couples.

The downturn in the New Orleans construction market has resulted in an interesting gender dynamic in New Orleans since women are now often finding themselves in a position of being the primary breadwinner of the household while the men wait at home for their next construction contract. In many Brazilian households, this has not been an easy transition. While women's employment can reduce dependency on men and enhance self-confidence for women, their new financial authority can also lead to antagonism between the sexes, particularly in married couples (Margolis *Little Brazil* 238). I have been witness to a case of domestic violence that arose when the wife was working long hours in housecleaning and the husband was unemployed in construction. The husband's frustration at his own unemployment, coupled with the fact that the wife had less time to devote to the cooking and cleaning of her own household, led to the husband's accusations that she was having extra-marital affairs during her absences from home. The conflict erupted into both verbal and physical abuse.

In terms of transnational managing of remittances, women tend to play a dominant role in the home community. Most single male migrants reported sending the money home to their mothers because the mother was considered to be the "most trustworthy" to manage their money efficiently. Migrants in serious (transnational) relationships reported sending money to their wives or girlfriends. Disagreements arose even in these "most trustworthy" cases, however. Carlos has not spoken to his mother in over six months because they got into a disagreement over the management of the funds that he sends home. Many long-distance relationships (Brazil-New Orleans) ended over similar financial disagreements.

Socializing in the Unique Post-Katrina Environment

The role that Brazilians played in the recovery of the city as well as the take-charge networking necessary for Brazilians to locate their jobs without an established enclave network meant that Brazilians came in contact with and often developed relationships with those native New Orleanians who had returned to their homes in those early months following the storm. Jimmy Huck, for example, a native New Orleanian who is the director of graduate programs at the Stone Center for Latin American Studies at Tulane, returned to New Orleans mere days after the storm passed. He managed to return to the Tulane campus while the city was still flooded to retrieve some important documents so that the Stone Center for Latin American Studies could begin operating at a satellite location at UT Austin. He was one of the first people back in the city and he commented that the first people besides himself who moved into his neighborhood after Katrina were Brazilian workers. The language that he heard among workers on Tulane's campus as he went to survey the damage at the Stone Center was Portuguese, not English or Spanish.

I talked with Jimmy informally about the early post-Katrina months in the city. I paraphrase our conversation below.

Jimmy: Those early months following the storm were really strange. Everyone was just so overwhelmed and sad. There was a real sense of camaraderie among all the people who were in the city at that time. I think that New Orleanians were really open to immigrants at first because there was this feeling of "we are all in this together." Anybody that was around to help was embraced. I had some neighbors who were Brazilian. I would have them over because I was home all the time working on my house. They would come over and help me sometimes, too. I don't really keep in touch with them the way that I used to. There are still a group of Brazilians that live in that same house. They are mostly different from the first ones that I knew, though.

Annie: Why do you think that you are not in touch with your new Brazilian neighbors?

> **Jimmy**: I think it is because there was something unique about that time immediately following the storm. Now I am busy and working. I am not home all the time. I became close to the first group because of the situation we were in. We were there together. My family was not there with me. I was not working. I was always at home. There were no restaurants or stores open then. There was a real sense of solidarity (Jimmy 7 May 2009).

The sense of solidarity that Brazilians also came to feel with New Orleanians during this time period has been essential in the development of the imagination of New Orleans' uniqueness. They have a special connection to the city, not only because they were able to earn money and achieve some of their financial goals there, but because their work was so central to the beginnings of a Brazilian community and to the renewal of New Orleans. The experience has provided Brazilians with a sense of ownership of their community.

Brazilians feel more invested in New Orleans than they did in other cities in the U.S.; if New Orleans is a city that they can call their own, it is because of the powerful role that they played in the city's wellbeing through their own physical labor. Their work directly helped New Orleanians in tangible ways. They worked alongside army trucks securing the streets. They cleared the streets and gutted houses, and some even pulled dead bodies from the debris (Frank 3 January 2009). They moved to New Orleans when it was, essentially, a ghost town and prepared the city for New Orleanians to move back home. Reconstructing the city became a personal project as much as a job.

Brazilians idealistically have expressed hopes to me that because of their efforts in reconstruction, they are a group with possibilities for receiving better treatment than they had received in other areas of the country where they previously lived. With respect to this, one interviewee responded,

> The government of Massachusetts does not act favorably towards the Brazilian community. There we went to the city governor with a list of over 10,000 names asking for help with certain problems within the Brazilian community and he didn't even listen to us. Here in New Orleans, we have not yet had the opportunity to ask

> for anything for Brazilians, but I think because Brazilians have been so important in helping the city become functional again that they will listen to us. The majority of the Brazilians here are hard workers. We are working to help New Orleans become even better than it was before Katrina. I hope that the government in Louisiana will see this. I would like to have more freedom, at least be able to obtain a driver's license. (Jackson 1 November 2006)

This interview was conducted in 2006. It is now 2010 and it seems unlikely that Brazilian immigrants are going to receive the political response to their solidarity with New Orleans that they were hoping for in the near future. Immigration law enforcement, in fact, is now more prevalent in New Orleans than it was in 2005. The double message to immigrants during post-Katrina is partially explained as being a part of the U.S.'s disjointed national immigration policy. While the early policy changes that fostered immigration into the recovery zone (August-Sept. 2005) happened outside the context of a national immigration debate, New Orleans is falling more within the national standards set for immigration enforcement now that the urgency of reconstruction has diminished.

Certainly, undocumented immigrants as well as employers looking for low-wage workers found post-Katrina New Orleans to be one of the most immigrant-friendly job markets in the country. While leniency in post-Katrina workplace law enforcement assured that contractors and other employers could benefit from cheap immigrant labor without fearing employer sanctions, it should be remembered that, even in recovery New Orleans, undocumented immigrants were afforded no peace-of-mind guarantees. Not only were immigrant rebuilders still subject to deportation, but also the Helms Burton Act that was supposed to assure they were fairly compensated for work had been suspended.[17] OSHA regulations that should have guaranteed baseline safety procedures in the workplace had also been removed. The message to immigrants in the post-Katrina environment was inherently contradictory, designed to ensure that rebuilding companies could exploit a cheap labor source at the same time that they distanced themselves from the politically unpopular consequences of an inevitable demographic change.[18]

Immigration and residency issues obviously combine with language and literacy difficulties to impact an individual's vulnerability in the face of disaster and the regulation of its aftermath. Disaster literature has mainly focused on immigrant vulnerability in terms of disaster recovery eligibility (Bolin and Stanford 96). While the fact that "illegal immigrants" are denied federal disaster assistance means that the undocumented workers who have relocated to New Orleans find themselves in an extremely vulnerable position for future disasters, Katrina also reminds us that disasters affect vulnerable first responders. Many first responders to New Orleans were recent immigrants, politically weak, lacking legal rights, and not culturally adept in dealing with U.S.

[17] Michael Piore has been the most forceful and eloquent proponent for arguing that international migration is caused by a permanent built-in demand for inexpensive and flexible labor inherent to the economic structure of developed nations. Wages not only reflect conditions of supply and demand, but are representative of the status and prestige of the jobs. In general, people believe that wages should reflect social status, and they have rather rigid notions about the correlations between occupational status and pay. Massey tells us that "the cost to employers of raising wages to attract low-level workers is typically more than the cost of these worker's wages alone; wages must be increased proportionately throughout the job hierarchy in order to keep them in line with social expectations" (Massey "Why Does Immigration Occur?" 37). This process is known as structural inflation. Since immigrants to New Orleans are less likely to be preoccupied with the social prestige related to certain jobs because they do not consider themselves part of the U.S. social network, hiring immigrant labor could be seen as a way to circumvent structural inflation. This has lowered wages in the construction industry in New Orleans, for example, but not changed the overall wages in the city. And the work that immigrants accepted, regardless of status— cleaning the streets, demolishing houses, cleaning houses are the activities that allowed New Orleans to recover.

[18] Disaster research has also shown us that the private sector's desire to cut costs often leads to an increased use of immigrant labor because these immigrants are willing to work for less money, receive less adequate benefits, and are less likely to file claims of abuse (Powers 28). Given the urgency of rebuilding and the inadequacy of working conditions, workers who respond to disasters often respond because they have little alternative opportunity in their current place of residency.

bureaucratic culture. They often found themselves living in precarious domestic and working circumstances upon arriving in New Orleans, with no outlets for accessing resources. Moving to New Orleans was particularly risky for this group of immigrants because there was not a network of more established hubs whom these first responders were following.

Even if the legal systems of New Orleans have not necessarily been favorably inclined to include immigrant workers in eligibility for local rights, Brazilians report that, socially at least, they do feel accepted in New Orleans in comparison with other areas of the country. Much of this acceptance arose out of this same unregulated time period immediately following the storm. There were more workers' abuses, but those workers also felt that they had unique financial and social opportunities. After all, the lack of regulation allowed some Brazilians to become subcontractors, managing all Brazilian construction crews, and Brazilians found themselves involved in New Orleanian social circles in unique ways largely because the migration patterns and interactions with New Orleanians were different in the post-Katrina environment. During an interview, I noticed that one Brazilian interviewee had a tattoo of the *fleur de lis*, the symbol of New Orleans, on her ankle. I asked her why she had decided to get that particular tattoo and she said that New Orleans was like her second home. For her, the symbol of the *fleur de lis* is inextricably linked to the aftermath of the hurricane and her solidarity with New Orleans that arose through the emotional ties created out of her hard labor rebuilding the city.

What Happens When Recovery Work Slows?

The unique post-Katrina environment in which immigrants could take advantage of the chaos of reconstruction to find work lasted for only a short window of time. As more sections of the city opened, people began to return to their normal routines. At the same time, as immigrant stories continued to flow about work opportunities, more workers began arriving in New Orleans and the price of labor dropped as a consequence.[19] Along with the reduced price of labor, the economic recession slowed recovery work. According to the U.S. Bureau of Labor Statistics, New Orleans fared slightly better than other parts of

[19] Nicholas Vaca refers to this immigration pattern of Latinos following disasters such as Hurricane Katrina to a "Latino tsunami" (18).

the country; in July of 2009, New Orleans had an unemployment rate of 7.4% while the U.S. average was 9.4%. Nonetheless, both private and public investment plans slowed down considerably. The tourism industry, New Orleans' main income source, was also affected since fewer people were vacationing in New Orleans. Since New Orleanians were investing less in construction projects and in housekeeping services and fewer tourists were staying in hotels, Brazilians began to question whether New Orleans could offer them long-term prospects for a better life in the U.S.

To deal with the downturn in their income, some Brazilians began diversifying the industries in which they worked, especially after 2007. There have been more Brazilians opting to work in the restaurant business in the evenings, for example, to supplement their construction paycheck. Some men are also working in warehouses packing goods or as delivery boys. Those who do not work construction say that they decided to change jobs because it was stressful working from paycheck to paycheck in the construction industry, not knowing when they would get their next contract. With restaurant and warehouse jobs, although they receive less money per hour, immigrants are always sure about the number of hours that they will work per week and they have a steady paycheck. Cristiano, for example, works at a furniture company loading delivery trucks during the day and at a sushi restaurant at night. These jobs both pay him $10 an hour. He used to make between $12 and $15 an hour working construction, but he was dependent on someone hiring him since he did not have the skills in construction or in English to negotiate a job on his own. He prefers knowing that he will have a paycheck each month, even if he is paid less than when he worked construction.

This downturn in the construction market has meant that, while there remains a Brazilian community in New Orleans, the numbers are smaller than they were at the height of Brazilian immigration to the city. I would estimate that in 2010 there were around 3,000-5,000 Brazilians living in the greater New Orleans area, as opposed to 5,000-8,000 during the 2005-2007 years. To estimate the number of Brazilians who have lived in New Orleans since Hurricane Katrina is difficult, however, because the community is quite transient. Most of the Brazilian men in the New Orleans construction industry work from contract to contract. When a job ends, they have the mobility to change locations because there is not an employer to whom they must be accountable. Because Brazilians themselves often work as subcontractors, there are many Brazilians who have come to live in New Orleans for a few months when one of their friends gets a large contract job and then return to another area of the country. There are even Brazilian workers who have come to New Orleans simply to visit friends and to partake in Mardi Gras festivities. They often work with their friends for the weeks that they come to enjoy Mardi Gras and then return to their previous city when the parties end. Needless to say, counting the number of Brazilians who have passed through New Orleans is very difficult. What is clear, however, is that the massive opportunities for employment that once existed in the post-Katrina recovery environment are here no longer. The Brazilians living in New Orleans find ways to cope with this reality.

A Brazilian immigrant who has been in New Orleans since September 2005 reported in an informal conversation on June 13, 2009, that he had not worked for more than two weeks. He was finally able to do some maintenance jobs for his landlord in order to pay his rent for the month. Brazilians from New Orleans have moved to Kansas City, back to Boston, or to Atlanta due to the downturn in construction employment.[20] Even though Brazilians tended to say that New Orleans is the city that felt most like Brazil, economic prospects dictate how Brazilians imagine their place within the city. In an interview with a Brazilian who lived in New Orleans and then returned to Boston, the interviewee said,

> I liked New Orleans. I earned a lot of money there. It is a very good place to live. When I first arrived it was great. But then there were so many people [Brazilians], and they kept coming and coming and coming. The community grew a lot. Then work started to slow

[20] Of those three cities, immigrants who moved to Kansas City seem to report more work opportunities. But during my research trip to Kansas City in June 2009, Brazilians reported a severe slowdown in construction work in Kansas as well. However, because there was still not a substantial immigrant labor force established there, prices for labor were still relatively higher than they had been in other areas of the country where Brazilians had previously lived (such as Atlanta, New Orleans, and Boston). In Kansas City, the cost of living was also lower than in New Orleans or Boston. Of the Brazilians I interviewed in Kansas City who had lived previously in New Orleans, the majority felt happy with their decision to move to Kansas, although they commented that they missed the lifestyle of New Orleans.

> down. There were a lot of people and little work. So I've returned to Boston (Chico 25 May 2009).

Some Brazilians are shuttling back and forth between New Orleans and another city where they also have construction job contacts. Brazilians from the Northeast, for example, often come to New Orleans for the winter months when construction work slows because of the cold weather up North. When summer comes, they return to areas such as Boston where they have a steady job and where the minimum wage is usually higher. During the summer months of 2009, there were many Brazilians in New Orleans who reported that they planned to spend the summer working in Boston; then they would return to New Orleans for the winter when work in Boston slowed. Brazilians in New Orleans, who hold unstable jobs in the construction industry, maintain ties between U.S. cities as a way to recover difficulties in the job market in their current location.[21]

A Brazilian immigrant who had arrived in New Orleans in 2005 and relocated to Boston in 2008 with the slowdown of the construction industry said,

> New Orleans was the place where I was able to really start my life in the U.S. It was a big financial push for me. I got there during a good phase in the job market. When I left New Orleans [for Boston] work had gotten weak... Many Americans in New Orleans wanted to rebuild their houses with money from the government.

[21] At the beginning of their migratory careers, and often throughout their stay in the U.S., immigrants satisfy the employers' need for workers who view bottom-level jobs simply as a means to the end of earning money with no implications for status or prestige (Massey "Why Does Immigration Occur?" 38). Most migrants begin as target earners, seeking to earn money for a specific goal that will improve their status or well-being at home in Brazil by building a house, paying for school, buying land, and/or acquiring consumer goods. Even low wages abroad are often seen as good wages by home country standards. And since they often do not consider themselves as part of the receiving society, immigrants do not necessarily seek a job for its prestige. These workers on the bottom of the payroll are expendable and may be laid off at any time with little or no cost to the employer. Indeed, the employer will generally lose money by retaining workers during slack periods. In Boston during the wintertime, for example, construction companies cut their payrolls, forcing workers in this sector to bear the costs of their unemployment. Thus, Brazilians in Boston migrate south during the wintertime if they were not able to accrue enough savings to make it through the slow wintertime in Boston. And they migrate north to Boston in the summer when the labor market in New Orleans is slow.

> But the money didn't come through, or they used the money that came through to buy a car, and they kept blowing us off instead of paying us. There was not any money. The government was not sending any more money down. Work went down. A lot of people started leaving. Not just in New Orleans, but all over the U.S. (Josué 4 June 2009).

Josué's interview mentions the difficult economic conditions in New Orleans following the slowdown in reconstruction, but he also acknowledges that the conditions are difficult in other areas of the country as well. There are Brazilians leaving Boston to return to Brazil just as they are leaving New Orleans because of the economic recession. But having ties to two cities in the U.S. diversifies employment options. Immigrants can go where the market is stronger at the moment, following the advice of immigrants currently residing in the other city.

Below is an interview excerpt with a Brazilian immigrant who spent time working in the recovery zone of New Orleans but who is currently living in the Ironbound neighborhood of Newark, N.J., a working-class neighborhood with a large Brazilian community. I was spending the day casually walking around Ironbound, waiting for an interview scheduled in the evening with a Brazilian from New Orleans who had returned to New Jersey. Simply walking around the streets of Ironbound and striking up conversations with strangers in 2009, I met four other Brazilians who had also spent time in New Orleans. And they mentioned to me other friends in Ironbound who had spent at least a few months working in New Orleans at some point between 2005 and 2009. Alex said of his experience in New Orleans,

> I lived in New Orleans for eleven months. I liked it because it was the only place that I have lived in the United States where I had a pay check at the end of each week. I earned a lot of money in New Orleans... I decided to leave because there was not much work anymore. The government stopped sending money for rebuilding and I was spending many days without any work. I decided to move to Florida... From Florida I moved to Maryland and then I was deported for a traffic violation. I spent a month in Brazil and then came back [through Mexico again] (Alex 1 June 2009).

Alex stated that New Orleans was the place in the United States where he had been able to earn the most money in the first months that he lived in New Orleans. However, he also said that it was the place where he had lost the most money, working jobs and then never receiving his payment. At one time, five of his family members lived in New Orleans. Now, only his brother-in-law remains. According to Alex, his brother-in-law loves New Orleans and won't leave, even if the work there is not very good. Alex adds that New Orleans was also the city where he had the most fun. He prefers the lifestyle of New Orleans to the lifestyle in Newark, but he also feels that he is more comfortable in Newark because he has more friends there and his employment options were currently more stable.

To Stay or to Leave

Brazilian pioneers to New Orleans have now been in the U.S., on average, between five to seven years, a time period that many immigrants project for their total stay abroad for their migration experience. As the last chapter illustrated, Brazilians in New Orleans live in New Orleans while constantly dreaming of returning to Brazil. By and large, the money earned in New Orleans is being invested in building projects in their home communities. The expectation seems to be that, one day, they will return home.

The decision about when to return to Brazil, however, often changes during the migrant's time in the U.S. The return often exists as a hypothetical plan whose exact date cannot be articulated but that will occur sometime in the future. Often even those who are able to articulate a date change their minds when that date arrives. And at times, the investment in Brazil may not even be linked to the return, but simply to the fact that Brazil is where they feel that the fruit of their labors will be kept safest given the fact that their legal status in the U.S. is often so precarious.

Those immigrants who have bank accounts in the U.S. express an increased level of integration (and perhaps willingness to stay) because owning a bank account shows both knowledge of an American banking system as well as sufficient comfort and ease in their community in the U.S. to be willing to trust leaving their money in a bank there. A bank account, of course, provides immigrants with possibilities for greater integration by allowing them to make purchases online, buy plane or concert tickets over the internet, or simply keep their money safe from home robberies. Those who do not have bank accounts tend to send their money in larger quantities to Brazil and more frequently, since it can be dangerous to keep large amounts of cash in their homes. Having to make the decision to hide money in insecure situations or send it to Brazil has the added consequence of making their ties to home and desire to return stronger.[22] Brazilians who live in the new New Orleans must weigh their employment options in New Orleans against their long-term goals for their time in the U.S. For some Brazilian immigrants, New Orleans has offered success, especially if they were able to exploit the opportunities for employment in the immediate wake of Katrina. For others who came down in later waves, the economic opportunities of New Orleans turned out to be more of a myth than a reality once the reconstruction market slowed.

Brazilians in New Orleans Today

Hurricane Katrina and its aftermath are the contexts in which Brazilian immigrants built their community's founding myth. As Brazilians remember and recount to future migrants the images of the demolished city and the stories (projected through the mass media and pioneers' own lived experiences), of their earning potential during those first few months, and the unique spirit of camaraderie that emerged from living in a disaster zone, Brazilians perpetuate future migration to New Orleans.

The media images portraying the catastrophic destruction of New Orleans post-Katrina and revealing it as a city marked by little political regulation and plentiful opportunity for employment motivated pioneer immigrants to come to New Orleans in large numbers. This

[22] Hiding money in the house also means that no one will know where the money is located. In most cases, this is a positive thing, but there are emergencies when it is necessary for someone to know where to find the money. For example, a serious car crash in New Orleans left one Brazilian immigrant dead and another in the Intensive Care Unit of the hospital for eight months. Neither of these immigrants had bank accounts. Friends of the victims (myself included) tried to find the hidden money to help send the body home to Brazil. We scoured the house from top to bottom, but we were never able to find the hiding place. We found the money of the Brazilian immigrant in the ICU stuffed in a slit that he had made in his mattress. With this money, we were able to buy a plane ticket for his sister, who lived in Connecticut, to come visit him. The money of the Brazilian who passed away is hidden somewhere in New Orleans, but its whereabouts remains a mystery.

migration multiplied as pioneer immigrants began spreading their stories of success in the informal and unorganized recovery market. Houses needed to be built, electricity needed to be installed, cars needed parts changed, and roofs needed to be repaired. Brazilians who arrived in New Orleans were given the space to rebuild a community through these activities, often learning the necessary construction skills as they went.

The Brazilians who arrived in New Orleans post-Katrina were themselves recent immigrants to the United States who had moved to New Orleans with relatively little social capital and skill, yet they were able to become the founders of a Brazilian community. This has given them a sense of agency and of belonging to New Orleans. They have a special connection to the city, not only because they were able to earn money and achieve some of their financial goals there, but because their work was so central to the beginnings of a Brazilian enclave, to the recovery of the city, and to imagining their own place as individuals within its social fabric.

Memories of living in this recovery zone and the roles that individuals played in the lives of one another have made the Brazilian immigrant experience in post-Katrina New Orleans unique from the experience of immigration to other places in the country. Those who arrived in the first wave of immigration arrived in a city that did not have resources for anyone, either immigrant or native. While those first few months were extremely difficult because the city lacked basic services, it lacked these basic services for the rich, the poor, the immigrants, and the non-immigrants. Everyone was in it together and individuals made the difference in the lives of neighbors.

Even though the infrastructure of the city had been destroyed, Brazilian pioneers enjoyed how their economic successes allowed them more social liberties. There was a spirit of adventure in the chaos that added to New Orleans being imagined as a lively and enjoyable place to live. In conversations with Brazilians who moved down to New Orleans in the first wave of immigration with no previous contacts and no idea about what they were to expect upon arrival, I hear a sense of nostalgia for those days. They talk about *churrascos* at each other's houses to network for jobs, parties in the Brazilian pizza restaurant and their inventions that managed to make life in New Orleans more livable even when the city had few resources available. The character of the Brazilian enclave in New Orleans was established during this time period and continues even through the slowdown in the economic market. If New Orleans remains economically viable as a work destination, Brazilians say that they want to stay because they feel connected to the city. Likewise, even if it is not economically viable, the image of New Orleans' unique character that developed during the post-Katrina environment will continue to influence how future migrants view New Orleans.

Brazilians who worked in New Orleans in 2005 and 2006 reported earning more money in New Orleans than in their previous cities of residence for similar work (Ibrahim 28 January 2008). And the fact that Brazilians were working and earning money meant that they expressed satisfaction with their lives in New Orleans, even though living conditions and access to resources were not at the standard of their previous cities. Brazilians in these special months post-storm were working and getting paid well. Because job opportunities seemed plentiful, Brazilians felt that they had the luxury of socializing more often. Brazilians living in New Orleans in 2005-2006 reported having more active social lives and spending more extravagantly than in New Orleans in 2009 since there is now more need to economize. The idea of New Orleans as a pleasurable city for Brazilians lives on in the memories of this "Katrina time."

It is a memory that is active and alive. Though the size of the Brazilian community fluctuates as individuals come and go, motivated by imaginings of possibilities of employment or lack thereof, the memory of Brazilians' role in rebuilding the city has become a survival strategy for the longevity of the Brazilian community in New Orleans. Remembering their past productivity within the context of Katrina reconstruction plants them firmly into the social fabric of the new New Orleans. "Katrina Time," the founding myth of Brazilian arrival in the city, places New Orleans in the imagination of the Brazilian community as an immigrant's "El Dorado." It is now in some ways a lost paradise, just always out of reach, that rests in their continued imagination of New Orleans' Katrina past and that influences the present and future. "Katrina Time" is a remembered and desired ideal, somewhat grotesque in nature because it arose out of the devastating ruin of the city, but nonetheless this ideal perpetuates Brazilian immigration to New Orleans even when the economic reality in the city today is quite different. Living on in the testimonies and memories of Brazilians, Hurricane Katrina marked New Orleans as a place where the Brazilian community will find economic and social prosperity just ahead, just over the horizon, or at least just after the next hurricane.

Race, Ethnicity, and Place for Brazilians in New Orleans

Not only did Hurricane Katrina mark a difference in the way that Brazilians integrated into the local community of New Orleans in comparison with other cities of residence in the U.S., but also the unique cultural and racial landscape in New Orleans existing prior to the storm became central to Brazilians' construction of their sense of belonging to the city. When Brazilians moved down to New Orleans after Hurricane Katrina, they entered into a racial and cultural environment distinct from other parts of the U.S. The historical particularities of the New Orleans cultural and racial landscape have "othered" New Orleans within the context of U.S. urban identity. Brazilians, as a group that has also been culturally and racially othered, found their place through the processes of hybridity and cultural mixture that have historically come to define New Orleanian identity. The interactions between Brazilians and the pre-existing local landscape are the process through which Brazilian migrants' own identity is imagined.

Migration Redefines Culture

Living outside of Brazil creates new relationships between immigrants and their home. In the novel, *First World, Third Class*, Regina Rheda describes the trials and tribulations of Rita, a middle-class Brazilian filmmaker who, discouraged by her employment options in Brazil, decides to try her luck in Europe. She moves to England as she awaits the paperwork for her Italian citizenship, which turns out to be a more complicated process than she expected. Living abroad requires that Rita rethink her relationship to her Brazilian citizenship as well as to her ethnic and racial identity. Rita had formerly expressed feeling a sense of superiority because she could pass for European rather than looking stereotypically Brazilian:

> Given her looks, she could pass for French, Spanish, Portuguese, or even Irish. Wasn't she European, after all? She felt superior to her friends, who were stuck in their miscegenated fate, doomed to unimportance, irredeemably rooted in Brazil's peripheral impotence (Rheda 95).

Yet the more time that Rita spends abroad, the more that she comes to question her own superiority as a white Brazilian and to venerate the *mulata* figure. For example, walking through the park, she watches the London School of Samba perform a relatively unskillful samba. However, the audience comes alive, "allowing their eyes to shine and their hips to sway" to the Brazilian rhythm. In turn, Rita, "swiveled a touch of pride in her pelvis. Not even the turquoise talent of the American from New Orleans had made as big a hit as this samba from back home" (Rheda 131).

At the same performance, Rita meets Baiana, a sensual, gregarious *mulata* who makes her living abroad by selling the embodied image of Brazil. When asked what she does for work, Baiana replies, "... a little bit of everything to do with the body. If you speak the language of the body, then you speak the language of the universe" (Rheda 132). Though Rita first looks condescendingly upon Baiana as a *malandra*, a trickster, Rita later becomes envious of Baiana, who seems to be having much more success than Rita both economically and with men by performing this image. Baiana's American boyfriend from New Orleans is the object of Rita's own desire and Baiana seems to be able to find both a job and a place to live in places where Rita can't. Writing home to a friend Rita says,

> None of the interesting men will look at me. And why should they? I'm a mess: No one gives a hoot for my Venetian features. I think things would be different if I were your standard-issue Brazilian woman, chocolate-skinned with photogenic hips, even if I were a trickster. Or if I were black, blonde, or Japanese. But what am I? A neutral, mediocre mixture... (139)

Rita comes to understand that her success (or lack thereof) could be contingent on how "Brazilian" others perceive her to be.

Among Brazilian immigrants, Bernadette Beserra has noted a similar phenomenon.

> Brazilians who are more Brazilian are better rewarded. Therefore, Brazilian immigrants soon face the challenge of turning into allegedly real Brazilians, which means, among other things, learning how to dance samba, making feijoada, dressing accordingly, playing soccer (for men), and so forth. Thus they deliberately work on their own exoticization (Beserra "In the Shadow…" 65).

The migration experience itself entails movement from one set of cultural norms to another. Gerard Kubik argues that persons can go through several different cultural profiles during their lifetime in a process of inner cultural reconfiguration (17).[23] The experience of migration often involves the unfolding of different forms of self-identifications. It is a process that happens quite unconsciously as one interacts with a set of unfamiliar cultural, linguistic, and social norms.[24] For immigrants, their cultural profile becomes imagined through the plethora of stories and the kaleidoscope of interpretations that come to mark their cultural identity in the context of the host community in which they find themselves. These stories, told about who they are, are constructed through comparing and contrasting the narratives' surrounding identity in the communities where they find themselves and in the communities where they have been before.

As ethnomusicologist Helena Simonett argues, culture is formed through discursive practices through which a plurality of voices is or-

---

[23] Since the twentieth century, there have been two main theories for the study of identity and immigration: retention theory and assimilation theory. Retention theory, advanced by theorists such as Melville Herskovits and Alejandro Portes, states that immigrant cultures, in spite of their apparent differences to the local country of residence, preserve many of the deeply rooted commonalities of their ethnic enclave that facilitate their retention of ethnic identity in a "generalized form" in the new social environment. On the other end of the spectrum, assimilation theory, outlined by Gans and Zhou, states that immigrants will slowly move away from their characteristic ethnic traits in order to incorporate and assimilate into the cultural environment of the host country.

[24] A language itself is a culture, just as nations, cities, and even families can be. For more about linguistics and identity, see Kátia Maria Santos Mota in *Becoming Brazuca*. She explains how language use is instrumental in immigrant career choices, in negotiations of power, in strategies of exclusion, and as an emotional space for proclaiming a sense of identity (329-332).

chestrated into common themes, idioms, and meanings (Simonett 11). Watching and engaging in the performances of the Brazilian community in New Orleans is like listening and entering into dialogue with the community "story," an entangled mass of stories of many individuals. I hope that the telling of these stories, spoken through words and gestures, can be parlayed into social justice by making us more cognizant of the role of immigrants in the reconstruction of both New Orleans and New Orleanian identity in post-Katrina New Orleans.

Brazilians Interpret New Orleans in Comparison to Other Areas of the U.S.

Brazilians claim that they feel cultural affinities with the city of New Orleans. To begin with, they focus on the mild climate, which they say makes life and work more enjoyable and permits them to work year round. But along with the weather, Brazilians described aspects of the social landscape that make them feel at ease in New Orleans. Brazilians described New Orleans as a cultural middle ground between the U.S. and Brazil. In answering the question about why they liked living in New Orleans, Brazilians usually responded by comparing their experiences in New Orleans with another city in the U.S. or in Brazil:

> For those of us who came from Atlanta, we felt like we were driving to Brazil as we drove down the highway (to New Orleans). The scenery is really similar. The people are friendlier. It is not like that in Georgia. In Georgia if they see more than four people in a car, they stop the car (Diogo 23 January 2009).

> There were a lot of streets around St. Charles that reminded me of streets in Belo Horizonte. The same kinds of trees lining the streets and everything. There is a street near downtown that looks exactly like Brazil. Each time I would go down that street I would imagine that I was in Brazil (Nene 25 January 2009).

> New Orleans culture is different from Boston. In New Orleans, you are freer to do what you want. It is more laid back. The climate in New Orleans is also similar to the climate in Brazil (Chicão 29 January 2009).

> At first I didn't like New Orleans. I thought that it was ugly and old looking. But I got used to it and found out how fun it is... New Orleans is my favorite city that I have lived in the U.S. because there is a lot more freedom there. You can live well, work a little, and have fun... After Katrina, New Orleans became a lot freer for the person to go out and drink and have a good time without being watched. New York is too big. Miami is horrible... New Orleans is great. You make friends easy. It is easy to meet girls (Charles 9 January 2008).

> Brazilians like New Orleans because it is perceived as being very similar to some cities in Brazil. There is much more freedom in New Orleans. Most of the Brazilians in New Orleans come there from the North of the U.S. In the North, the laws are much more strict. You can't hang out on the street with the car stereo blasting. You can't drink on the street... In New Orleans it is very relaxed. Brazilians drive drunk; they have parties all night long. For Brazilians who like parties, New Orleans is the best place to live. The Brazilian community in Boston is much bigger, but they don't have the same freedoms that they have in New Orleans (Fabio 12 February 2008).

The above excerpts from interviews reveal that Brazilians have liked living in New Orleans because they think that it is culturally more similar to Brazil than are other cities in the U.S. The consensus among Brazilians who have spent time in New Orleans (both currently and those who have moved on) is that New Orleans is a city where, overall, Brazilians can be *a vontade* (at ease) and feel *liberdade* (freedom). This does not mean that Brazilians always like New Orleans more than other places of residence. Especially for those who arrived in New Orleans in the first months after Katrina, New Orleans was not an easy city to live in.

> The truth is, when I first arrived in New Orleans [in December, 2005] I thought the city was horrible because when I arrived everything was still closed, nothing was functioning. Everything was difficult for us. The city was ugly. It didn't have any plants or flowers. We are the ones that planted trees and flowers in the city again. Girl, I planted a lot of grass in New Orleans! (Thais 8 July 2009)

Brazilian immigrants who have lived or who are living in Florida, for example, often say that when they have money, they prefer living in Florida because of the physical beauty and the access to the beaches and upscale clubs. Some prefer Massachusetts because the organization of the city and the larger Brazilian enclave is more in line with what they imagined their immigrant experience to be. The overwhelming majority, however, claim that for sheer quality of life reasons, they prefer New Orleans because it is more casual in enforcing laws against immigrants and in its social life. All of this, of course, is dependent on the job market. The social sphere comes second to job opportunities, and downturns in the job market often result in Brazilians becoming more critical of New Orleans. Also, the laid-back atmosphere of New Orleans described in these 2008 interviews speaks to the context of post-Katrina New Orleans. Law enforcement was more relaxed on issues of immigration because government officials were preoccupied by trying to bring some sense of normalcy back to the city.

Performances of a City

Brazilians also refer to the performative aspects of New Orleans when drawing comparisons between Brazil and New Orleans in relationship to other cities in the U.S. The very architecture and spatial organization of New Orleans allow for certain types of performance. When I ask Brazilians what city in Brazil most resembles New Orleans, they often answer Salvador when they have in mind the African influence in the city, the festive street culture, and the friendliness of the city. Fred Góes, Rockefeller Scholar at Tulane University from 2003-2004, writes,

> New Orleans has a lot more in common with Bahia than with the rest of the United States in terms of hospitality, human warmth, kindness, spicy food, the rhythm and swagger of the African descendents, and the magical enchanting cosmic energy, that only the word '*axé*' is able to explain (Góes 14).

To a lesser extent, Brazilians highlight Salvador and São Luis, Maranhão, for the importance of reggae in the local culture, which immigrants also tend to compare to New Orleans. Three interviewees commented that people in São Luis and Salvador were similar to the people in New Orleans because both places had strong connections to Jamaica. They were, in all likelihood, making a reference to the Black Power movement that unites the Black Diaspora experience as a whole. An awareness of the large African American presence in New Orleans— rather than a common musical tradition— is probably at the root of this interpretation: After all, reggae is not a cultural expression for which New Orleans is well known. Rio de Janeiro is also often compared to New Orleans because the carnaval tradition in the Rio de Janeiro sambadrome seems somewhat similar to Mardi Gras krewe traditions; both are spectacles to be watched rather than participatory carnivals. Although both Rio and New Orleans have neighborhood block parties that beckon the public to participate, they are best known for the spectacle of their carnival. Salvador is better known for its participatory carnival but, ironically, with the resurgence of street carnivals, Rio's carnival is becoming just as participatory as the carnival of Bahia, which now has mechanisms such as private boxes (*camarotes*) and cords (*cordas*) as ways to "privatize" the mainstream carnival experience for those with money. It's important to note that these comparisons between New Orleans and the cities of Rio de Janeiro, Salvador, and São Luis are based on immigrants' stereotypical understandings of Brazilian urban place, since Brazilian immigrants themselves have often never visited these cities.

Immigrants also drew comparisons that came very much out of their lived experiences. One respondent saw New Orleans as being most similar to Teresina, Piauí. Piauí is one of the poorest states in Brazil. New Orleans reminded him of Teresina because it is a state capital that has a small town, rural feel. This response is influenced by the fact that the respondent is from Tocantins, the neighboring state to Piauí. Thus, his lived experiences in Brazil make Teresina a more likely answer than Salvador, Rio, or São Luis, three cities that he has never himself visited. The immigrant explained that he made this comparison because when he was driving through Mandeville, one of the suburbs of New Orleans, he saw a family riding around in a horse-drawn carriage. It was a simple carriage of the kind used to carry wood and other materials around a farm. For him, this was a representation of the simplicity and the rural ambiance of the city of New Orleans. New Orleanian suburbs, where many Brazilians find themselves working and living, are greatly influenced by Louisiana rural life. This is an aspect of New Orleanian identity that is often overlooked in the homogenous descriptions of the New Orleans party culture. One Brazilian told me that the first time that he had ever ridden a horse was in New Orleans when his employer took him out to the family farm for the weekend. The closeness of the rural-urban setting is both familiar and comforting to many Brazilians, whose interpretation of the present is necessarily influenced by lived experiences of the past in both Brazil and in New Orleans.

The Latin Side of New Orleans

There is also an understanding of New Orleanian culture that has often invoked comparisons with Latin America's laid-back atmosphere, even though, in recent history, there has only been a large community of Latinos in the city after Hurricane Katrina. Latin American intellectuals have even claimed New Orleans as a Latin City located in the U.S. (Donato 219). Brazilian writer Oswald de Andrade wrote that "in North America we have a sister region— Latin, Catholic, and *mestiça* Louisiana. With her we can get along and communicate" (Andrade 51). Brazilian intellectual Fred Goés, who lived in New Orleans as a Rockefeller Scholar at Tulane University from 2003-2004 while studying comparisons between Brazilian *carnaval* and Mardi Gras, explained that New Orleans is

> ...where the U.S. is part of the Third World, where misery and inequality are evident, as was observed in the aftermath of Katrina; where segregation, as covered as it may be, lets its centuries-old wrinkles appear. There, as a Latino, I felt at home (Góes 146).

This description of "Latin" New Orleans speaks to the general cultural sensibility of the city and not to a population of Latinos. In fact, New Orleans has been one of the least "Latin" cities in the country in terms of recent immigration history. Except for a relatively large pre-Katrina Honduran community that began immigrating to the city to work in the shipyards in the 1960s, a Latino presence was minimal before Hurricane Katrina.

The "Latin-ness" of New Orleans was largely a holdover from the 19th century. As a Southern port city, New Orleans had historical connections with Latin America, in particular, with the Caribbean. The first Spanish-language newspaper in the United States, *El Misisipí,* was published in New Orleans in 1808. New Orleans and Havana, Cuba were, before the U.S. embargo, sister cities, both as business partners in the shipping industry and as two ever-exchanging cultural hubs. As a port city in the Gulf of Mexico, New Orleans was constantly receiving flows of culture, goods, and people from the Caribbean and other parts of Latin America. This process was heightened even more after the Haitian revolution, when many refugees from Saint Domingue settled in New Orleans (Lachance 104). But a declining economy in recent history meant a city with dwindling work options that were insufficient for a substantial immigrant population.

After Katrina, however, Brazilian and Hispanic immigrants alike began to arrive in New Orleans, and they began to interpret New Orleans as having "Latin tendencies." Brazilians noted New Orleanians as being more warm and open in comparison to other parts of the country. They commented on how they saw neighbors talking with neighbors when they were working in different neighborhoods around the city and how people in the streets greet one another. Though New Orleans has achieved notoriety for its violence, poverty, and strained race relations, New Orleans is also well known for having hospitality, a party culture, and easy access to performance in the public space. These are some of the characteristics that separate the social experience in New Orleans from the experience of other cities in the U.S. In describing New Orleans, a Brazilian worker said,

> The people in New Orleans seem very Latin. They like to party. They are very happy. They have more free time. For me, being in New Orleans is the same thing as being in Brazil. They [New Orleanians] are more Latin, happier, more open. Even the police are better prepared to get along with immigrants. They are used to dealing with people who like parties and like to drink. They don't treat you as bad. In the North it is different. They will stop you and humiliate you. I love New Orleans. To have a good time, the best place to live in the U.S. is New Orleans. Those who like to live life with happiness have to live in New Orleans (Carlos 2 June 2009).

Carlos describes the "Latin feel" of the city and the friendly police officers who reinforce the perceptions of New Orleans' relaxed atmosphere in this interview. He mentions that there is something about the spirit of the city of New Orleans that feels "Latin." So much so, in fact, that Carlos says that the way that people and space interact in

New Orleans is the same as in Brazil. This comment communicates his remarkable level of comfort with the city more than communicating a particular similarity between the two places. Following LeFebvre, the "feel" of any space is based on the historical ways in which that space was used. The processes that contribute to a city's ambiance relate to the rhythm and flow of the city; these are not necessarily quantifiable qualities, but qualities that are, nonetheless, significant and historically based.

Carlos notes that his interaction with the police in New Orleans is part of the reason why he sees New Orleans as being more open and free—the police are more accustomed to dealing with tourists, more accustomed to turning a blind eye to revelry. Brazilians that I interviewed expressed the opinion that there was a greater flexibility in the enforcement of laws in New Orleans compared to their experience with other parts of the U.S.

These responses, however, remind us that there is a very human element to the construction of space in New Orleans. Police officers are the regulating foot soldiers of a city culture who ensure that people move along and perform their daily activities in an orderly fashion that is in line with the expectations of the city. Their numbers and their attitudes affect how people interact with the space of the city. In the case of Brazilian immigrants, their responses to police officers affect the extent to which they engage with New Orleans' urban and social environment in secret or in public and whether their social habits are accepted within the spatial and cultural makeup of New Orleans. Carlos' interview seems to reveal that Brazilians feel as if they can move freely in public social spaces in New Orleans, since the police are less likely to become agitated when Brazilians socialize in ways that would not be considered acceptable in the rest of the U.S. (Having open containers of alcohol on the street is a prime example.)

However, interpreting New Orleans as a place where anything goes must also be analyzed through the context of the Katrina disaster. Carlos sees the New Orleans police as being socially better equipped for dealing with immigrant populations. But being better equipped to handle immigrants was definitely not the reality of New Orleans post-Katrina if we make comparisons to other cities in the U.S. where immigration has a longer history. New York, Los Angeles, and San Francisco are, in fact, international cities with a much larger immigrant presence and with more experience dealing with a multicultural population. After Hurricane Katrina, the lack of resources in New Orleans in comparison to the social ills of the city are reasons why police were actually *not* well-equipped for handling the immigration issue. And as we move farther away from the Katrina disaster, law enforcement has become stricter about immigration issues.

Carlos makes a comparison between immigrants and tourists to the city, but these experiences are, in fact, quite distinct. With an overworked police staff that was struggling to maintain order in a half-abandoned city ranked by the FBI in 2008 as the Murder Capital of America, there were more pressing issues at hand than deporting the undocumented immigrants who were rebuilding neighborhoods. The incapacity of the police force to deal with issues of immigration right after the storm actually transferred into these undocumented Brazilian workers feeling more accepted, though this was, by and large, a false belief. Because New Orleans had never before in recent history been a city with a large immigrant population, often police officers simply did not know what to do when they pulled someone over who was driving without a license. It was often easier to pretend that the incident never occurred rather than decide how to handle the situation. "New Orleans is the place where I felt the most comfortable in the United States. The police pulled me over in New Orleans and I was driving just with my driver's license from Brazil. They asked me what I was doing and then let me go. This is great for us" (Vinícius January 2, 2009).

Although Brazilians reported cases of police abuses in post-Katrina New Orleans, in general, Brazilians reported feeling more comfortable with New Orleanian police officers than with the police in other cities in the U.S. While the Brazilians that I interviewed are aware of their precarious position as undocumented laborers, they also said that they rarely found themselves under direct threat of deportation in New Orleans in comparison to experiences in other U.S. cities. Brazilians illustrated this point by claiming to have been stopped several times by New Orleans police officers for minor offenses such as driving with expired license plates, a broken tail light, or swerving while driving. And in each instance, while the Brazilian claimed to speak little English and not have a proper driver's license, police officers let them drive away. That is, although their presence in the city and behind the wheel of a car were technically illegal, they were not actively discouraged right after the storm. But, as we move farther and farther from August 25, 2005, police regulation of undocumented immigrants continues to increase. Carlos, the first respondent quoted above, was deported in 2010 after being stopped for a traffic violation after a night of partying at a local bar frequented primarily by Tulane University undergraduate students. In 2011, Louisiana had the highest number of immigration detentions of any state in the United States.

The Big Easy

Brazilian descriptions of life in New Orleans after Katrina, however, seem to embody the irony of New Orleans' nickname, "The Big Easy." While immigrants interpret New Orleans as an inviting city used to dealing with "outsiders," their descriptions also represent the underlying tensions of this nickname in a city that is "stressed out" with issues of unemployment, violence, and devastating hurricanes.

The phrase "the Big Easy" is drawn from the slang vocabulary of African-American musicians in New Orleans and is used to imply an attitude that New Orleans is a sexually promiscuous city, with lax civil laws, and a laid-back majority black population. The term is thought to reference an obscure jazz hall of the early twentieth century, but it became popular in the 1970s when the term appeared as the title of a crime novel by James Conaway and in the writings of *Times-Picayune* columnist Betty Guillaud. In Guillad's writings, the phrase is used to draw attention to a variety of leisurely activities in New Orleans and to the permissive attitude of local officials who could be bribed away from enforcing the law (Stanonis 243).

Brazilians in New Orleans are privy to the effects of centuries of race and class inequality that masquerade as a tourist paradise. In *Laughter out of Place*, Donna Goldstein explains how laughter is often used as a critique of social power injustices in Brazil. "This humor was a kind of running commentary about the political and economic structures that made up the context within which the people of Rio's shantytowns made their lives— an indirect dialogue, sometimes critical, often ambivalent, always (at least partially) hidden, about the contradictions of poverty in the midst of late capitalism" (Goldstein 2).

The "easy" character of New Orleans, like the episodes of humor that Goldstein documents in the Rio *favela*, are marked with a sense of irony. Brazilians who live in New Orleans come to see first hand that New Orleans is a community that has suffered many abuses, both those caused by the hurricane and by a government that seemed to have abandoned the city. A popular New Orleans T-shirt reads, "It ain't easy in the Big Easy." Implied in this commentary is that residents of New Orleans are often living in communities where structures of power are unpredictable and beyond their own control. Brazilian immigrants find something oddly familiar in this social environment and in the tactics used by New Orleanians to cope. For reasons not so far removed, they decided to leave their home towns, just as many downtrodden New Orleanians did after the storm. But on the other hand, New Orleanians party boisterously, they celebrate Carnival, they play music, and they dance, all in the face of their disaster. Brazilians have often described New Orleans to me as being a *cidade do povo* (a city of the masses), a phrase that invokes everything from folk, to people, to a city that belongs to the subordinate classes. Immigrants themselves, leaving a class of subordination in Brazil, come to trace their own individual histories of subordination onto the *povo* of New Orleans. In this sense, Brazilians come to understand and apply the full irony of the nickname "Big Easy" in their descriptions of New Orleans.

New Orleans as a City of *Malandros*

In an interesting description of the cultural makeup of New Orleans, post-Katrina, Brazilian observers often commented that the work environment post-Katrina revealed New Orleans to be a city of *malandros* in comparison to their other cities of residency in the U.S. A *malandro* in Portuguese is a person possessing *malandragem,* a wily, clever, cunning figure who invents ways to beat the system (or at least to get around it). *Malandragem* is thought of as a characteristic of Brazilian culture and refers to having the cunning and street smarts to succeed even when the system is against you. A person with *malandragem* is considered to be a bit of an opportunist, a hustler, and perhaps even to possess a bit of a Robin Hood spirit. In a work context, Brazilians often felt that the New Orleanians who employed and worked with them were *malandro*s, finding ways to take advantage of Brazilian labor and paying them little, in installments, or with bartered items such as cars or construction tools. Brazilians saw New Orleanian coworkers also finding ways to survive by testing the system. Though *malandragem* is an etic [outside] rather than emic [inside] category for describing New Orleanians (since New Orleanians do not describe themselves as *malandros*), Brazilians, nonetheless, use the term to refer to the New Orleans social world that they are observing.

Malandragem has several levels of significance and can even have criminal connotations.[25] Roberto Da Matta proposes that, in the Brazilian social system, laws apply to the notion of the "individual" and not to actual "people." *Jeitos* (ways of getting around the system) and *malandragens* are forms of "personalizing the law in order to become a person" since the universal rules and laws of Brazilian society are too drastic and impossible for people to actually follow (184). In the 1920s the *malandro* image became part of Brazilian urban culture to describe those people who refused to buy into the unjust working relationships of capitalism and, thus, made their own rules. In this sense, the *malandro* was an urban hero (Calvani 122).

It is the urban setting that necessitates and develops a person's *malandragem* in Brazil and in Brazilians' interpretations of New Orleanians as *malandros*. Though the archetypal *malandro* figure is usually linked to the samba world and pictured wearing a linen suit with a top hat, snakeskin shoes, and some glittering jewelry for good measure, it is possible to imagine that the typical dress of New Orleanians parading with Social Aid and Pleasure Clubs during a second line parade bear points of comparison. Though samba is not playing during the second lines, brass bands are perhaps one of the most traditional musical representations of black New Orleanian neighborhoods; they provide the appropriate musical soundtrack to Brazilian interpretations of the New Orleanian *malandro* as well. Brazilians, whether they seek out second lines or not, come in contact with the image of the second lining New Orleanian that holds affinities with the archetypal *malandro* on the streets and in the stores where they shop. The ludic and capricious cunning of the *malandro* figure is seen in Brazilian interpretations of typically New Orleanian characters, both in their dress and in their interactions.

---

[25] While most Brazilians adamantly state that they do not engage in drugs or criminal activity, they say that they do come into contact with this environment in the neighborhoods where they work. Finding out about the illicit activities Brazilians engage with in New Orleans is complicated by my gender. I have less access to this information because Brazilians are often reluctant to talk to me, a woman, directly about both drugs and prostitution. Though these may be issues among some members in the Brazilian community in New Orleans, I am not qualified to comment on them.

There are obvious differences in the *malandro* image in the two contexts: The *malandro* figure in Rio de Janeiro culture is imagined as a very individualistic figure, while the second-lining *malandro* of New Orleans is linked to a community that is inventing, hustling, and creating ways to survive. There are no moments in Brazilian culture when all *malandros* come marching out together in their matching *malandro* linen suits, for example. However, the commonalities in the social environments in which these figures arise become points by which Brazilians interpret a greater cultural understanding of New Orleans. In the aftermath of Katrina (in a city that had some of the highest rates of poverty and unemployment in the country even pre-Katrina), New Orleans has a culture of inventing ways to survive that stem from the politics and social relationships created through the manipulations of the social system. These manipulations become visible in the daily politics of labor, social interaction, urban navigation, and the overarching pace of life in New Orleans. The Brazilian interviewees by describing New Orleans, in comparison to Boston, Atlanta, and even Florida, as less rigid, less strict, and more open, were also describing a system in which *malandragem* could flourish. The people of New Orleans were considered to be friendlier, more upbeat, more humble, happier, and also more conniving than Americans in other cities. The performance of *malandragem* takes a different form in New Orleans than in other cities in the U.S. (and definitely a different form than in Brazil), but a community with a history of inventing ways to survive speaks to Brazilians' cultural understanding on a personal level.

The *malandragem* of the city of New Orleans in Brazilian interpretations is very much linked to Brazilian understanding of the *liberdade* (freedom) of the social world. Bourbon Street, for example, is infamous for being a space where acting disorderly is not only accepted, but also expected. While far from being another Brazil, New Orleans and its people may bear a resemblance to Brazilian conceptualizations of daily life under the banner of *malandragem* in the form of the *liberdade* (freedom) that this lifestyle offers. *Liberdade* seems to describe a feeling of not being restrained by a strict system of law enforcement, of being able to bend the laws, or having "unwritten social norms" that allow for more flexibility in social movement. In the interviews I conducted, typical examples provided of the *liberdade* of New Orleans included being able to drink on the street, having access to parties and bars that were open twenty-four hours, being able to get out of a ticket by "having connections," and feeling less police surveillance while driving or socializing in public spaces in comparison to other areas of the country.

This comparison is potentially cumbersome, as Brazilians almost unilaterally agree that New Orleans may have *liberdade*, but it is not like the *liberdade* that they feel at home in Brazil. The characteristics of the *liberdade* of New Orleans, then, are mostly tied to its similarities to Brazil in comparison to other areas in the U.S. where public drinking is not allowed, where bars and restaurants close at 2 a.m., where favors and patronage are not routine methods for circumventing the law, and where the local police are more strict in their assumptions about "orderly conduct" in public and in enforcing documentation. Also, as we have already seen, the extent to which New Orleans is unregulated was also very much contingent on the moment in time in which Brazilians arrived. Hurricane Katrina caused such a breakdown in social, political and juridical structures that law enforcement did provide a greater sense of *liberdade*. And, in a community suffering so much pain and destruction, moments of joyous partying were especially embraced, as those were also moments of hope within the crumbling city of New Orleans. The uniqueness of this Katrina Time in New Orleans in nearly every way influenced Brazilian ideas of their own place in the city.

New Orleans' Black/White/Creole Landscape

New Orleans' social environment that allows certain leniencies in interpreting work and social relationships has also developed, to some extent, out of the particularities of its racial landscape. New Orleanians have developed tactics for circumventing the strict black/white dichotomy of the rest of the U.S. while at the same time living in a city heavily influenced by the segregationist traditions of the Deep South. The racial makeup of New Orleans becomes a point by which Brazilians mark the difference of New Orleans from the other cities where they have lived in the U.S., and in ways that create affinities between racial norms in Brazil.

According to the U.S. Census Bureau's 2007 population estimates, the proportion of the Orleans Parish population that is African-American fell from 66.7 to 60.2 percent between 2000 and 2007. Simultaneously, the proportion of Orleans Parish's population that is Hispanic (of any race) increased from 3.1 to 4.5 percent. In other words, during this time period, the percentage of Hispanics in the Orleans Parish population grew by more than 45 percent, while the percentage of African-Americans in the Orleans Parish population dropped by nearly 10 percent. Even so, New Orleans has continued to be a black— or at least a "Chocolate"[26]— City even though the demographics have changed since Hurricane Katrina.

Many attribute the historically large percentage of African-Americans in the city, at least partly, to the periods of French and then Spanish colonialism. New Orleans represents an example of a racial landscape unique to the U.S. but similar to other parts of Latin America, including Brazil. For generations, New Orleans was labeled as the most "African" of U.S. cities. Gwendolyn Midlo Hall points out, "The largest slave plantations of the antebellum South were in Louisiana. Slave participation in the Civil War began and was most extensive in Louisiana. The bitterest battles of Reconstruction, as well as the first mass migrations north after its end, occurred in Louisiana" (Hall 60). The black population in New Orleans was an urban population and was dense because the swamp restricted the city's expansion.

New Orleans was a Catholic city in a Protestant U.S., and this had repercussions for how processes of creolization and identity-formation took place in New Orleans. Periods of both French and Spanish colonial rule implemented many customs and transnational contacts that are unique to New Orleans. The four decades that New Orleans was under Spanish rule were instrumental in giving New Orleans the African heritage that the city has today. According to Gwendolyn Midlo Hall, the French and Spanish slave trade to Louisiana as well as the chaos of being colonized by three different nations made Louisiana

---

[26] Chocolate City was first used by the funk band Parliament in relation to Washington, D.C. The above reference, however, alludes to Ray Nagin's famous speech on Jan. 16, 2006, at the Martin Luther King Day celebration at New Orleans City Hall in which he used the term "chocolate" to describe race relations in New Orleans. Christopher Dunn suggests that Nagin's subsequent defense of this statement ("How do you make chocolate? You take black chocolate, mix it with some white milk and it becomes a delicious drink. That is the chocolate that I am talking about") is revealing of the way that racial relations are often imagined differently in New Orleans. Nagin emphasizes a connection between blackness and *mestiçagem* in this commentary (Dunn "A Roma Negra" 125) .

"arguably the most Africanized slave culture in the United States" (Hall 65). There is no Congo Square (the main square of the French Quarter where, in the colonial era, slaves where allowed to congregate, play music, and dance on Sundays), for example, in any other city in North America. And the Tremé neighborhood in New Orleans, made famous in the HBO series "Tremé," was a neighborhood of free blacks as early as 1770. This meant that African cultural traditions were maintained in a way that they were not elsewhere in the United States (Flaherty 32).

New Orleans is also a city that celebrates its mixed cultural heritage as being symbolic of the city's identity. We often think of New Orleans as a "creole" culture, or a "gumbo."[27] This metaphor was used to signify that New Orleans was a place of racial mixture, a melting pot where the influences of different cultures came together. The term "creole," introduced to Louisiana in the late eighteenth century during Spanish rule, is the disputed symbolic representation of the racial mixture of the city. The word "creole" has been redefined over time for social and political reasons and has many meanings. Jennifer DeVere Brody argues that there is an inherent slippage between race and national origin in the term "creole" because someone could "acquire" a creole identity. For example, a "creole" is typically used to describe someone who was born in the Americas but whose parents, of whatever race, were born in Europe. However, it was also possible to *become* a creole by staying in the colonies long enough. The slippage between race and national origin, of living at home and abroad, has allowed for much leeway in how the term is used today (Brody 113).

In the colonial and early national period, the term was independent of race. "Creole" referred to the culture and cuisine of the largely French-descended, but also heavily African-influenced, native-born population. But when Reconstruction ended in 1877, Jim Crow Laws of separate but equal and American apartheid brought this term into question. In the nineteenth century, the term "creoles of color" emerged, suggesting that creole identity did not entirely transcend race and the meaning of the word "creole" changed radically across time and place. The discourse surrounding the meaning of the word "creole" in New

[27] The word "gumbo" is an Angolan word that came into the Louisiana lexicon sometime in the nineteenth century. Though it is a matter of speculation how it arrived, Ned Sublette notes that travel writers from the nineteenth century were already calling New Orleans culture a gumbo (Sublette 17).

Orleans is related to a Caribbean discourse in which the term was more of a cultural marker linked to language, religion, and culture, rather than to race. It was not until the Anglo-Americanization of New Orleans during the nineteenth century, that the term creole became racialized.

Although the creole was symbolically important as a representation of the uniqueness of New Orleans, the myth of unity through racial mixture does not hold up to the reality on the streets. It did not in the nineteenth century and still does not today. While New Orleans seems to be a city of great racial mixture and though creole culture has emerged as a marker of New Orleanian identity, modern race relations in New Orleans still follow the traditional U.S. racial classification system of black/white that are a stubborn legacy of the U.S.'s segregation history. New Orleanian Creoles of color became black and the segregation practices of the Deep South left their mark.

The creole culture has thus emerged as part of New Orleanian African-American culture. A strict black/white dichotomy is clearly visible in the physical spaces of neighborhoods in New Orleans. These racial dichotomies of the South became even more blatantly visible in the devastation caused by Hurricane Katrina. Ironically, even though New Orleanian culture can be described as a "gumbo," in many ways, New Orleans is one of the most segregated cities in the U.S. because race, poverty, and opportunities for social growth are inextricably linked in the city's urban development. Look no further than the New Orleans public school system in which 83% of the students are African-American and 99% of those students qualified for free/reduced–price lunch in 2005-2006.[28] Neither the African-American nor the creole of color gained social mobility from the symbolic position of the creole as representative of New Orleans' uniqueness.

A Brief Overview of Brazilian Racial History

Brazil's racial landscape holds points of comparison with New Orleans. First, I want to make clear that it is very problematic and, in fact, impossible to accurately compare racial relations of an entire country to those of one city, especially when crossing national boundaries where race as a social construct has evolved quite differently. In

[28] See Teach for America statistics: http://www.teachforamerica.org/corps/placement_regions/greater_new_orleans/schools.htm

fact, the difficulty in such a comparison is especially true when describing the racial landscape in Brazil for the Brazilian immigrants now living in New Orleans. Brazilian theorists and intellectuals who have researched racial thought in Brazil have mostly created an understanding of race relations based on the major urban centers in Brazil. Brazilians living in New Orleans, however, are usually coming from rural areas of Brazil, from states with a far different racial makeup and racial understanding than those areas that have pushed racial theory in Brazil. Nonetheless, having a brief overview about how Brazil as a nation has approached the topic of race is important for understanding Brazilian racial interpretations of New Orleans. We must keep in mind, however, that local communities in Brazil hold different social constructs in their interpretations of race that must also be factored into the analysis.

Among close friends in the Brazilian community here in New Orleans, I am often referred to as "nega" or "neguinha," which literally means, "my little negress." An ex-boyfriend who is Brazilian used to call me "preta" (black woman). I am blonde and blue-eyed. Anyone who has any familiarity with race relations in the U.S. knows that the use of "negra" to refer to a white, especially to a white woman, seems out of place and even inconceivable in U.S. society. But in this example rests the idea that the way that race is conceived and talked about in Brazil is, indeed, different from the U.S. Being called "nega" does not always speak to the color of someone's skin, but can also refer to the affection that the speaker has for that person. In most cases, "Nega" has a positive connotation of affection. This expression is so common in Brazil that few people are actively aware of a racial consciousness when they speak it. In the U.S., however, this word has been highly racialized and politicized.

Brazil and the U.S. are the two largest countries in the Western Hemisphere— both in terms of total population and in terms of African Diaspora population (Telles 13). Modern race relations in Brazil can be broken down into three stages or schools of thought. The first stage began in the early 1930s. Gilberto Freyre's influential book *Casa-grande e Senzala* (1933) *(The Masters and the Slaves)* inspired in future generations of sociologists the idea that Brazil was a racial democracy, alleging the absence of racial discrimination. Though Gilberto Freyre's writings included the terms "ethnic democracy" and "social democracy" (*Sobrados e Mucambos* 1936), the term itself did not appear in

Freyre's writings. The first use of "racial democracy" to describe Brazil was published in an article by Roger Bastide in the *Diário de S. Paulo* on March 31, 1944. "Racial democracy" does not enter into academic literature, however, until 1952 when Charles Wagley uses the term in his "Introduction" to the edited volume *Race and Class in Rural Brazil* (Guimarães 139).

The acceptance of, the debate over, and finally the rejection of "racial democracy" through analyzing Afro-Brazilian discrimination have marked the different periods of racial thought in Brazil. Finally, in the 1950s and 1960s, especially because of the writings of Florestan Fernandes in São Paulo, race in Brazil began to be seen as a powerful determinant in one's location in the class structure in Brazil and, thus, was an important means of maintaining and reproducing the capitalist system.

> In the first two stages of Brazilian racial thought, the culture of legal segregation of the races in the U.S. had been used as a point of explanation for the difference between Brazilian and United States' racial relations. In fact, segregation was used to claim that Brazil had a more "humane" or cordial system of racial relations (Telles 4).

Brazil has historically been famous for not only accepting but exalting miscegenation. The mulatto figure was symbolically important as a symbol of national identity during the Vargas government (1930-1945). Vargas promoted Afro-Brazilian culture, represented through the mulatto figure, as part of the national identity campaign aimed to cross regional and class differences within Brazil. Samba, capoeira, and candomblé were all cultural forms developed in the Afro-Brazilian community and incorporated as representations of the Brazilian nation. There are few parallels to this cult of hybridity in the U.S. That is unless, of course, we consider New Orleans as being symbolically representative of U.S. national identity. Jazz, for example, was not widely used as a popular symbol in nationalist projects in the U.S., though in New Orleans jazz is imagined as central to U.S. cultural identity. Like the mulatto whose symbolic power for identity formation united the Brazilian nation with little actual social mobility for the mulatto, the creole has likewise been so represented in New Orleans. This fact becomes important for the way that Brazilians come to see themselves, a culturally and racially mixed group, fitting within the fabric of New

Orleans identity.

Carl Degler proposed that the difference between racial relations in Brazil and the U.S. can be summed up by the fact that in Brazil the "mulatto" is not considered black and in the U.S. he is (Degler xii). According to Degler, it is this difference in the way that the "mulatto" is understood that makes the racial experience in the two nations so different. In Brazilian society, distinctions are made based on a variety of colors rather than on a U.S. black-white dichotomy. Degler argues that the mulatto has a more privileged position in Brazilian society than Afro-Brazilians because Brazilian political movements have given the mulatto a prime location in nation-making projects; the mulatto was symbolically paramount in understanding what it means to be a Brazilian. However, as Nelson do Valle Silva notes, there was not much difference in the social mobility of blacks versus mulattos in the city of Rio de Janeiro in the 1960s and 1970s (42-43). For mulattoes in Brazil, just as in the U.S., race has played a factor in their lack of social mobility. Degler's comparison of the mulatto figure as exceptional in Brazil is, thus, problematic.

In Brazil, though the mulatto may be symbolically significant, the figure is still marginalized socially and economically. Also, as the U.S. moved away from a system of segregation in the 1950s and 1960s and moved toward a system of systematic institutional integration, this new direction made comparisons of Brazil's racial relations as being superior over the U.S. seem awkward.

> The United States has remained a bi-racial society but has moved from legally barring non-white participation in the power structure to forcing non-white entry into that structure, even if only in token numbers. Meanwhile, the Brazilians are left with the legacy of whitening. Now, as before, the surest means for a Brazilian of African heritage to gain upward mobility is to possess a whiter skin than his parents. The North Americans have embarked on a social experiment the Brazilians have never contemplated: the active promotion— with government funds, laws, and personnel— of equal opportunity (Skidmore *Black Into White* 212).

Though Brazil does not have a tradition of formal racial segregation, it does deal with issues of structural racism in ways much like the U.S. That is, racism is so engrained in the institutional systems that it becomes difficult to pinpoint it. The U.S. approach assumes easily identifiable ethnic groups. All civil rights legislation and "affirmative action" plans are based on this assumption, making it easy to understand why the "mulatto" would be considered black in the U.S. Brazilian legislation, however, is based on the idea that, in racial terms, all citizens are equal in regards to their access to resources. Special provisions for citizens based on race and "affirmative action" programs have been met with obvious skepticism in Brazil, since in a nation with a history of varying categories surrounding race, such provisions are almost impossible to administer and enforce.

Brazilians' Insertion into New Orleans Racial Landscape

Combining the U.S. black/white dichotomy and New Orleans' particular history surrounding the exaltation of the creole figure, Brazilian immigrants in New Orleans are confronted with a racial landscape that in many ways resembles Brazil and in others is quite distinctive. This affects their understanding of their social environment in New Orleans. New Orleans is a city in which racial symbols of mixture represent place and community in everything from performance culture (jazz and blues, Mardi Gras Indians, zydeco, second lines), food (gumbo, jambalaya), and the people that they see on the streets every day. Because of these factors, Brazilians tend to conceptualize New Orleans as a very diverse and accepting city. From a Brazilian perspective in which race is based on a complex color spectrum and where miscegenation has been central to identity, multicultural New Orleans appears more like Brazil than most other areas of the South which have not incorporated symbols of racial mixture as being indicative of local culture.

But the harsh systems of legal racial segregation in the United States have caused New Orleans to evolve quite differently than cities in Brazil. Brazilians are very conscious of the racial division in neighborhoods in New Orleans, for example, even if they are unaware of the historical reasons why these divisions have occurred. Also, Brazilians note that the poor in New Orleans are mostly African-American. Yet Brazilians do not often understand the nuances of structural racism in the city that cause such trends. Plus, they have been conditioned by Brazil's myth of racial democracy to be less conscious of race, often being unable to see the structural violence based on race in Brazil, let alone in the U.S. And even though, culturally, Brazilian immigrants report having more in common with the African-American culture in New Orleans in terms of the way extended families and social networks fill the gaps left by city, state, and federal governments in New Orleans, they do not report feeling a sense of communion with the African-American community. In fact, they feel quite distant. Brazilians, as a whole, tend to express more difficulty integrating into the African-American community than they do into the Anglo community in New Orleans.

Brazilians find themselves navigating systems of structural racism in the U.S. with little knowledge of the root causes, having been socialized in another racial and cultural context. Sales argues that Brazilians bring a certain "cultural baggage" with them when they immigrate to the United States based on their experiences in Brazil (*Brasileiros Longe de Casa* 91-114). While Sales does not mention race explicitly, race cannot be separated from this notion of "cultural baggage."[29] The act of immigration to the U.S., however, begins to heighten racial consciousness among Brazilian immigrants since they must contend with different social constructions for understanding race.

While watching the Brazilian *telenovela, América,* with me in New Orleans, a Brazilian immigrant commented that when watching *novelas* in Brazil, he had never been conscious of racial choices in the programming. But now as he watches, he sees the characters with a new perspective that has been influenced by his time abroad. He went through the characters on the screen: "She looks white. She looks Hispanic. She looks Brazilian. She looks American. He looks American." His decisions were based on phenotypical characteristics that have been used to define his experience of living the past seven years in the U.S. Before immigrating, he would never have thought of the characters in such terms; they had all simply looked Brazilian to him. He now views these actors racially in the way that Americans would interpret them.

As a final project for my seminar on Brazilian immigration to the United States, Katie Chang, one of my students at Tulane University, conducted surveys about racial identification among Brazilians who attended a Brazilian Health Fair that had been organized as the

[29] For more about racial attitudes among Brazilian immigrants see *Fronteiras Cruzadas: etnicidade, gênero e redes sociais* by A.C Martes and S Fleischer and Cileine de Lourenço's contribution to *Becoming Brazuca.*

Service Learning component of our course. In describing how immigration had changed their perceptions of race, many Brazilian respondents (those whom Katie labeled as looking "Latino") felt that their race was viewed differently in the U.S. in comparison to Brazil. Some responses from the surveys: "[In Brazil] race was not important, I thought I was white," "I started to see race when I came to the U.S.," "America is very racist." Those Brazilians who find themselves somewhere in the middle on the color line, as that color line is articulated in the U.S., reported the most striking differences between their perceptions of race in Brazil and in the U.S.; this is because they have gone from being able to pass as white to being considered "black" or "Hispanic." These interviews revealed that Brazilians are, in fact, confronted with new black/white racial dichotomies in New Orleans. At the same time, they tend to see New Orleans as a cultural and racial "other" where they may better fit in.

New Orleans is a city where the majority of the people that Brazilians interact with in their workplace and in the places that they choose to shop and to eat are also not white. Ironically, Brazilians admit a greater connection to New Orleans because of the influence of African-American cultural heritage on the city; they report this African-American culture bears similarities with their own Brazilian heritage. At the same time, they express distance and an inability to find common ground between themselves and the African-American community in New Orleans, which tends to be a close-knit community not used to welcoming outsiders, a tactic of self-protection in the wake of U.S. race relations.

How the Hurricane Affected Racial Understandings

The people who surround immigrants in their daily lives necessarily influence immigrants' opinions about race, but those opinions often lack full context or understanding. In an Oxfam study of New Orleans race relationships post-Katrina, researchers discovered that Latino immigrants often held stereotypes of African-Americans as not being hard workers specifically because they were not aware of the institutional structures that kept African-Americans from returning to work right away after the Hurricane. African-Americans from New Orleans were dealing with the red tape involved in making FEMA and insurance claims. Moreover, the schools for their children had not yet opened in the areas where they found work, precluding them from settling down in these neighborhoods. Immigrants were often in contact with African-Americans on the lower end of the socioeconomic spectrum since immigrants often work low-end jobs. Issues of race and class were convoluted in Brazilian perceptions of the New Orleanian African-American community.

Brazilian affinities towards African-Americans as well as their prejudices against them are in part results of the structural violence that surrounds race in New Orleans.[30] According to Oxfam representative Ilana Scherl, Brazilians were not included in their study of Latino perceptions of race in New Orleans precisely because there seemed to be a difference in perceptions of race between Brazilians and other Latino groups, but Oxfam could not include Brazilians as a separate group because it would have been too costly. So, a comprehensive study on race relations in New Orleans that includes Brazilian immigrants has yet to be done. Some of the attitudes expressed in this Latino-focused survey, however, probably ring true for Brazilians as well. Even Afro-Brazilians have expressed to me that they have found it difficult to integrate into the African-American community in New Orleans because of cultural differences rather than skin color, suggesting that there is something deeply ingrained and structural about the way race is interpreted between cultures.

[30] On June 16, 2009, Oxfam published a study entitled "Building Common Ground," which looked at shared attitudes and concerns between the African-American community and the Latino community in Post-Katrina New Orleans (http://www.oxfamamerica.org/files/building-common-ground-en.pdf). 90 percent of African-American and more than 80 percent of Latino respondents rated affordable health care, affordable housing, job opportunities, and crime as "very important" issues to their survival and well-being in New Orleans. The survey revealed that the two communities suffered many of the same fears and obstacles in the social sphere. The majority of African-American and Latino respondents identified experiencing discrimination based on the way they talk, their education level, and their appearance. The survey also revealed, however, that both communities felt wary toward the other and did not recognize these factors as an obstacle for the other group. While both African-Americans and Latinos see discrimination affecting their own community, each group perceives the other community as experiencing fewer problems in the same areas. For example, both African-Americans and Latinos said their own education levels represented a "major" factor in the discrimination they experienced, but when asked how major a factor discrimination based on education was for the other group, the perceptions were that the discrimination was less pervasive. The same held true when each group was asked about the discrimination the other experienced concerning social and economic success.

Racial Understanding of New Orleans Linked to Home in Brazil

Brazil is the country with the largest number of people of African descent outside of Africa, yet, as I began this discussion of race, I noted that the Brazilian interpretation of race in New Orleans has the added difficulty that the majority of the immigrants in New Orleans are coming from rural environments in Brazil where Afro-Brazilians are not, in fact, a majority. My interviews reveal that there are many Brazilians who do not attempt to adapt to New Orleans culture or to the structures of classification in the U.S. at all, especially those immigrants coming from rural areas in Brazil's interior. There are many Brazilians whose daily routine is simply going to and from work seven days a week to be able to earn enough money to return to Brazil as soon as possible. They live with other Brazilians and work for a Brazilian subcontractor. Their social context is often so different from other New Orleanians that they feel unable to find common ground. Along with language barriers, the social differences between rural and urban environments seem insurmountable. Those heavily involved with the Brazilian evangelical church in New Orleans also have few social interactions with local New Orleanian culture because of their religious choices.

The cultural similarities between Brazil and New Orleans are more applicable in Afro-Diasporic cities such as Salvador (which is 85% Afro-Brazilian) rather than the immigrant hometowns of Conceição do Araguaia, Pará or Colorado do Oeste, Rondônia. What a Brazilian from Rondônia has in common with a Brazilian from Salvador is little more than an imaginary line drawn to demarcate Brazilian territory. And if that line had been drawn 300 miles east, there would be little at all uniting them. These Afro-Diasporic cities in Brazil, however, are important in national Brazilian cultural imagining. Even though immigrants from Bahia are in the minority in New Orleans, they are slightly more visible because *baianos* are disproportionately involved in the Brazilian music groups that have made the most significant cross over into the local New Orleanian community. Bahians who are friends of these musicians are also more likely to attend such events and mix with other spectators, increasing the visibility of *baianos* in the cultural scene of New Orleans.

Overwhelmingly, however, as we have already seen, the Brazilians in

New Orleans come from rural or semi-rural backgrounds in the Center-West of Brazil, though the specific towns and villages vary greatly. And in these sending communities in Brazil, the number of people attending the local rodeos often outnumbers those at soccer matches; the music playing on the local radio is *sertanejo* and not samba. Needless to say, these towns break the stereotypes of symbolic Brazilian nationalism. This difference between the rural inner Brazil and its more celebrated coastal cities is perhaps most striking when we look at the racial make up of these rural sending towns. In the Brazilian cities and towns with relatively large numbers of immigrants living in New Orleans, very few had a sizeable Afro-Brazilian population. In fact, the 2000 Census data indicates that less than 10% of the population living in any of these locations identified themselves as "black." Conceição do Araguaia had the largest percentage to identify as black with 9% of the population; Turvânia had the lowest percentage with only 1% of the population. We must remember, however, that racial categories in Brazil are quite different from the U.S., and even those Brazilians who identified as "white" in Brazil are often considered non-white on the U.S. color spectrum, convoluting issues of race during the migration experience. A large portion of the Census respondents also identified themselves as *pardos* (mixed-race), indicating that they fit somewhere in between on the color spectrum in Brazil, not to mention in the U.S.

	Belo Horizonte, Minas Gerais	Governador Valadares, Minas Gerais	Manhuaçu, Minas Gerais	Padre Paraíso, Minas Gerais	Goiânia, Goiás	Turvânia, Goiás	Colorado do Oeste, Rondônia	Conceição do Araguaia, Pará
White	1,199,070	105,743	42,131	3,464	625,922	3,884	11,469	12,631
Black	180,056	16,075	4,899	986	41,202	77	1,349	4,069
Amarela	4,312	361	73	12	3,386	0	96	16
Parda	833,668	122,686	19,310	12,931	411,663	1,150	8,749	26,309
Indígena	7,588	629	246	16	2,290	1	51	127
Sem Declaração	13,831	1,637	464	65	7,915	22	178	235

Figure 11: Table of 2000 Census Data on Race from Migrant Sending Cities

So while the majority of the Brazilians in New Orleans classify themselves as being white in Brazil, phenotypically, many of them bear resemblances to the local New Orleanian community in that a significant percentage of their community appear to be of mixed ancestry. Brazil's racial history of *mestiçagem* can be seen to parallel New Orleans Creole culture; both are famous as locations of distinctive racial mixture. However, I would argue that being able to "pass" for New Orleanian is possible for only some Brazilians— mainly those who come from cosmopolitan areas of Brazil and who can present themselves as being more multicultural and, thus, more "blendable." Regional differences between Brazilians are significant because Brazilians from some areas of Brazil have more ease blending into the local New Orleanian cultural setting than others do.

Vignette of Gustavo: A Brazil/New Orleans Commentary on Race

In order to illustrate how differences in racial categories between the U.S. and Brazil and structural racism have influenced the daily interactions that Brazilians have with the New Orleanian social scene, I present a vignette of Gustavo, a dark-skinned Afro-Brazilian from Salvador, Bahia who moved permanently to New Orleans after coming to the city to do window restoration in 2006. He says that integrating into the African-American culture of his African-American (New Orleanian) wife has been a challenge. Gustavo had lived in Boston in 2006 and was planning to return to Brazil after his last job in New Orleans because work had slowed for him and he had recently divorced his Brazilian wife.

In his first trip to New Orleans, he stayed for three weeks to work on the window project. He did not like New Orleans because he arrived six months after Hurricane Katrina and he was shocked by the lack of resources, by the flies and mosquitoes, and by the destruction that he witnessed. After finishing the window job in New Orleans, he went to Miami to say goodbye to some friends before moving back to Salvador. While in Miami, however, he got another call from his friend in New Orleans asking him to do another restoration job, so he decided to return.

During this second trip, he discovered Casa Samba, a Brazilian Samba School run by African-Americans. There, he met his future wife, an African-American native of New Orleans who dances with the group. He decided to stay. His new social connections through his wife changed his perspective on New Orleans; he said that he began to feel many similarities between New Orleans and his hometown of Salvador. Obviously, Gustavo has forged cultural bonds with the African-American community through his personal social and domestic life. Because of his skin color, one could assume that his acceptance and integration into the African-American community in New Orleans would have been rather easy, especially given the familiarity with African-American culture that he gained through his marriage. However, even Gustavo spoke of the difficulties of integrating into the New Orleanian African-American community:

> When I go to work in an African-American neighborhood, it is really hard. They accept me unless I start to talk. As soon as I start talking, everything changes. If I am in a neighborhood where there are both blacks and whites, like in Metairie, I don't feel as much discrimination. But, yes, I have experienced discrimination from the African-American community here in New Orleans. I have had people tell me that I am not black; I am of "African descent." This guy said to me that "black" means someone who was born here in the United States. Black people from other countries outside of Africa are people of "African descent." For him, "black" only refers to people who were born here…
>
> My boss put me to work in a condominium complex that was all African-American. He put me there because he thought that there would be a better chance that they would accept me coming into their homes because I was black rather than if two white guys were to come in. He thought they would treat us better. Everything would go well in the morning when I arrived and they thought that I was an African-American. But as soon as I spoke, they started to be suspicious.
>
> I was in one neighborhood and this guy came up and asked me if I was faking my accent. He thought that I was an undercover police officer. He had to explain to me what the word "undercover" meant. I had heard the word "undercover" before, but this was the day that I really learned what it meant. I said, 'Are you crazy? I am from Brazil!' He said, 'I don't know. But if I catch you speaking in English without an accent you are going to have some problems with

us here.' I said, 'No. Don't worry. I am not a cop. You won't have any problems' (Gustavo May 13, 2009).

Gustavo's difficult interactions with African-Americans in New Orleans suggest many complexities of the Brazilian experience in the city. On the one hand, Gustavo has found obvious points of connection to the African-American community. He is married to an African-American woman and he says that he has been well received into her family. He comments that he thinks there are many similarities between the culture of his Brazilian family and hers. He says that he feels as though her family and friends are particularly interested in learning about his culture and mentions that they have even expressed an interest in going to Brazil. Because of his marriage, in 2009 when this interview was conducted, he interacts more with people in the New Orleanian African-American community than he does with Brazilians during his daily life. But Gustavo also describes how even though he often feels that there should be a sense of unity and acceptance based on race between himself as an Afro-Brazilian and African-Americans in New Orleans, African-Americans receive him with a sense of skepticism because of language and cultural differences. He does not fit within their racial scheme and they do not know how to place him. So, while we may think of mestizo Brazilians, especially Afro-Brazilians, as having a greater possibility of acceptance into the African-American community in New Orleans, it is obviously not as simple as this.

These interactions between Brazilians and African-Americans on the community level are especially interesting in terms of how Brazil is viewed in the realm of cultural performance. Casa Samba, for example, a Brazilian cultural performance group run by African-American New Orleanians, is often hired specifically to do events in New Orleans that draw attention to the transcultural connections between Brazil and New Orleans, especially with emphasis on the African Diaspora. On the stage, the Brazil-New Orleans Afro-Diasporic connections seem favorable. On the community level, however, the culturally significant and historically resonant criteria for categorizing race make close friendships across ethnic lines difficult.

An Afro-Brazilian colleague of mine who enjoys participating in New Orleanian culture and is herself engaged to a New Orleanian (black) creole commented that she often feels as if she is an infiltrator into the New Orleans African-American cultural scene. She loves to frequent cultural events such as second lines and parades by the Mardi Gras Indians, but she comments that she is always an "outsider" at these events. She compared going to a second line to going to a samba circle in Rio. During the course of the music, everyone is friendly, but when the party ends, all the partiers go back to their own houses. In the seven years that she has lived in New Orleans, my informant has never been invited to the home of anyone that she met through a second line event. So, while she may be participating in black New Orleanian culture as a spectator, she feels that assimilation is not an easy process. Culture and language seem to be more important markers of assimilation than race; culture speaks louder than color concerning who is accepted or not accepted as part of a particular group.

Being In Between Categories

Brazilians are a hard group to classify both culturally and racially since many do not self-identify with the term Latino and since many have a physical appearance that fits somewhere "in between" on a U.S. racial color line. They may pass as New Orleanians or as Latinos, but they often do not self identify with either. Labeling Brazilians as Hispanic or Latino, as they are often labeled in U.S. official documents, poses two problems: First, race is a social, economic, and political construct. This is evident in the different understandings of racial categories in Brazil and the U.S. Secondly, the term "Hispanic," as a U.S. social, economic, and political construct, does not incorporate Portuguese speakers in its root definition. Thus, few Brazilians self-identify with Hispanic since the term implies Spanish and not Portuguese descent. "Latino" is perhaps a little bit more acceptable since Latino is a reference less to history than to the geographical place of origin. It is not incorrect since Brazil is located in South America, but the word holds no descriptive power to a label of race, a social category used to classify people according to arbitrary but, nevertheless, culturally significant and historically resonant criteria.

In New Orleans, Brazilians' racial invisibility (both the fact that they don't identify as Hispanic and the fact that many can pass for New Orleanians) has at times worked in their favor, sparing them from the brunt of racial discrimination. On Nov. 3, 2006, a town hall meeting was held to discuss the growing immigrant community in

New Orleans and what was reported as a subsequent growing racial tension. A community member commented that two reasons for New Orleanian resentment of the immigrant community are lack of education and fear of a group of people whose customs and habits are unfamiliar to them (Town Hall Meeting 3 Nov. 2006). The media often exacerbated the portrayal of Hispanic immigration by publishing articles that presented the Hispanic presence in a negative light. News stories often went for shock appeal and concentrated on lootings, immigration conflicts, and job abuses. Few stories appeared about the rich cultural additions made by Latinos in the New Orleanian community. David Meeks of *The Times-Picayune* said that when the paper did a bilingual cover story on the front page about the Spanish-speaking immigrant population, he received complaints for two straight weeks from New Orleanians who were opposed to immigration (Town Hall Meeting 3 Nov. 2006). By "immigrant," in both the town hall meeting and in *The Times Picayune* articles, most people referred specifically to the Hispanic community.

Although it may be problematic for Brazilians to be the invisible minority in terms of finding access to resources, their invisibility has benefited them; most New Orleanians are completely unaware of the size of the Brazilian population currently working in the city. Brazilians are thus shielded from the brunt of the anti-immigrant debate. There has been hardly any media attention on Brazilians, except when they are lumped under the term Hispanic, a community with which Brazilians do not self-identify.

The one exception to this invisibility was an article published on Jan. 20, 2008: "Brazilian Boom: Attracted by construction jobs and an easygoing lifestyle, more and more Brazilian immigrants are settling in New Orleans. But it's too soon to say whether the enclave will put down permanent roots." In the article, *The Times Picayune* presented a very positive portrayal of the Brazilian immigration experience to New Orleans. Brazilians were praised for their entrepreneurial endeavors, their cultural likenesses to New Orleans lifestyle, and their role in the reconstruction process (Nolan). The article separates Brazilians from Hispanics by explaining how "Brazilians tend to be skilled construction workers rather than day laborers" and comments on their large numbers in ESL classrooms. In this single positive post-Katrina immigration story, Brazilians are purposefully separated from Hispanics.

It is, in fact, appropriate to separate Brazilians from Hispanics since, in general, the Brazilian community remains separated from the Hispanic community in living arrangements, work networks, and in the public imagination. There are individual cases of Brazilians befriending, dating, and sharing housing with Hispanics, but these cases are the exceptions that prove the rule. In general, Brazilians have tended to remain a separate community. Thus, when Brazilians interpret their acceptance into the New Orleanian community, they usually say that they feel less racial discrimination than they felt in other areas of the country and less than their Hispanic counterparts report. (I found the first point to be especially the case among Brazilian immigrants coming to New Orleans from Georgia and Florida, where racial tensions seemed to be more pronounced.) When Brazilians do express feeling racial discrimination in New Orleans, they often report that it is because they have been falsely identified as being Hispanic. Gustavo says,

> Brazilians still have a certain amount of credibility here. There have been times when I have been working and I started talking Portuguese with my partner. Most people in New Orleans don't know the difference between Spanish and Portuguese. They ask me if we are Hispanic. 'No.' They say, 'Ah, because if you were Mexican I was going to ask you to leave my house. I don't want Mexicans, Hondurans, anyone who speaks Spanish in my house because they might rob me or do a bad job.' Americans here still accept that the Brazilians are different. They have a certain amount of credibility as being hard workers. This happened to me more than one time. It was not that the person always had something negative to say about Hispanics, but you can tell (Gustavo 13 May 2009).

This interview shows that Gustavo was able to distance himself from internalizing racial discrimination by considering that he was not a part of the Hispanic community. He sees himself as being accepted precisely because he is Brazilian and not Hispanic. In truth, most likely the significance of difference is not on Gustavo's "Brazilian-ness," but is simply a function of the client's dim understanding of Brazil's geographic and cultural identity. When Gustavo says that he is not Hispanic, he is Brazilian, the client has little idea how to interpret this because, until that moment, Brazil was not on the client's radar of stereotypes. Thus, lack of knowledge of Brazil means the client has not even developed an opinion for or against Brazilian immigrants. In fact, as mentioned above, he does not even recognize what language is being spoken. Gustavo, however, interprets this scene as proof of the perception that Brazilians have more credibility as hard workers. So a moment that could have turned out with Gustavo feeling discriminated against was actually transformed into a moment of feeling a sense of Brazilian identity and acceptance— "No, I am not Hispanic."

New Orleans as an "Othered" Landscape

Though Brazilians have interpreted the cultural and racial landscape of New Orleans in a myriad of ways, what seems to be consistent is that Brazilians imagine New Orleans as being an "othered" city. Thus, Brazilians, as a culturally and racially "othered" group themselves, have found that they have been able to fit easier within the social structures of New Orleans. Emily Clark claims that New Orleans should be imagined as being "at the heart of American identity" rather than seen as being "othered" (Clark 32). She asserts that through the rhetoric in the news following the devastation of Hurricane Katrina, it was possible to deduce that at the heart of the national response to Katrina was a belief that the people of New Orleans *do* occupy a foreign country" (Clark 27). Clark argues that the slow response to Katrina was based on the opposition of a false dichotomy between an American history and identity and a New Orleanian history and identity, i.e., the government responded slowly to New Orleans because New Orleans is seen as not being fully "American." For Clark, the way that New Orleans is imagined, as an exotic creolized place where life and law operate differently from the rest of America, is more a construction of government officials and the tourism industry than it is a result of a process of historical development that is, in fact, unique from the rest of the U.S.

Clark is right to point out that the "othering" of New Orleans is very much related to the images created to attract tourists. There are layers of exaggeration in the way New Orleans is imagined to fit an economically attractive cultural profile. The city is set up for tourists to have the type of relationship with New Orleans that they come looking for. Bourbon Street is a prime example of marketing the music, sex, diversity, and anything goes party atmosphere of New Orleans to an exaggerated degree. The way that many Brazilians interact with the city of New Orleans, in fact, is often as a tourist would interact with it because it is the city's public spaces that are most accessible to them. So for the same reasons a tourist sees New Orleans as the exotic "other," so do Brazilians to some extent. And, at the same time, they interpret, as outsiders, what they perceive as "New Orleans is like Brazil," making connections to the food, the culture, the music, the people, and perhaps, unconsciously, to the identity-building projects in both locales that exaggerate the idea of the exotic in the making and marketing of identity.

However, Clark's argument that New Orleans is othered simply through the bureaucracies from above is a subject for debate. While Clark is right to note the importance of culture from above, more emphasis must be given to the agency that local New Orleanians have had in building New Orleans' culturally unique image. Looking at New Orleans culture as simply a product of government and the tourism industry seems to overlook the influence of local New Orleanians in the creation of the local character of the city. New Orleans' distinctiveness also arises from the people who live here, and not simply from the discourses surrounding the marketing of the city.

I agree with Clark that, yes, the "othering" of New Orleans has been an aspect of marketing New Orleans to the tourist, and New Orleans is, in fact, more American than we think. However, I would nevertheless contend that understanding New Orleans' uniqueness also means conceptualizing New Orleans' transnational ties with both Cuba and St. Domingue in the eighteenth and nineteenth centuries, rather than imagining New Orleans as a U.S. city disconnected from the rest of the world. From this perspective, New Orleans is at the heart of American identity precisely because it is an alternative example of cultural evolution that has partaken of the cultures of an *entire* American hemisphere. For this reason, New Orleans, it could be argued, is the most American of cities. The complexities of the transnational relationships in New Orleans in its founding era, especially the influences of these relationships to the social constructs of race, is imperative to understanding the distinctive spirit and character of New Orleans. Along with this history, the people of New Orleans themselves, through popular culture and their own battles of everyday resistance, have been active agents in making New Orleans a culturally unique place. Brazilian immigrants' interpretation of New Orleans as "a little piece of Brazil in the United States" or as a "Latin" city portrays its unique cultural evolution based on historically constructed social and racial categories in New Orleans that do, in fact, differ from other parts of the U.S.

Post-Katrina Brazilian Identities

Living outside Brazil often requires Brazilian immigrants to be more auto-critical, both in terms of their Brazilian identity and of their identity as immigrants. In an interview, a Brazilian immigrant who moved to New Orleans after Hurricane Katrina commented to me that Louisiana now feels like home to him:

> Louisiana, for me, is home. It is like being born in a place. Even if it is a region that is very humble with little comfort, that is where you are born. And you love that place. For me, Louisiana is this. It is my home. I love this place. Moving here was like being born again… New Orleans was a rebirth. All that we went through in the difficult times [were] to get to where we have gotten today…" (Gilson 30 June 2009).

For Gilson, moving to New Orleans was a rebirth, the creation of a new identity. The formation of a new self unfolded through the struggles to make a place for himself, adapt to a new set of cultural norms, and create a new sense of community with which to identify, all while dealing with the wreckage left by Hurricane Katrina. Homemaking in New Orleans involved "tucking away thoughts of difference" and finding symbolic moments of solidarity with both other Brazilians and with New Orleanians. The spirit of solidarity that arose out of the crisis of New Orleans reconstruction and the distinctive racial and cultural landscape of the city in comparison to other cities in the U.S. allowed Brazilians to construct a place for themselves in New Orleans. Even though the comparisons of culture and race in Brazil and New Orleans rest very much in the realm of imagination, Brazilians find ways of bridging the actual cultural gaps between their two homes by making such comparisons.

In some ways, Brazilians have come to feel a connection with working class New Orleanians, black, white, and creole. Especially in the aftermath of Katrina, locals and immigrants alike were dealing with similar day-to-day issues of getting by and surviving. Because immigrants and working-class New Orleanians continue to deal with similar issues of poverty and structural marginalization, and because both groups tend to seek ways to enjoy life even in hardship, Brazilians express feeling a sense of kinship with the locals, even though this kinship is experienced mainly through observing from afar. These factors together create a unique racial and cultural landscape that Brazilians must navigate as they form a sense of their own place as immigrants within the cultural mix of New Orleans.

Brazilian perspectives on the racial and cultural landscape of New Orleans expressed in this chapter show us that migration causes us to question our interpretations of categories used to classify who we are. Brazilian immigration to New Orleans illustrates how local categories of classification become complicated by transnational flows as displaced peoples (Brazilians and New Orleanians alike) cluster around imagined ideas of home, community, and urban space that may or may not be anchored in actuality. The process of mediating these diverse flows of racial and cultural understandings becomes part of the imagining of the Brazilian enclave character in post-Katrina New Orleans. We must consider how viable it will be, once reconstruction ends, to have a large immigrant community in a city that has been historically poor and working class.[31] Answers to this and other questions will be revealed with time and will influence the way that the Brazilian immigrant community continually reinvents itself.

[31] Louisiana has one of the weakest economies in the United States. This, as we have seen, is one of the main reasons why there was not a large immigrant community in New Orleans before Katrina— the economy offered them no huge draws. Becoming part of the makeup of the Louisiana economy post-Katrina, Brazilians experience divisions of wealth that are very similar to the world that they left behind in Brazil. New Orleans is a city with some of the greatest contrasts between the rich and the poor in the U.S. In most places in the South, the rich and the poor are separated geographically, but, in New Orleans, you can walk down a neighborhood block with houses half falling down and with the spray paint markings of Katrina still visible. Then, two blocks later, you can find yourself standing in front of mansions so beautiful that tourists come to New Orleans year round just to gaze at them. This is a social phenomenon that Brazilians understand. Brazil is a country that has one of the widest disparities of wealth worldwide: The richest 10% control more than 50% of all wealth and the poorest 10% less than 1% (Gannon 100). Braziliain *favelas* [slums] sit back to back with the residences of the upper echelons of Brazilian society. Choosing to live in New Orleans long-term could mean a negative change in their economic earnings for some immigrants, in comparison to other cities; Brazilians seem conscious of this. But I think that many of these immigrants still hope to stay, motivated by their imagining of New Orleans as a more pleasurable and welcoming experience— as a halfway point between their lives in Brazil and the life that the immigrant experience offers them.

Brazilian Enclave Spaces Emerge in Post-Katrina New Orleans

Idelber Avelar, a professor at Tulane University, has a blog entitled "O biscoito fino e a massa." In this blog, he talks about issues of politics, literature, and music as they relate to his personal experience as a Brazilian living in the U.S. On July 12, 2007, Idelber wrote a poignant blog explaining how the experience of living abroad has made him feel even more Brazilian because, when he is far away from home, he begins to idealize the concept of home in ways that he did not while living in Brazil.

Idelber describes the experience of embodying multiple relationships with his own Brazilian identity depending on his geographical location and on the people who are around him as a "ping-pong" effect; he constantly switches how he chooses to identify based on the cultural contexts where he finds himself. Obviously, Idelber writes from a perspective that is notably different from the Brazilian working class immigrant.[32] But the "ping-pong" of the Brazilian imaginary experienced by Idelber articulates similar sentiments of expatriation expressed by the Brazilian working class immigrants in New Orleans as they choose to recreate spaces in New Orleans that remind them of home in Brazil.

The physical spaces that Brazilians choose to occupy in New Orleans create an enclave community existing between homeland and the current "home" in New Orleans. An immigrant's identity, while always malleable, rests at this "ping-pong" between two imagined nations: one

[32] Idelber has a Ph.D., is white, has been speaking English since pre-adolescence and was not leaving a desperate living situation when he left Brazil. He did not go into thousands of dollars of debt as a final gamble at economic prosperity.

defined by his or her daily life and experiences in Brazil and the other constructed in trying to remember the absent spaces of Brazil while in the U.S. Immigrant enclave spaces allow Brazilians a safe space to play the "ping-pong" identity game.

Brazilians have adapted and invented spaces within a New Orleanian social sphere that both consciously and unconsciously reference Brazilian perceptions of the local community and the diversity of the Brazilian community within the "new" New Orleans. The Brazilian community in New Orleans is influenced by immigrants' connections to Brazil, their work life, and the cultural and racial landscape in New Orleans itself. Brazilians' sense of belonging is not fixed, but is multifaceted and is constantly "refurnished" through specific migrant performances that tie Brazilians to each other in spaces that are culturally relevant. Brazilian immigrants constantly perform the rituals of conformity and nonconformity to the hegemonic understandings of Brazilian identity within their enclave spaces. This chapter will outline those spaces that Brazilians have marked as particularly "Brazilian spaces" in post-Katrina New Orleans, and will illustrate how Brazilian performances within these spaces become the foundations of the community character.

Brazilian Identity Performances within Enclave Space

The construction of national identity depends on political, geographic, and linguistic categories. However, even though these categories must exist in order to demarcate nations, their borders are inherently porous. The national border has never been a stable container of identity, since the border has always been permeable and the cultures on either side have shifted over time. Enclaves of co-ethnics living abroad show us that such categories can no longer capture the elastic boundaries of the nation. There is no such thing as a fixed or static Brazilian national identity because identity is always imagined by a regionally, racially, and socioeconomically diverse group of Brazilians.

Enclave spaces take into account the experiences common to all Brazilians in the U.S. as well as the regionally diverse lived experiences of Brazilians coming from various parts of Brazil. The yellow, green, and blue of the Brazilian flag have a heightened ability to unite the Brazilian community in the U.S. at the same time that those colors represent a sense of increased diversity in Brazilian experiences. Upon arriving, many Brazilian immigrants come to self-identify with a Brazil that really had little relevance to their previous lived experience in Brazil, but that becomes important for their experience as Brazilians living abroad. The nostalgic immigrant finds a sense of unity behind the exaltation of these symbols.

Arjun Appadurai uses the word "ethnoscape" to define the shifting world of people in which this plurality of cultures co-exist and interact with one another. These ethnoscapes are not spatially bound, but reproduce across transnational ties. Appadurai explains an ethnoscape as "culture" that is in its adjective form; the term "cultural" emphasizes the fact that culture really lives in the realm of differences, in contrasts and comparisons between one group and another. Brazilian culture is not a noun or an object, but it is a process that continually evolves through discourse (Appadurai 33). To talk about the cultural, we are referring to differences that are observable in relation to some other embodied object or culture. Therefore, culture (the cultural) for Brazilian immigrants speaks of differences within enclave identities that are constantly in the process of making and remaking.

The Brazilian ethnoscape now includes a cultural connection between a place like New Orleans and Minas Gerais, for example. We see the veracity of this connection not only in the increase in a flow of people between the two regions, but in an increase in the media flows between Brazil and New Orleans as well. The *Jornal Nacional do Globo*, the Brazilian primetime news channel, came to New Orleans to do a news story on Brazilian immigration and aired a four-minute news program on Brazilians in New Orleans on April 6, 2006 during the 8 p.m. timeslot. The fact that Brazilian immigration to New Orleans made primetime news in Brazil in 2006 is a testament to the changing ethnoscapes of a city and a nation. At the focus of the news story were Brazilian musical performers and the Brazilian owners of stores, restaurants, and churches because these are the most meaningful markers of an enclave community. The Globo news channel has continued to return to New Orleans periodically to provide updates on the Brazilian community in New Orleans and will, presumably, continue to come as long as a significant Brazilian community presence continues.

Performing Brazil in Enclave Spaces

Brazilian immigrants find themselves inevitably represented and perceived, either by Americans or by Brazilians from other regions of Brazil, in ways that they were not familiar with in the past once they arrive in the U.S. According to Judith Butler, identity is not an idea that is free floating, but is a result of daily, embodied performances. "Identity is performatively constituted by the very 'expressions' that are said to be its results" (Butler 25). In the case of Brazilian immigrants, these expressions can be in line with nationalistic understandings of Brazilian culture: samba, soccer, and *carnaval*. Or they can offer alternative, yet no less Brazilian, expressions of culture: *sertanejo*, rodeos, and Brazilian Pentecostal churches, for example.

Butler notes that these alternative ideas of culture are sometimes referred to as being "subversive" of dominant cultural paradigms. However, as she also insists, placing a judgment on what is and what is not considered to be a subversive performance should always happen within context. For example, among Brazilians coming from rural areas of Brazil, *sertanejo*, rodeos, and Pentecostal churches may actually be imagined as "mainstream" expressions since what is considered mainstream is in dialogue with normative social practices located within the context being described. Butler says,

> I am not interested in delivering judgments on what distinguishes the subversive from the unsubversive. Not only do I believe that such judgments cannot be made out of context, but that they cannot be made in ways that endure through time ("contexts" are themselves posited unities that undergo temporal change and expose their essential disunity). Just as metaphors lose their metaphoricity as they congeal through time into concepts, so subversive performances always run the risk of becoming deadening clichés through their repetition and, most importantly, through their repetition within commodity culture where "subversion" carries market value (Butler xxi).

Brazilian identity is created by what Brazilians do at particular times, rather than through an assumption that all Brazilians inevitably are or behave in a certain way. Samba, soccer, and *carnaval* may seem natural to our understandings of what Brazilian culture should be because the national representations of Brazil are seen as transcending cultural differences. But alternate understandings of Brazil are actually the norm within the Brazilian enclave community in New Orleans.

As Brazilians continue to settle in the suburbs of Metairie, Kenner, and Chalmette because of cheaper rent prices and closer proximity to job sites, Brazilians have fewer direct physical contact with the cultural traditions of New Orleans that share the most affinities with Brazilian mainstream culture (second lines, Mardi Gras, and the party life of the city). I have noticed that even those Brazilians whom I had known to participate in New Orleanian culture fairly regularly when they were living in Uptown and Downtown New Orleans in the months after Hurricane Katrina seemed to lose those connections once they moved to the suburbs. Pure distance became an issue for deciding where to socialize as well as for knowing when and where different events were taking place. On the other hand, I have already emphasized that most Brazilians in New Orleans are coming from rural areas of Brazil. Moving to the suburbs put them in closer proximity to rural Louisiana in terms of both geographical and cultural proximity. They are living closer to the lake for fishing, the woods for motorbike racing, and Brazilian churches for a necessary support network.

Alternate Ideas of Brazil within Enclave Spaces

Alan Marcus asserts that the spaces that Brazilian immigrants reproduce in the U.S. offer new ideas of Brazil that are often unnoticed by Americans (Marcus *The Context*... 20). In Brazilian cultural spaces in New Orleans, the regional traditions of the central west of Brazil are more present than the images of Brazilian nationalism. This fact comes to influence the development of the Brazilian enclave character and the spaces that become community landmarks. The poster on the wall in the local store "Brazil Connection" in 2007 shows a picture of cattle grazing in a pasture. There are no pictures of Rio de Janeiro's Corcovado or Pão de Azúcar anywhere in sight since the cultural symbols of Brazil for Brazilians in New Orleans are linked to Brazil's interior rather than to symbols of Rio de Janeiro. When Brazilians in New Orleans ask me about my experiences in Brazil, they ask me if I have eaten *piqui* fruit, gone to a rodeo, or seen the Rio Araguaia because these are the symbols that represent the place of their longings rather than the standard images of Brazilian national culture. Exploring the spaces created by Brazilians to mark their Brazilian enclave in New Orleans reveals how the Brazilian community has imagined and constructed its identity with an eye on the particular New Orleanian social sphere as well as on alternate understandings of what it means to be Brazilian.

In this chapter, you will note the absence of overt political groups as well as the absence of commentary on the role that local universities have played in defining the Brazilian enclave character in New Orleans. I will quickly acknowledge, however, that the universities have played an important part in the intellectualization and the politicization of Brazilian identity in New Orleans. For example, historically African American Xavier University has set up cultural exchanges between Xavier and Brazil's Unipalmares, the first historically black university in Brazil. Tulane University hosted BRASA IX, a conference dedicated to the promotion of Brazilian Studies, in March of 2008. In Tulane's first graduation ceremony after Hurricane Katrina in March of 2006, the faculty honored Gilberto Gil, world-renowned musician and Brazil's Minister of Culture, with an honorary Ph.D. The strength and visibility of Tulane's Center for Latin American Studies and the Spanish and Portuguese Department have also meant that there are a group of students and faculty, myself included, with interest in learning about and supporting the Brazilian community in New Orleans.[33] Proximity to Tulane has helped the Brazilian community forge bonds with students and scholars and has greatly increased Brazilians' access to social

[33] Tulane is home to the Stone Center for Latin American Studies, one of four continuously funded Latin American National Resource Centers in the country, and it has long occupied a critical position as the only Latin American National Resource Center in the Deep South (AL, AR, LA, MS, and TN). Nationally, few institutions of Tulane's size compare in number of faculty, students, library resources, and research support for the study of Latin America. In the period 2000-2005, Tulane University awarded 88 Ph.D.s with Latin American foci in Spanish and Portuguese (25), Anthropology (19), Latin American Studies (15), History (6), Business Administration (5), Political Science (4), Sociology (3), French (2), Economics (1), EEB (1), Geology (1), Parasitology (1), Public Health (1), and Social Work (1). Along with these impressive numbers, Tulane has currently the second-highest rated Latin American Studies undergraduate program in the country. Many students, including myself, have come to New Orleans because of the academic resources available to study Brazilian culture. Until Katrina, however, these interests were theorized by comparing the two separate worlds of Brazil and New Orleans. Now, these worlds are starting to converge and students have taken advantage of the opportunities to be involved with the developing Brazilian community in New Orleans.

and cultural capital. Brazilian bands have played for numerous events for the Latin American Studies Department at Tulane University. (I must admit that I, myself, often set up these contracts, but I was only allowed to do this because there was a wider departmental interest in musicians who could bridge the gap between the university and the local immigrant communities.)

While the universities have been very important in the debate surrounding Brazilian identity and culture, they are not included in this chapter because the seminars and exchanges are sporadic and are also attended by a small and less diverse segment of the Brazilian population. This should not be understood, however, as being of lesser importance, especially since these academic events often influence the ideas of those people in positions of influential power in defining Brazilian identity to a wider audience. However, this chapter will focus specifically on performances within the Brazilian enclave imagined and created by Brazilian immigrants themselves since the disaster of Hurricane Katrina.

Private Spaces of the Brazilian Enclave

The most effective attempts at Brazilian enclave organization in New Orleans post-Katrina occurred in spaces that allowed for grass roots networking within the community, where Brazilians could reinterpret and reappropriate the enclave culture in their own unique ways. Private gatherings with other Brazilians provided a sense of structure to the unstable process of continual cultural reinterpretation. The liminality of gathering spaces separated in both place and time from U.S. culture is, in fact, a brief escape from the alienation that many Brazilians could experience in New Orleans because of language barriers or immigration status, regardless of how accepting that they claimed their New Orleanian community post-Katrina to be. Perhaps the most constant form of performing and reinforcing this sense of group cohesion are private events organized by and for Brazilians in their own homes.

Private Churrasco Parties

The homes of individual migrants in New Orleans provided and continue to provide protective spaces for Brazilians to feel at ease as they learn to reinvent themselves within their New Orleans environment. At home, Brazilians can socialize in a familiar language and with familiar social cues and customs. Private gatherings such as *churrascos* that were communicated through networks of friends were perhaps the most common Brazilian identity scenes in the early months of Brazilian immigration to New Orleans. *Churrascos*, informal parties revolving around the familiar cultural tradition of roasting meat and listening and dancing to familiar music, served to unite the community and create a network for finding employment, housing, and other necessary resources. They were also a way to communicate information about the local New Orleanian culture. Brazilians learned how to deal with the ins and outs of the social and legal systems through shared experiences and advice from their friends. Even though private gatherings include a relatively small number of Brazilians at each event, these moments play a crucial role in introducing new people into the community and in maintaining both regional and national traditions.

Within these intimate circles, Brazilians discuss and create categories of identification: "New Orleanians are…," "Brazilians are…," "Brazilians from Rondônia are…" In interviews, Brazilians expressed remarkably similar responses when asked to define New Orleans as a city and as a community for Brazilian migrants to plant roots. As the previous chapters explained, New Orleanians were defined as friendly, open, partygoers, and were often a bit *malandro* like Brazilians. The city of New Orleans itself was always described as a good city to live in, with a climate similar to Brazil and with a less rigid social and political organization that allowed immigrants more freedoms. Brazilians were described as hard workers and friendly. The fact that responses among my interviews tended to be so similar reflects, to a great extent, the fact that Brazilians openly discuss and debate issues of identity as they pertain to themselves and to others when they are together in private social settings. These conversations become extremely influential to the whole community's imaginings of self and place within New Orleans by articulating and sharing what become common understandings.

At a *churrasco* in 2008 that lasted late into the night, a Brazilian immigrant commented, "I love New Orleans. Only in New Orleans could we have this party this late at night and no one complains." There was a group of about 15 to 20 Brazilians at this event in the private home of a Brazilian immigrant in the suburb of Metairie, La. This comment speaks to the fact that the respondent felt as if New Orleans was a city that was welcoming to him because it allowed him a space to socialize freely with his Brazilian friends without fear of impinging on the cultural sensibilities of New Orleanians. Thus, the privacy of the event provided him a needed space to express himself as a Brazilian and the acceptance of the event by New Orleanian neighbors helped him conceive of New Orleans as a tolerant space for Brazilian culture.

The *churrasco* mentioned above also performed another social role common in the Brazilian enclave space because the people at the *churrasco* were organizing a *consocio entre amigos* (fraternity of friends). *Consocio entre amigos* is a common practice among Brazilians in New Orleans through which, each month, members of the *consocio* put a certain amount of money, usually between $50-$100, into a joint pot. The amount of money varies depending on the particular needs of the individuals who join it. The pot of money goes to a different member of the *consocio* each month, allowing immigrants to be able to possess a large sum of money quickly. If they need to pay off a debt or make a down payment, they are able to get the cash to do it on their particular month of receiving the pot. Thus, social gatherings such as this *churrasco* are a way to strengthen friendship ties that also hold significant economic consequences for the community.

Private gatherings among friends are mostly attended by other Brazilians, but not exclusively. Inviting New Orleanians that Brazilians meet through work or in New Orleanian social settings are ways to build friendships and social ties with Americans in a comfortable Brazilian space. Maxine Margolis comments in her research on the Brazilian community in New York that when there are Americans at such gatherings, the event tended to be segregated by nationality. In the New York context, the Americans would gather together in one room and the Brazilians in another. She also comments that rarely did she see Americans dancing during such an event (Margolis *Little Brazil* 185).

In my experience in post-Katrina New Orleans, however, in private gatherings where both Americans and Brazilians were present, there was much more mingling than what was described by Margolis in New York City. Rarely have I been to a social gathering in the privacy of someone's home where I noticed a stark divide between Brazilian and American guests. The one exception to this are language barriers that often cause conversations to have a disproportionate number of one or the other nationality, but, in the course of the party, with the dancing, the drinking, and the merry-making, there were no obvious divides between Americans and Brazilians. In fact, when there is dancing, it is likely to act as a bridge between Brazilians and Americans. The difference in the New York and New Orleans context is perhaps a combination of the gender ratio inequality in the Brazilian enclave in post-Katrina New Orleans which was not equal (Brazilian men need American women present in order to dance) and the performative nature of New Orleanian local culture in which locals may be more comfortable using dance and music as a common language.

This acceptance of American guests has been particularly evident in celebrations of the *festas juninas* in the homes of Brazilians in New Orleans. The *festas juninas*, June festivals, take place at the beginning of the Brazilian winter (the U.S. summer) as a celebration of rural life and as a way to give thanks for the rains in the Brazilian northeast. During the São João festivities, Brazilians organize to cook typical São João dishes and dress up as *caipiras* (country bumpkins).[34] Women will paint freckles on their face, a gap between their teeth, and wear checkered dresses and pigtails. Men will wear straw hats and dress up as farm boys. They all dance *quadrilha* around a bonfire. (*Quadrilha* is a folk dance with rotating couples that dance together in a type of square dance, often revolving around the *casamento matuto* [mock wedding] of two people.)

Festas juninas have been held yearly in private home settings in New Orleans since 2006. In 2008, a group of about forty Brazilians and ten Americans practiced *quadrilha* dancing once a week for a month leading up to the São João festivities. The fact that there were Americans

[34] The term *caipira* is used in two different ways: First, it is a descriptive term to refer to someone of mixed-race who comes from a rural background. Similar slang words often used as synonyms are *gente da roça* (people of the fields) and *gente do mato* (people of the woods). The second use is a pejorative means of ridiculing someone who seems simple-minded, is shy and awkward in unfamiliar social situations, who lacks schooling, or has a strong rural dialect. The *caipira* imagery used in São João festivals is derived from the character Jeca Tatu, protagonist in Monteiro Lobato's book of short stories published under the title *Urupês* (1914) (Pierson 108). The highly popular radio and television figure Amacio Mazzaropi is credited with turning Jeca Tatu into the archetype of the *caipira*. Mazzaropi played a comic and simple-minded Italian immigrant *caipira* living in the interior of São Paulo in all the films that he starred in after 1958 (Dennison and Shaw 12). The freckled-face pigtail image of the *caipira* women also seems to be derived from the female characters in Mazzaropi films.

present is indicative of how the New Orleanian Brazilian enclave has found ways of integrating Americans into their Brazilian social life in comfortable home settings. Recreating Brazilian cultural activities in private space in New Orleans fills a particular desire to unite Brazilian experiences with lived experiences in the U.S.

Figure 12: Festa Junina, New Orleans, 2008

Virtual Spaces

The Brazilian enclave in New Orleans is also increasingly defined by virtual spaces. Technology has created virtual communities, which are often central and quite encompassing of an individual's sense of place. Television and the internet are paramount in creating the universal visual images that immigrants associate with their community. They are also the mediums by which transnational relationships continue to be established and through which members of the enclave can create bonds of commonality with each other. Brazilians can follow their sports teams from afar, be keyed in on national Brazilian news, and watch their favorite Brazilian soap operas. The result of this media access is that technology provides ample fodder for conversation with other Brazilians who are watching similar virtual experiences, also aiding in the formation of a community in New Orleans.

Brazilians commonly have computers with at-home broadband Internet connections, webcams, and televisions with satellite hook-ups so that they are able to stay connected with their communities in Brazil and in other parts of the U.S.; these also allow immigrants to document their time in New Orleans for themselves and others.[35] Media supplies an opportunity for Brazilians to have visual images of their particular enclave community. For those communities with large Brazilian populations, television footage provides information about the local community through news coverage and advertisements. The footage of Hurricane Katrina helped motivate Brazilian migration to New Orleans and created the image of New Orleans as an immigrant El Dorado. But besides major news such as Hurricane Katrina, advertisements and news about the Brazilian community in New Orleans are on Brazilian news channels sporadically, since the community is still relatively small and unestablished in comparison to other Brazilian communities in the U.S. The lack of advertisements about the Brazilian community in New Orleans can affect how Brazilians construct their community in New Orleans as being different, unique, and smaller than larger Brazilian communities in other parts of the country.

However, the most important virtual mode by which Brazilians in New Orleans see visual representations of their enclave and maintain their connections to Brazil is through the Internet. Orkut,[36] an online networking site, is the technological hub of the Brazilian community in New Orleans. Orkut, similar to MySpace or Facebook,[37] is increasingly the home of Brazilian immigrant profiles in which personal messages as well as advertisements and notices for labor services can be posted. While the site was designed within the framework of an American company, over half of the approximately 45-million user profiles on Orkut are now Brazilian. The only non-English language

[35] These services are increasingly affordable. For instance, many Brazilians purchase a cable package that includes two Brazilian TV networks, Teleglobo and Brasil-Record. Divided among the number of people living in the house, the price each immigrant pays for this television package plus their internet connection can be as little as $10-20 a month per person.

[36] Orkut is the name of a Turkish software engineer who designed a social network service in the free time contractually allotted to him as an employee of the U.S. company Google, Inc.

[37] More Brazilians in New Orleans are joining Facebook as a way to communicate with American friends. This is an example of how members in the Brazilian community are becoming more anchored to their local space.

used by the site is Portuguese.

A person on Orkut may have anywhere from a dozen to a few hundred friends, met or unmet, real or imaginary, and be part of any number of communities. Not only through cyber communities, but also through personally selected cyber friend groups, Brazilian immigrants use Orkut to define their enclave community in New Orleans. As Brazilians create profiles and assemble photo albums about lived experiences in New Orleans to share with friends, Brazilians are themselves creating the images associated with the Brazilian enclave community.

Granted, each profile is different, highlighting different aspects of lived experience in New Orleans; Brazilians have albums of the destruction of Katrina, their completed construction projects, their social lives, fishing trips, or their church groups, for example. And while these images vary among the different members of the community, those who view the albums come to understand the Brazilian enclave experience in New Orleans through the amalgam of posted images. The internet can bridge gaps between physical spaces and even help establish a physical space as being Brazilian by labeling it as such. New Orleans has become a Brazilian enclave community in part because Brazilians have documented it as one through Orkut.

Orkut was particularly instrumental for Brazilians who first arrived in New Orleans because upon arrival there were not yet any Brazilian-specific locations where they could post news and advertise events in the community. Before immigrants got their bearings, the computer was the sole source of mass networking; it also provided a means for communicating about Brazilian spaces that arose as the community grew. Through Orkut, Brazilians advertised rooms to rent, new businesses, church services, cultural events such as dance classes or bingo games, cars for sale, health and beauty services, restaurants— and the list goes on. "I meet a lot of Brazilians living in New Orleans through Orkut. Just this week I had six people request to be my [virtual] friend who I had never seen before but who live in New Orleans" (Francielly 6 January 2009).

There are some thirty "communities" for Brazilians interested in New Orleans on Orkut, be it as tourists, backpackers, or residents, with anywhere from over 1,200 members, to just two. Their subject matter runs the gamut. "Bourbon Street— New Orleans," the largest, is essentially a discussion board for Portuguese-speakers to post advertisements related to their favorite restaurants or suggestions for clubs to go to when newcomers visit the city. Another, "The Hot Brazil Show," was opened to publicize a Brazilian music series organized by Shaka Corbin, a Guyanese native who lived in New Orleans and who in 2005-2006 promoted a Brazilian music series. The site is currently inactive because Shaka moved to New York a few months after Katrina. His Brazilian assistant, however, has since opened a similar site called "Ge Productions." There are Portuguese-language fan sites for the New Orleans Hornets and the Saints. There are many sites that are not serious. For example, there is a vampire fan site and a "Eu quero saquear new orleans!!" ("I want to loot New Orleans!!") site, which fantasizes about coming to New Orleans in time for the next major hurricane to plunder the city.[38]

The most relevant Orkut group to this study is "Brasileiros em New Orleans" ("Brazilians in New Orleans"), which was created after Hurricane Katrina. There are more than three hundred and seventy five members in the group, though this is a fraction of the people who actually visit it. Conversation threads on the site say a great deal about the extent to which the site is not only a facilitator for the Brazilian community in New Orleans, but also a cyber community itself. There are occasional postings with announcements of live Brazilian bands performing in New Orleans, gatherings to watch soccer matches, invitations to newly opened Brazilian churches, announcements for bingo games, dates revealing the opening of new Brazilian stores, ads for salon and beauty care, and personal ads. Brazilians who have never been to New Orleans can request information about the city from another Brazilian's perspective. There is even a Brazilian who posted a thread wanting information on New Orleans for a play he is producing about Hurricane Katrina in Rio de Janeiro. English classes are offered by both independent bilingual Brazilians and by official start-up agencies through the Orkut group.

Brazilians, however, tend to be most active on Orkut within their own group of cyber friends whom they personally accept as part of their virtual community rather than from these fan pages. Brazilians often send out advertisements directly to the "scrapbook" pages of their friends where the advertisement is sure to be read rather than posting them on community webpages. As I am writing this, I am receiving an

[38] To find these communities, simply go to the Orkut main page and search these names under the "Communities" option.

advertisement for a bingo game, a church service, and someone selling Nike Shock running shoes in New Orleans on my Orkut scrapbook page. Orkut also has a feature to create a promotion page that will be sent as a pop-up to all virtual friends. If someone wants to advertise a baby shower only to his Orkut friends, for example, he can fill out the promotion pop up and it will be displayed briefly on all of his friends' pages.

Thus, Orkut is a convenient way for Brazilians in New Orleans to reach out to a large number of people. The photographs and advertisements of life in New Orlean, as well as the ability to communicate with all those other Brazilians in New Orleans who have Orkut, have been instrumental in solidifying group cohesion. Rarely do Brazilian events happen in New Orleans that are not somehow communicated, either before or after, through the internet profiles of at least a few of those Brazilians present. Thus, Orkut becomes part of the Brazilian enclave experience while it simultaneously aids in creating it.

Thematically relevant, though he is not listened to widely within the Brazilian community in New Orleans, is the fact that singer Bizadão, currently of Pompano Beach, Fla., wrote the song "Email dela" ("Her email") about the role that the internet has played in forging transnational relationships between Brazil and the United States. The song tells the story of a Brazilian immigrant who logs on to the computer in the middle of the night to communicate with his girlfriend, who is, presumably, back in Brazil. He sings about the difficulty of having a relationship via the internet: "A internet é contra a natureza, passar a noite inteira sem botar a mão." (The internet is unnatural, spending the whole night together without touching.) But he nonetheless eagerly awaits communication with her as the pinnacle of his love-life experience. The song lyrics go, "I want to see her email. I want to open her email. 'Let me see your email and I will let you see mine.'" In these provocative and ironic lyrics, the emailing experience permits a couple to create a vicarious sense of intimacy since their email texts are the closest thing to physically touching one another. "Opening her email" becomes the climax of their relationship.

Forging relationships that exist merely in a virtual form are common in the Brazilian enclave in New Orleans. Sometimes these relationships evolve to become physical relationships when the immigrant returns home or if the other person is able to move to the U.S. I have been to two weddings for Brazilians in New Orleans who met a spouse over an internet site. In one case, the wife came to New Orleans from Rio de Janeiro to marry her husband. In the other case, the wife came from Medellín, Colombia. In both cases, the couples did not know each other beforehand. So not only do virtual networks maintain established networks, but they also create new relationships.

Electronic media make both the local and the global seem like two sides of the same coin. While on the one hand, media can create distance from the viewer and the community, it can also compel transformations within those same communities, be it through increased migration, the success of new businesses, or new romances motivated by online communication. Due to the rapidity through which electronic media moves through the daily lives of immigrants, media became a resource for Brazilian self-imagining within the context of New Orleans before other resources were available.

Brazilian Stores

Figure 13: Brazilian Store beside Cajun Grill franchise, Causeway Blvd, Metairie, La.

As the Brazilian community grows, Brazilian stores become another outlet to advertise services and events occurring within the Brazilian community in New Orleans. Not only do these stores serve as a meeting place where Brazilians can meet other Brazilians and converse in Portuguese, but the stores also provide bulletin board space for advertisements that pertain to the Brazilian community. Since New Orleans became a place with a community of recently arrived Brazilians overnight, many of them transitory and without much support, the Brazilian stores began to provide a space for networking. There has been a wave of Brazilian stores coming through New Orleans, though most of these stores have been short-lived, staying in business for less than a year. Since 2006, there have been at least five Brazilian stores that have opened and closed in New Orleans. In August of 2009, two Brazilian stores were still open: The Brazilian Market and Brazil Connection.[39] Today, only the Brazilian Market remains.

Brazilian Market[40]

The Brazilian Market was the first Brazilian store to open in New Orleans and has become an important reference point for the Brazilian community. Greyze Viera, owner of the Brazilian Market, moved down to New Orleans in April of 2006. Greyze is a long-time resident of the U.S., coming to pursue a course in agronomy in Minnesota in 1988 and later taking business administration courses in Boston. Before moving to New Orleans, he lived in Atlanta for thirteen years

[39] According to the owners of the store, Brazil Connection, it was God who told them that they should come to New Orleans. Storeowners Mauro and Arianne bought a Framingham, Mass., Brazilian store that was going out of business and moved the whole store, merchandise, shelves, coolers, and signs, down to New Orleans in 2008. *Igreja do Avivamento* (World Revival Church) further reinforced their sign from God when Mauro was asked to assist Pastor Fabiano as a church organizer in New Orleans. Mauro moved to New Orleans in December 2008 and divided his time between the duties of the church and the store. Members of the congregation frequented the store to give him constant business. However, the Brazil Connection closed down in September 2009 because it was not making enough profit. I do think that it is possible for more than one Brazilian store to be successful in New Orleans, but location is key. Brazil Connection was located on the same street as the more established Brazilian Market, but the Brazilian Market is located right off the interstate while Brazil Connection was farther down Williams Boulevard. The two stores were constantly competing. The most profitable location for a new Brazilian store in New Orleans today is Chalmette. There are many Brazilians living in the Chalmette area because of lower rent prices as well as construction job opportunities. Because of distance, people living in Chalmette rarely go to the Brazilian stores located in Kenner. Opening a store in Chalmette would cater to a different clientele of Brazilians and would have more chance of success.

[40] The narrative of this section comes from my interview with owner Greyze Viera conducted on July, 6, 2009.

where he managed a construction company and exported machine parts for *Editora Abril*, a Brazilian magazine publishing company that distributes popular Brazilian magazines such as *Veja*, *Nova*, and *Estilo da Vida*. In March 2006, Global, a money-wiring agency that Greyze had also worked for in Atlanta, sent Greyze to New Orleans to investigate the potential for the New Orleans market. Global rented an office space in the New Orleans suburb of Kenner, La., and Greyze became their representative for the money-wiring service transmitting funds from New Orleans to Brazil. Within this space, Greyze also opened the Brazilian Market. In 2006, Brazilians were making a lot of money in New Orleans, and so the market for a money-wiring agency with Portuguese-speaking employees was profitable. When he first arrived, Greyze was also working as a construction contractor with his partner, but they soon decided that both parties would benefit if they ended this partnership. Greyze took on full responsibility for the Brazilian Store and his partner continued in construction.

Greyze was the pioneer in setting up an import business between Miami and New Orleans for Brazilian products. When he first arrived, he had to make a trip to Miami once a month to get new merchandise. Now merchandise is shipped directly to his store. Having a Brazilian store in New Orleans was one of the first symbols of the Brazilian presence in New Orleans; it is a space that provides cultural products that help Brazilians deal with longings for Brazil. Greyze says that 2006 and 2007 were very profitable years for the Brazilian Market. In 2009 and 2010, however, the reality is much different. The economic crisis and the slowdown of construction in New Orleans has meant that fewer people have money to spend and fewer Brazilians are in New Orleans. Those Brazilians who are in New Orleans have become more accustomed to New Orleanian foods and lifestyles and have diversified their shopping and eating habits. More Brazilian stores have also opened, and, though none have had the longevity of the Brazilian Market, there has been constant competition; as one store closes, another one opens.

Until the end of 2007, Greyze had a satellite store location in Slidell, also rented through the Global money-wiring agency. According to the wiring registry in Slidell, which kept thorough records of bookings, there were 285 Brazilians sending money home to Brazil from Slidell at the end of 2007. This number dwindled, however, making it unviable economically for Greyze to keep his satellite location open. In order for the Brazilian store in New Orleans to be profitable, Greyze has had to diversify his business since 2007.

The store now also functions as a restaurant, selling Brazilian meals and *salgados* (Brazilian finger foods). According to Greyze, the restaurant is actually the service that generates his largest profit. But the Brazilian Market also finances cars, provides car insurance, and helps with CPF *Cadastro de Pessoas Físicas* (Registration of Physical Persons) issues in Brazil.[41] And, of course, the Brazilian Market continues to wire money to Brazil. Greyze says that the diversification of the offerings of the Brazilian Market is what has kept his business afloat. And, in fact, without his side import/export business with *Editora Abril*, he thinks that he would no longer be in business.

A Brazilian store, like many other small business ventures, is often much more significant as a community marker than it is as a business endeavor. Whether or not the Brazilian Market is economically profitable, however, for now it does provide a space for Brazilians to reproduce a Brazilian migrant identity based on their enclave experience in New Orleans and their homes in Brazil. Brazilians can buy canned *piqui* (a fruit commonly used in Brazilian cuisine in the North and North West of Brazil), passion fruit juice, or Brazilian candy at the same time that they can make contacts about work and social opportunities in New Orleans.[42] All communities need physical landmarks and the Brazilian Market is this for the Brazilian enclave in New Orleans.

---

[41] The CPF is a taxpayer number needed for Brazilians to make any financial transactions or investments in Brazil. Thus, any Brazilian immigrant who plans to invest in Brazil must keep his CPF up to date.

[42] Almost any Brazilian in New Orleans can tell you how to get to the store; there have been two health fairs organized for the Brazilian community in New Orleans, and they have both taken place in the parking lot of the Brazilian Market for this very reason.

Figure 14: Brazilian Market, Kenner, La.

Brazilian Night Spots

Brazilian nightspots are also crucial landmarks for the Brazilian community. They are important scenes for processing the image of Brazil through the music, dance, food, and drink that immigrants associate with their home experience.[43] Lisa Lowe has argued from the perspective of Asian Americans that cultural production reveals fissures and gaps that have illegitimately tried to cover up the existence of immigrants (or homogenized their culture) in U.S. society (Lowe 11). That is, immigrants perform their existence even if they do not exist legally or if they are politically invisible. So, even though Brazilians get lumped together with Latinos/Hispanics in the political sphere (if they are to politically exist at all), there are performative spaces where heterogeneity can be expressed and a critique of homogenizing discourse can be explored. In Brazilian nightspots, marked by their liberating social atmosphere, Brazilians can perform in contexts familiar to them. The Brazilian community itself plays the role in deciding which music, food, and drink are chosen as customary.

[43] See Linger's description of the Brazilian restaurant scene in Japan in *Becoming Brazuca* (183).

The only consistent, weekly Brazilian party night in New Orleans is that at Rotolo's Pizzeria. Before exploring Rotolo's as a Brazilian nightspot, however, the "Katrina story" of the Rotolo's Pizzaria in Jefferson Parish, run by long-time Brazilian immigrants Nalu and Rogerio Paivas, needs to be told. Perhaps no other narrative in this book reveals with more clarity both the impact of Hurricane Katrina on the Brazilian community and the Brazilian community's importance to New Orleans.

Rotolo's Pizzaria: Enter Hurricane Katrina[44]

When hurricane Katrina hit New Orleans on Aug. 29, 2005, Rotolo's Pizzeria had only been open since the previous May. Both Rogerio and Nalu had invested much hard work and everything they owned into making their business a success. They could not afford for a hurricane to destroy what they had given everything to build. They had already tasted the defeat of a failed business with their melon farm in Brazil, and they were prepared to do whatever it took to make sure that Rotolo's did not fail. The whole family decided to stay in New Orleans during Katrina and ride out the storm in Nalu's brother-in-law's house, which was the family house located on highest ground. Unlike them, their brother-in-law, Rob, a native of New Orleans, was accustomed to dealing with hurricanes.

As soon as the high winds had died down, the family went to survey the damage to the restaurant. Rotolo's was still standing, though there had been roof damage and damage to one of the interior walls. The restaurant was also out of electricity. They tried to check on their house the same day, but the water was already rising so high that their car could not get there. Rob had a boat, and so they took the boat around the city as far as they could to view the damage, but, since it was not a flat-bottom boat, there were many areas that they could not pass. They headed back to Rotolo's to see what could be salvaged of the restaurant instead.

Rogerio realized that with no electricity, the over $5,000 worth of food stock in the freezer was going to go bad, so he went with Rob to FEMA, which had set up tents in Zephyr Stadium in Metairie,

[44] What follows is based on an interview with Rogerio and Nalu Paiva, owners of Rotolo's Pizzaria, Metairie, on July 29, 2009.

to donate the food. Rogerio arrived at FEMA with free food but he left with a job contract made in the parking lot and signed with only a handshake. FEMA had contracted a catering company to feed the soldiers and rescue personnel that they were housing, but the catering company needed at least a week before it was prepared to serve so many people. Rogerio was contracted to make breakfast, lunch and dinner for the 600 people living in FEMA tents at Zephyr Stadium until the catering company could begin.

There was no electricity anywhere in New Orleans, so Rogerio and his family had to go to the Rotolo's franchise in Baton Rouge to prepare the food and then deliver it to Zephyr Field three times a day. The same day that Rogerio was given the contract to provide food for the relief workers housed at Zephyr fields, Rogerio and his family went to Baton Rouge to begin the preparations for the next day's meals. They left Baton Rouge at 2 a.m. with two vans full of food, more than 600 calzones, and their two children sleeping in the backseat of the car underneath a pile of napkins.

For the next week Rogerio and Nalu invented ways to feed the workers when there were almost no resources available. Mitch, the owner of the Baton Rouge franchise, helped them call around to other restaurants and stores in the area trying to get enough supplies to be able to feed so many people, since nothing could be prepared in New Orleans because there was still no electricity in the New Orleans Rotolo's.

They worked long hours with little sleep. Rogerio recounts that on several occasions he almost fell asleep at the wheel driving food back and forth from Baton Rouge to New Orleans. They remember fondly, however, the gratitude of all the army officers who thanked them for being so resourceful and figuring out a way to feed their troops. Rogerio remembers that it was never easy; they were constantly inventing. Coffee, for example, had to be made with water from the city. There was simply no way to get potable water for so many people every day and to prepare all of the food. But Rogerio and his family drank the city water right alongside the rescue workers. Often the officers, who always ate after the troops, found that there was nothing but pasta left by the time the end of the line came around. Nalu and Rogerio made urgent calls to Brazilian friends in other areas of the country to come down and help them deliver food and make runs for needed ingredients.

Rotolo's regained electricity on the fifth day after the hurricane passed. It was one of the only buildings in the whole area with electricity; the relief electric workers gave the Rotolo's business priority because they were providing rescue food services. By the end of the week, the catering business contracted by FEMA had come with reinforcements and Rogerio and Nalu were able to reopen Rotolo's restaurant again. As soon as the restaurant was reopened, anyone who had not evacuated flocked there. Everyone was jubilant to see a business up and running again and eager to hear any news about what was going on. Those in New Orleans had little contact via cell phone, TV, and radio because the communication lines were so severely damaged.

Rogerio and his crew had special passes to be able to travel through the city because they were providing relief assistance. Once Wal-Mart got electricity back, Rogerio was able to go looking for cooking ingredients there. Wal-Mart closed every night at 11 p.m. because of fear of looters, but Rogerio was given the number of the manager who would open up especially for him because he was considered part of the emergency relief crew. Rogerio remembers how bizarre it was to serve pizzas to soldiers while their machine guns rested on the chairs beside them.

The restaurant was open for less than a week when Rotolo's got an order for 100 pizzas to be sent to Tulane University. Rogerio went to Tulane University to deliver those 100 pizzas to the U.S. Texas Marshals. He walked into the library to find armed soldiers sitting around the studying tables with the library stacks of books behind them. They were grateful to get the pizza, their first meal of the day. The U.S. Marshal general pulled Rogerio aside and asked if he would be able to solve one of their problems: They needed someone to feed the 1,780 soldiers who had been sent to New Orleans to watch over the city. It had been a huge challenge for Rogerio to be able to make meals for 600 FEMA employees. Now he was being asked the impossible— to feed 1,780 soldiers. But he agreed.

By dinner time of the following day, Rogerio and his crew were delivering meals to U.S. Marshals housed at Loyola University, Tulane University, the city zoo, the Convention Center, and Children's Hospital. His daughter Mariana, 15, slept on a mattress in Rotolo's Pizzeria because she had to wake up every night at 2 a.m. and crack 3,060 eggs to make enough pizza dough for all of those people. Ovens in both New Orleans and Baton Rouge were constantly baking pizza for the soldiers. Rogerio recalls the eerie feeling of traveling at night through a city the size of New Orleans and not seeing any signs of life except for people in army uniforms. When he received the contract with the U.S. Marshals, Rogerio had to close the restaurant to the public again in order to complete the orders. People would come knocking on the door in the evenings after he had finished serving the soldiers begging for just one cheese pizza. Usually, however, there were not even enough leftover ingredients to make it.

On Sept. 24, 2006, Hurricane Rita ravaged Lake Charles, La., and the U.S. Marshals were called to respond. Rotolo's got a call from the same company that had contracted them to work for the U.S. Marshals in New Orleans, asking if they would be able to provide 5,000 lunches per day for two weeks to relief workers at Lake Charles. Rogerio said that there was no way that he could prepare hot meals for that many people, but that he could prepare cold meals. So every day, Rogerio and a group of his Brazilian workers traveled to Baton Rouge to prepare cold meals that they would then take to Lake Charles. The work was non-stop. Once the contract had ended with the Marshals at Lake Charles, Rotolo's reopened its doors to the public of New Orleans as one of the few functioning restaurants in the area.

Rotolo's becomes a 'Super-Hub' for Brazilians

At this point, Nalu and Rogerio's restaurant became a contact point for Brazilians arriving in New Orleans. Nalu and Rogerio comment that there were times when a Brazilian would arrive at Rotolo's straight from some other area of the country because they had been given the name of the pizzeria from a Brazilian friend who told them that the people at Rotolo's would be able to tell them where they could find work.

While this was not always the case, the pizzeria became a meeting point for Brazilians, where Brazilians could socialize, speak in Portuguese, and feel comfortable. The pizzeria was also a place for networking. Those who came down searching for jobs could meet other Brazilians who were looking for workers or who knew about openings in the company where they were working. Those Brazilian laborers who were also musicians began playing at Rotolo's, at first only for tips.

Then, when the restaurant became popular on Saturday nights, Nalu and Rogerio began paying the bands $200 a night. The first group that approached the couple about playing at Brazilian night was a *sertanejo* (Brazilian country music) group. Nalu was skeptical at first that the public would be interested in listening to that style of music, but little did she know, the Brazilians who came to do construction work in New Orleans were from the areas of Brazil where *sertanejo* was mainstream. Saturday nights at the pizzeria became highly popular. Nalu even had a Brazilian woman cooking typical dishes like *vaca atolada* (Brazilian beef rib dish) and *feijoada* (stew of beans, meat, and pork) for Brazilian nights during the first few months that the pizzaria began their Brazilian nights.

The success of Brazilian night at Rotolo's Pizzeria has mirrored the ebbs and flow of the Brazilian enclave community in New Orleans. The first two years after Katrina, Brazilian nights at the pizzeria were packed. Nalu talks about the World Cup of June 2006 as being the moment that she fully realized just how many Brazilians were in New Orleans. Brazil played France in the quarter final of the World Cup 2006— and the pizzeria had standing room only to watch the game. I also vividly remember the 2006 World Cup. I was in Brazil at the time doing field research on my Master's thesis. I received a telephone call from a group of Brazilians living in New Orleans when the game was over. Brazil had lost to France and the immigrants, heartbroken, were burning their Brazilian jerseys and their Brazilian flags in the parking lot of Rotolo's Pizzeria. Jackson took the phone and said to me, "Annie, I am no longer Brazilian. I am from New Orleans."

Soccer is more than just a sport to Brazilians, and the disappointment of the World Cup was even more difficult for those living away from Brazil. Far away from a home that for most immigrants had already failed them by not offering economic possibilities, Brazilian immigrants had wanted to believe that Brazilian soccer was a national event by which they could unite behind their country. They were devastated when Brazil lost. But what was interesting about that moment to me was the fact that not only did my friend want to distance himself from his Brazilian background, but that he wanted to ally himself with his new home, New Orleans. The World Cup loss actually had the effect of uniting the crestfallen Brazilian enclave community in New Orleans. And Rotolo's provided a space for that new cultural identity as Brazilian New Orleanians. The restaurant became a super-hub for networking for jobs, for finding friends, for holding Brazilian parties, and for knowing the pulse of the Brazilian community and the realities of their economic and social prospects in New Orleans.

Rotolo's has continued to be an important enclave landmark for performing Braziliain identities even now that New Orleans is in a stage of relative normalcy. According to Rogerio, Saturdays are usually his best business nights. In fact, in 2006-2007, at the height of Brazilian immigration to New Orleans, the number of weekend clients totally overwhelmed the wait staff, especially due to the language barriers of the waitresses. There is now a Brazilian wait staff to help serve the Brazilian clientele on Saturday nights. An environment like Rotolo's speaks directly to the diaspora experience. The community dictates musical choices, which events are viewed on the television in the bar (mostly soccer and boxing matches and occasional rodeos), demand for special events such as bingo games to raise money for the community, and even the normative ways that Brazilians interact with one another.

Performances of identity in the pizzeria are specifically grounded in diverging regional representations of Brazil. On a grassroots level, the identity performances in Rotolo's locate both performers and listeners in a particular Brazil that is rooted in regionalism but that speaks to a universal experience lived by all Brazilians in the New Orleans enclave. Patrons may drink a *caipirinha* while wearing a Saints jersey; eat an American-style pizza Brazilian-style, covered in ketchup and mayonnaise; or they may practice their English skills while teaching an American how to dance the Brazilian *forró* (perhaps never having danced in public at home, but the diaspora experience creates a need for closeness to both Brazil and to other people). At play in such performances are nationality, Brazilian regional constructions of identity, social class, and local context. There is often a dissonance between these constructs of identity, yet the enclave space allows room for performative discourse.

Musical Choices During Brazilian Nights

Rotolo's Pizzeria became an important location for Brazilian musicians to play Brazilian music for the Brazilian community nostalgic for an imagined "home." Songs of nostalgia for those lost or left behind are of paramount importance to the repertoire of the Brazilian performer. But "home" has not typically been imagined through samba at Rotolo's. Rio-centric versions of nationhood often tend to ignore the rural and agricultural roots of much of Brazil where the majority of Brazilian immigrants to the U.S. are from. *Sertanejo* music represents "home" for a large majority of the Brazilians living in New Orleans, invoking a sense of nostalgic longing for Brazil's countryside. *Sertanejo* music has at its forefront the history of manual labor, the land, and the rural past as a central part of its musical identity.

It is an alternate view of Brazilian national character. Dent suggests that there is also a racial component to this rural music because *sertanejo* focuses much less on the centrality of Africa in the image of the Brazilian nation and more on the racially mixed countryside worker (Dent 460). The racially-mixed countryside worker is consistent with the racial profile of Brazilian immigrants in New Orleans who tend to see themselves as racially-mixed but who do not, as we have seen, tend to embrace Afro-Brazilian culture as representative of "home." *Sertanejo* music is perhaps especially fitting for the migrant experience because *sertanejo* is usually sung by a duo, emphasizing the importance of figurative brotherhood, a necessary component of the migrant experience.

The Brazilian *sertanejo* duo Zezé di Camargo and Luciano, for example, sing the song "The day that I left home" ("No dia em que eu saí de casa"). The song is about a son who has grown to become a "bird" ready to flee the nest and explore possibilities for a better life away from home. I have heard versions of this song sung by almost every group of musicians whom I have seen come through the pizzeria (with the exception of the Som Brasil *pagode* band, which is run by American aficionados of Brazilian culture and not by Brazilians): "The day that I left home my mother called me to her side… Wherever you go, you will always be in my thoughts and in my prayers… But she knows that once they have grown, children become birds and want to fly." (O día que saí de casa minha mãe me disse: 'Filho vem cá… Por onde você for eu sigo com meu pensamento sempre onde estiver …Mas ela sabe que depois que cresce o filho vira passarinho e quer voar.) Although this song was written in the context of a rural to urban immigration movement in Brazil, it has come to be one of the anthems of Brazilians living in the United States. Thus, the focus on migration and the nostalgic longing that such movement invokes is important in bridging the migrant experience to understandings of Brazilian identity as it is imagined within the Brazilian diaspora.

On many a Saturday night in Rotolo's pizzeria during its post-Katrina hey-day, this song hit a chord deep in the heart of the Brazilians present. When the local *sertanejo* group played this song, with *cachaça* cups in hand (or *guaraná* for those who don't drink alcohol), the whole audience sang together, remembering with "*saudades,*" a bittersweet longing, all those loved ones that they left behind in search of a better life through their migration to the United States. The loss of home merges with the loss of family in this song, as in many other *sertanejo* hits. The intertwined singing voices of the duo point to migration as an experience that creates a person who is lacking some combination of family, love, and/or home. Being "complete" relies on being able to return home (either permanently or simply to visit). Since opening for Brazilian nights in 2006, Rotolo's has served as a location where amateur musicians have been able to form duos (and sometimes extended groups) to perform music of "home."[45] These musicians work in the construction industry and do not tend to see playing music as their profession. They play because they themselves miss the music of their homeland.

The first band to perform at Rotolo's Pizzeria in New Orleans post-Katrina was Banda Bandida. Their first gigs were at informal *churrascos* and they later began playing in the pizzeria because of their popularity in informal local Brazilian social circles. In most instances, Banda Bandida played only for tips, playing for about a year in New Orleans during 2006-2007. The story of Banda Bandida begins with Reginaldo, a construction worker from Goiânia who came to New Orleans from Boston to work in 2006. Banda Bandida is representative of how the performance circle of Brazilians in New Orleans post-Katrina was mostly made up of construction workers who took up music as a pastime because there was no Brazilian music scene for immigrants when they first arrived. Reginaldo plays the accordion; he became involved with the Brazilian Assembly of God Church in New Orleans, which gave him money to buy an accordion so that he could play in the church band. Answering an advertisement for an accordion in a Bra-

[45] Interestingly, *sertanejo* music is played only within the Brazilian enclave spaces. When Brazilians make their music public, during Mardi Gras blocos, for example, Brazilians are more likely to play *axé* and funk music than *sertanejo*.

zilian newspaper in Boston, he went back to Boston to buy an accordion and to help a friend finish a construction job there in April of 2006.

The person selling this accordion was Edilson, a Brazilian contractor and bandleader of the group Banda Bandida that was already formed in Boston. Edilson had been thinking himself about moving his family to New Orleans to try his luck in the construction industry there. After talking with Reginaldo, Edilson and two other members of Banda Bandida, who worked in Edilson's construction crew in Boston, decided to move down to New Orleans to work in the post-Katrina construction industry. Banda Bandida was then reassembled in New Orleans playing both *sertanejo* and *forró* hits. Their music was very danceable and the lyrics spoke of everyday situations of life, work, love, and heartbreak. During the heyday of the pizzeria, Banda Bandida would pack in full crowds of Brazilians who would dance and sing along with the band.

The breakup of Banda Bandida was a gradual process. First, two of the members moved back to Brazil. Both of these return migrants are from the Goiânia area— Goiânia and Goianilândia. Then a third band member moved back to Boston because his wife did not like living in New Orleans. She found New Orleans difficult because there were so few other Brazilian women there at the time and because she was working for a demolition company, doing a "man's job," according to her. In Boston she had a schedule of houses to clean and was much happier. A fourth member, Johnny, also moved back to Boston to begin the *sertanejo* duo Johnny and Leo. Johnny and Leo have become successful playing for the larger Brazilian community in Boston and have even recently been offered a music contract in Goiânia. Music is now Johnny's full-time job, and the duo tours to other Brazilian communities in the Northeast. They are debating whether or not to return to Brazil to accept the contract, since returning to Brazil gives them no guarantee that they will be able to return to the U.S.

As Banda Bandida group members moved away, new people came down to New Orleans to take their place. Slowly, new musicians began taking center stage and new *sertanejo* duos emerged as performers at the pizzeria. Again, these performers tended not to be professional musicians, but construction workers with a musical hobby. The pizzeria provided a place for them to become performers because *sertanejo* and *forró* music were needed niches with the arrival of the Brazilian community post-Katrina. One of these singers who has been performing at Rotolo's since 2006 told me that having the opportunity to become a performer at Rotolo's gives him a sense of purpose and provides him with a sense of belonging within his Brazilian community. He feels as if he is able to give back to his community by providing a time when compatriots can listen to familiar music in a comfortable social setting. Rotolo's has been paramount to his own feelings of connection to New Orleans. Shy and quiet in person, he explained that Rotolo's has been a social space for him to network for both friends and work connections. "I owe much of my happiness in New Orleans to Rotolo's," he said (Emerson 19 July 2009). Emerson hopes to be able to live in New Orleans long-term and has no plans of returning to Brazil, even though construction work has slowed for him.

The owners of the pizzeria, Nalu and Rogerio, have created an atmosphere where Brazilians can feel at ease and where important community building events can take place. Brazilians who take advantage of this space come to feel a sense of self-agency within their enclave community. The pizzeria has hosted bingo games, fundraisers, baby showers, wedding parties, and birthday parties for Brazilians. Community members become the organizers, and Rotolo's provides the space. The bulletin board on the wall of the pizzeria shows photographs of some of these moments of Brazilian *communitas*. These personal photos of Brazilian nights and social occasions instill a sense of ownership for Brazilians in the Rotolo's community. Rotolo's keeps a mailing list of more than 250 people and an Orkut page to send updates on events there to the larger Brazilian enclave as a way of documenting Rotolo's as a tangible marker of the community. Mass media is, thus, an important means through which imagination takes shape and through which Rotolo's becomes both a lived and a virtual space of the Brazilian community in New Orleans.

Nalu and Rogerio's Rotolo's franchise became so popular among a Brazilian crowd that, in 2010, they decided to break from the franchise and open their own restaurant, "Coco Bamboo," at the same location. Coco Bamboo continues with the pizzeria theme; however, they now incorporate more tropical items onto the menu, using the Brazilian identity that had been constructed through these years as a Brazilian hub to market their business. Construction skills learned during Katrina were also put to use. Rogerio ordered wood and stone from Brazil to do the interior decoration of the restaurant, giving it a feel of his homeland inside. Free from the franchise, owners Nalu and Rogerio are now able to expand their social offerings to the Brazilian community as well, though the success of Brazilian nights has never reached the same intensity as those months of post-Katrina camaraderie.

Other Brazilian Night Spots

There have been other attempts to create alternate space for Brazilian nightlife in New Orleans, though none have remained as successful as Rotolo's Pizzeria. The owners of these spaces are typically construction workers who saw the opportunity to open a business marketed specifically to the Brazilian community. In most cases, they had minimal experience as small business owners. When they discovered that a business was a full-time job, and the time came to choose between their job in the construction business and their job as a small business owner marketing to an unstable Brazilian community, most chose to continue in construction.

Álvaro Junior opened the Brazilian club "The Chat Room and Suingue Brazil" in the summer of 2006 when there were many Brazilians in New Orleans working in reconstruction. Álvaro had initially moved to New Orleans on Sept. 7, 2005, with a 4-month contract with an American roofing company in New Orleans. Joe, the owner of this roofing company, had been visiting family in Boston a few months before Hurricane Katrina and had seen Álvaro's work there. The two roofers had swapped business cards, unaware that they would ever meet each other again. But after Katrina hit New Orleans, Joe called Álvaro to see if he would be interested in coming down with a crew of workers to put tarps on roofs.

Álvaro came down with a crew of four men to see if the work was as plentiful as others claimed. Indeed, Álvaro began putting roofs on five to six houses a week, making the money in one week that it usually took him a month to earn in Boston. During the first year after the storm, Álvaro claims that he was earning an average of $25,000 a week even after he paid his workers. While I think that this claim is exaggerated, it is clear that New Orleans provided a plentitude of work options for roofers in 2006. Álvaro decided to stay in New Orleans when his four-month contract ended and he began working as a subcontractor. Through these connections in the construction industry, he decided that there was ample space to expand the Brazilian nightlife options in the city and to make a profit. Because of his work in construction, he had the capital to do it.

According to Álvaro, he decided to open the club because he felt that there was a need for social spaces in New Orleans where Brazilians could relax and socialize without fear of police or confrontations with Americans. He claims that he and his colleagues spent almost every weekend on Bourbon Street or at Rotolo's Pizzeria in 2006. He also admits that he had to bail one of his friends out of jail almost monthly, usually because he drank too much and got into confrontations on Bourbon Street. When asked why he thought Brazilians were always in trouble on Bourbon Street, Álvaro said that "it took a while for Brazilians to understand the rules of freedom that functioned on Bourbon Street. They weren't used to that sort of freedom and they didn't understand the limits" (Álvaro 9 August 2009). While Brazilians cited Bourbon Street as a space that offered liberties for social life comparable to Brazil, it was also true that certain kinds of unruliness were not tolerated, and Brazilians had to negotiate the appearance of social liberty with the reality of law enforcement.[46]

Taking this into consideration, Álvaro decided that opening a night space for Brazilians was a needed niche. He rented a space in an abandoned section of Tulane Avenue (3200 Tulane Ave.), a rough downtown neighborhood far from mainstream night spaces, and opened "The Chat Room and Suingue Brazil." Due to its location in a derelict neighborhood still half-boarded up after its ravaging by Katrina, it was not a space chosen to attract an American clientele. The neighborhood was purposely selected as a space that would not conflict with more mainstream American night locations, a space where Brazilians could be Brazilian without worrying about how outsiders interpreted them. One interviewee said, "They [the owners] felt as though they couldn't use a space that Americans use because they were afraid they would not be accepted" (Gilberto 13 November 2006).

During the time that the club was open, this space represented an

[46] At a meeting about hurricane evacuation plans for the Brazilian community, I informally asked a police officer there about the contexts in which he most frequently arrested Brazilians. He said that fighting on Bourbon Street and driving while intoxicated were the most common reasons why Brazilians were jailed. Fighting was usually motivated by too much alcohol consumption in social areas where Brazilians are perhaps more socially on edge and defensive.

attempt at recreating a transnational Brazilian place that was separated in time and space from the local New Orleanian community. Americans were invited, especially women because of the unequal ratio between men and women, but the motivation was specifically to fill the need for a Brazilian cultural space. The music choices were mostly *samba pagode* and *axé*.[47] Though both *samba pagode* and *axé* are musical forms that are not necessarily popular in the regions of Brazil where the majority of Brazilian immigrants in New Orleans are from, these two music genres were chosen by the club organizers because both *samba pagode* and *axé* are musical forms that do not require a partner of the opposite sex and are "festive" music. It allowed Brazilian men who were in New Orleans without wives or girlfriends the space and opportunity to express themselves through movement even in a predominately male group. In these Brazilian cultural circles, I noticed that even men who were not dancers in Brazil, often coming from regions of Brazil where samba is not part of the local culture, would sometimes dance s*amba pagode* in New Orleans because the steps embodied their sense of inclusion in a Brazilian enclave.

Connecting to cultural practices that mark Brazilian nationalism for those away from Brazil is a way of performing feelings of nostalgia for home as well as a renewed relationship to the homeland experienced through migration. Also, samba and *axé* music are played during Carnival time in the home areas of Brazil for the majority of the immigrants in New Orleans. Thus, these rhythms instill a sense

---

[47] *Samba pagode* is a slightly slower derivative of the Carnival-style *samba enredo*. *Samba pagode* is defined, not as a musical genre, but as a cultural practice when groups of friends gather informally for a party and play samba music. *Samba pagode* does differ from the *samba enredo* of carnival in its instrumentation (banjo, tantã, repique-de-mão, etc) (Galinsky 127). According to Philip Galinsky, the *pagode* movement in Rio de Janeiro emerged as a form of resistance to the commercialization and corruption of the Afro-Brazilian *escolas de samba*. The *pagode* style blended "traditional elements of the samba that had been somewhat neglected up until that point with a modified instrumentation and a modern, innovative sound" (Galinsky 120). Even though different styles of *pagode* have gained success across social classes and race in Brazil, *pagode*'s lyrics and rhythmic style associate it most closely with the working class and the Afro-Brazilian experience (Galinsky 141). *Axé* is an energetic popular dance music from Salvador, Bahia. According to Perrone and Dunn, the term "suggests a calculated bid for recognition in the world-music market by appropriating the Yoruba term for 'life-giving force' as an adjective and the English noun" (Perrone and Dunn 28).

of freedom and an escape from the normal routine. Brazilians have imagined New Orleans as a place different from the normal routine of immigration; thus the music becomes a way of celebrating their connection to their local situation as immigrants in New Orleans as well.

"The Chat Room and Suingue Brazil" stayed open only four months. The owner of the club was vague in his interview about the reasons for its closing. In the interview, he claims that the club was a good financial investment for him, saying that the club was always packed and Brazilians spent a lot of money there on Brazilian drinks. His reason given for closing was that the club took too much time away from his personal life. However, he also mentions that his clientele preferred to go to places where they would mix with New Orleanians because the majority of the Brazilians in these early months of post-Katrina New Orleans were only men. This second comment seems to suggest that the club business was not as profitable for him as he had imagined. Whether the reasons for closing were more personal— the club interfered with his personal life and his work schedule as a subcontractor— or whether there was not a large enough Brazilian community to support such a business, what is clear is that the Brazilian enclave in New Orleans does not congregate solely in Brazilian night spaces. The New Orleans Brazilian community tends to be more integrated into the New Orleanian night scene than other Brazilian enclaves in other parts of the U.S. There is both a desire for Brazilian spaces and a desire for spaces where Brazilians can feel more connected to New Orleans.

A second failed attempt at a Brazilian nightspot in New Orleans was opened during the 2007-2008 year at Carnaval restaurant on Canal Street close to the French Quarter. A Brazilian *churrasco* restaurant serving buffet food "by the kilo" turned into a nightclub on Saturday nights.[48] The owners of Carnaval, like Álvaro, were also construction contractors in New Orleans. They approached the restaurant business as a side job and as a place for their wives to work. However, the owners were not prepared for the amount of investment in time and money needed to begin a small business venture before any real profits would be seen. After a year, the owners decided that they were making more money in the construction business than the restaurant/nightclub business, and they sold Carnaval to a Honduran im-

[48] Brazilian nights tend to be on Saturdays because most workers in both the construction and housecleaning industries work on Saturdays, and so think of Friday nights as part of the work week.

migrant.[49] Because Brazilians had once frequented the restaurant, the Honduran owner continued with a few Brazilian items on the menu in order to maintain at least a portion of that Brazilian clientele for almost a year after its transition. (Customers could order a *guaraná*, a *caipirinha*, and sometimes eat a *feijoada* on the weekends, for example.)

For the year that Carnaval was open, it hosted local Brazilian bands and DJs. Again, none of these musicians were professionals but were members of the Brazilian community performing in the context of post-Katrina New Orleans. A Brazilian rock band called *Saia Rosa* (the Pink Skirts) made their debut at Carnaval restaurant and had a following of young Brazilians in New Orleans for several months. This group is particularly interesting in illustrating that many of the Brazilian immigrants who moved to New Orleans were young adults who socialized as other 20-year-olds would when far away from home and in an environment where they were experiencing new liberties for the first time. They approached their New Orleans immigrant experience in very much the same manner that college students in the U.S. approach their first years in college. New Orleans was a place where they worked hard, partied hard, and tested the limits of their social world.

The Pink Skirts got their name when the band members, who at this time were not yet a band, made a bet that whoever refused to jump off the bridge of the downtown Riverwalk into the Mississippi River had to wear a pink skirt for their night out in the French Quarter. Two of them jumped off, but Flavison did not believe that his friends would actually jump and remained on the boardwalk. That night they bought a small pink skirt with the symbol of the New Orleans *fleur de lis* on it, and Flavison had to wear the skirt all night as they went bar-hopping between Frenchmen Street and Bourbon Street. The next week, the group of friends traveled to Panama City for a weekend at the beach. They had so much fun watching Flavison in his pink skirt that they all decided to buy pink skirts and go out on the town in Panama City.

[49] Although the restaurant owners did not mention this as their reason for selling the restaurant, it should also be noted that there were several fights that broke out on the premises between Brazilian clientele who had had too much to drink. I was present at one of these fights in which a Brazilian customer smashed a bottle across the face of another Brazilian customer who was taunting him about his lack of desirability to a Brazilian woman present that night. These fights caused increased police patrol of the area, which resulted in more reluctance among Brazilian customers to attend the Saturday night events.

Figure 15: The Pink Skirts in Panama City, Fla.

Figure 16: The Pink Skirts at Carnaval Restaurant, New Orleans

That same weekend they also began rehearsing their band, and they decided on the name "Pink Skirts" because it invoked an experience that had symbolically united them as a group of Brazilians exploring and creating their community in New Orleans. The Pink Skirts band sang rock in Portuguese, English, and even some Spanish— their musical choices reflecting their transnational experience. Typical of the experience of migrant mobility, however, they disbanded after a few months when some members moved away to other areas in the Gulf South to work construction and the drummer returned to Brazil. Even though their musical skills were hardly highly developed, they also had one of the largest followings of any of the Brazilian music groups to play in New Orleans, evidence of the fact that many of the immigrants in post-Katrina New Orleans were themselves young adults, who were enthusiastic about following a local Brazilian garage band that gave festive voice to their own youthful experience and community.

Brazilian nightspots in New Orleans are evidence of how performances of different imaginings of both Brazil and New Orleans have been important for the Brazilian community. The fact that many of these clubs have been short lived and the performers themselves quite transitory residents is very representative of the Brazilian community in New Orleans as a whole in the early years of the Brazilian enclave formation in New Orleans. I do not think that these failed business endeavors and the constant rotation of performers necessarily means that the Brazilian enclave in New Orleans is failing. In fact, I would say quite the opposite. These changes are the inevitable fluctuations that are part of a transnational community. The fact that some immigrants leave while new ones come, in a constant circular flow between nation and homeland, reveals that the New Orleanian enclave is in the process of establishing itself. The community is continually being reinvented within these enclave spaces to account for the changing personalities within the diaspora.

Outside of enclave spaces, in 2006-2008, when the Brazilian community was at its height, Brazilian nights were also held occasionally at clubs that were normally marketed to an American clientele. However, unlike enclave spaces mentioned above, professional Brazilian musicians almost always played at such events. Sometimes musicians were local, but often bands were from other parts of the U.S. These events took more time and organization to prepare. Event organizers made fliers, sometimes event T-shirts, and sold tickets ahead of time to assure good attendance. Tickets were sold to both Brazilians and Americans and the events were, thus, frequented by more Americans than the weekly Brazilian nights held in enclave spaces. These hybrid Brazilian-American spaces seemed to be where Brazilians felt more at ease to bring their international friends, mostly Americans but Hispanic as well, since the events had less of the *boteco* (drinking hole) atmosphere and more of a cultural performance environment. The spaces where such events occurred were chosen not simply as being spaces for communing with other Brazilians, but as spaces to celebrate the liveliness of Brazilian culture, whether the audience is Brazilian or not. Such events are, thus, easier for outsiders to interpret. More recently these Brazilian events have been less frequent in New Orleans. The events were expensive to organize for a Brazilian community that was often not large enough to support it. And many of the Brazilians that organized these events in 2006-2007 have since left New Orleans or have joined Brazilian evangelical churches and no longer move in party circles. The growth of the evangelical cultural scene in the Brazilian community in New Orleans is quite substantial and has changed Brazilian social life dramatically.

Brazilian Churches

The emerging Brazilian religious community is perhaps the most significant tangible marker of the transnational Brazilian community in New Orleans. As the congregations of these churches grow, they have significantly influenced the Brazilian community's social options. Though the Brazilian churches have changed locations frequently and church members have come and gone as immigrants in New Orleans move to different neighborhoods, to different states, or return home to Brazil, the churches themselves have remained active and are currently more prosperous than the Brazilian nightlife scene in New Orleans, providing an alternate interpretation of the character of the Brazilian community. The social outlets for immigrants outlined in previous sections celebrated Brazil and Brazil/New Orleans connections through food, music, dance, and merry-making within enclave settings. The Brazilian churches, however, construct Brazilian spaces linking Brazilians to both their communities in Brazil and in New Orleans by providing a pious social life that revolves around the worship of God. The church space allows Brazilians to maintain ties with Brazil through sermons that speak directly to the Brazilian immigrant experience and that allow migrants access to a useful social networking group that can increase their personal success while in New Orleans.

Ana Cristina Braga Martes has noted that the reasons that Brazilian immigrants join a church in the United States are often more socially motivated than they are religious. Evangelical pastors in Boston have commented that it is easier to get Brazilians involved in churches in the U.S. than in Brazil because there is less distraction in Boston (Martes "Os imigrantes brasileiros e as igrejas em Massachusetts" 119). New Orleans, as a city that has defined itself by the social distractions available twenty-four hours a day, would seem quite different from Boston. However, while New Orleans does offer a plethora of social options, it does not offer many social options in Brazilian-specific social settings. Thus, churches have become increasingly important as Brazilian enclave spaces in New Orleans for Brazilians who yearn for the comfort and security of living within a larger Brazilian community.

The largest Brazilian church in New Orleans is the Assembly of God Church *(Assembléia de Deus)*, which has also been documented as the largest denomination of Brazilians in Massachusetts (Martes *Brasileiros nos…* 97). Today, The Assembly of God Church in New Orleans has approximately 150 members and is an important church in the Brazilian Diaspora in the U.S. The New Orleans congregation is substantial enough that every two months singers and/or pastors from Brazil come to hold special worship sessions in New Orleans. The church has even provided space for the Brazilian consulate to make its visits from Houston to New Orleans when providing services for Brazilians in the area.

As Ana Cristina Braga Martes notes, whereas evangelists had once sent missionaries to Brazil to help the afflicted and the downtrodden, Brazil is now sending missionaries to the United States ("Os imigrantes brasileiros e as igrejas" 87). The motivations for joining a church are not that different from immigrants' motivations to come to the United States: Both are life changes that help individuals reach their fullest potential both personally (spiritually) and financially. It is a common rule among the Brazilian Pentecostal churches that members should tithe 10% of their paychecks to the church. But this money is seen as an investment in their futures. By maintaining the house of God, immigrants imagine that God will then repay them by increasing their own personal wealth.

The Brazilian Worship Setting

The majority of the migrants in New Orleans are Protestant Christians. Although Brazil is often imagined as being a Catholic country,

Brazil actually has the second-largest practicing community of Protestants outside the United States and the largest community of Pentecostals in the world. Within migrant communities, these numbers tend to be even more pronounced (Freston 255). Even when moving to the U.S., the most Protestant country in the world, Brazilians still find themselves seeking out Brazilian religious settings rather than joining Protestant Anglophone churches.[50] The reasons for seeking out Brazilian churches are not purely based on language. In areas such as Framingham, Mass., for example, where a sizeable Portuguese population and a Portuguese religious community were already in existence prior to the arrival of Brazilian immigrants, Brazilians have still tended to seek out Brazilian instead of Portuguese religious contexts (Freston 258).

New Orleans is a city with strong gospel traditions, a performative style of worship, and eloquent and forceful preachers, especially in black Protestant churches. Yet, Brazilians still seem to prefer the Brazilian Protestant worship style to New Orleanian religious settings. When asked why he felt that Brazilians did not attend Anglophone Protestant churches, Pastor Everton said,

> The American Pentecostal Church and the Brazilian Church serve the same God. But I serve a Brazilian church… As a leader of the Brazilian church, I have received my direction from God about how to run the church. The director of an American Pentecostal church has also received instruction about how to run his church in order to best reach his community… There will always be differences between them because the Brazilian instinctively has a manner of being and a manner of thinking just as the American also has his own instinctive way of being. As a Brazilian, I do not see myself going to an American church. And it is not because the American Church is not a wonderful church. It is because I am Brazilian. The customs of my church are Brazilian. It is easier for me, the way we worship, the language, these things all influence me to continue to frequent the Brazilian church rather than the American church. There is something about the way Brazilians worship. Brazilians are

[50] The Evangelical churches serving the Brazilian community in New Orleans are *Assembléia de Deus Brasileira em LA*, *A Família de Avivamento em New Orleans*, *Igreja Cristã do Brasil* and *Ministério Emanuel*. Catholic services for Brazilians are held in the Church of St. Anthony of Padua.

> more scandalous (*escandaloso*) with their worship of God. Brazilians call out to God more often. Brazilians pray and sing louder. They cry more. The spirit of God comes into our lives. It is what makes us cry, makes us euphoric (Everton 30 June 2009).

As Everton explains, the Brazilian church is important not only as a space for the worship of God, but also provides a Brazilian cultural space in which Brazilians can interact with their faith and with other Brazilians in their own cultural context. Crying, shouting, screaming, and speaking in tongues, which may be seen as out of context or even "escandaloso" to those outside of evangelical church circles, are common in Anglo evangelical circles as well, but these practices become means for communicating the particular experience of being a Brazilian immigrant connecting to God in Brazilian churches. Sermons are filled with illustrative stories and anecdotes specific to a Brazilian cultural context. Brazilian services in the U.S. often justify the situation of living clandestinely in the U.S. That is, in the way that the word of God is interpreted in Brazilian churches, the condition of being "illegal" in the U.S. is not seen as being illegitimate. In fact, the interpretation is quite the opposite. The experience of coming to the U.S. to help family and make a better life is supported and actually praised. The church becomes a vehicle both to legitimate the immigrant experience and to socialize Brazilians into a hybrid Brazil-New Orleans social world where people within the church can network for needed resources.

The Founding of Brazilian Churches in the Aftermath of Katrina

Pastor Everton of the Assembly of God Church was the first Brazilian pastor to arrive in New Orleans after Hurricane Katrina; he came a mere eighteen days after the storm. He held his first (outdoor) service on Sept. 23, 2005, with five Brazilian workers in attendance. When Hurricane Katrina hit, Pastor Everton had been in the U.S. for three months living in Florida, waiting for "the word from God about where he should move to open his own congregation" (Everton 30 June 2009).

During the first years in New Orleans, Pastor Everton rented and worshipped in two different hotel convention rooms in the New Orleans area.[51] However, in both cases the management of the hotels asked the church to leave after a few months because the worship services were so loud that they disturbed the guests. Also, in the first space, the Conference Center of a Travel Lodge hotel in Metairie, the church's prohibitions about drinking alcohol also conflicted with the Brazilian restaurant/bar run out of the same hotel. The weekend church services lasted until 8 or 9 p.m., and those people who frequented church were encouraged not to participate in the music and drinking that was occurring just next door. The bar began losing clients because those people who were members of the church did not attend and those who were not members did not want to be looked down on by the churchgoers and so stayed away as well. The bar closed because of lack of clientele soon after the church started services there in 2007.

According to Everton, the first years for his church were very difficult because finding space to rent in New Orleans was nearly impossible with such a limited number of functional buildings left standing after Hurricane Katrina. When Everton was turned away from the hotels, he then started renting a house specifically for church functions. However, the house was soon too small for the number of people attending services. He then met Pastor David Lima, the pastor of a Baptist church in Kenner, La., who allowed Everton's congregation to use the space in the Baptist church. Everton says, "David Lima was a father figure for us at the beginning" (Everton 30 June 2009). Finally, in 2008, Pastor Everton was able to secure a worship space in a building that had formerly housed an American Pentecostal church that had closed.[52] This building on West Esplanade Avenue in Kenner is now the home of the Brazilian Assembly of God Church, the first Brazilian church in the New Orleans area.

There was no Portuguese Catholic Mass in New Orleans until 2007, two years after the evangelical churches began their services. Unlike the Pentecostal churches whose services are run by Brazilian immigrants themselves (many of them also undocumented), the Catholic Mass in New Orleans is performed by an American priest who noticed the growing numbers of Brazilians with spiritual needs. Unlike the Evangelical Brazilian pastors who work to meet the spiritual needs of the Brazilian community alone, Father David Dufour divides

---

[51] The hotels were the Quality Inn and Travel Lodge, both located in Metairie, La.

[52] *Assembléia de Deus Brasileira em LA*, 523 West Esplanade Ave., Kenner, La.

his time between three different communities. He currently performs Mass in English and Spanish as well as Portuguese.

Figure 17: First Brazilian Church in New Orleans

Father Dufour explained that, after Hurricane Katrina, he noticed more Brazilians showing up for his Spanish Mass located at Our Lady of Divine Providence Church in Metairie. The Brazilians who came to Mass in Spanish began asking about the possibility of a Mass in Portuguese, so Father David spoke with the Archbishop about providing a Mass for the Brazilian community. Father Dufour had met with the Hispanic Apostolate and found that the majority of the Brazilians who had signed up for the Hispanic Apostolate's ESL classes lived in Metairie, Kenner, and Uptown New Orleans.[53] After the Archbishop gave permission to proceed, the first Brazilian Mass in New Orleans was performed in the winter of 2007 at St. Anthony of Padua Church, centrally located for the Brazilian

[53] As data from ESL classes confirms, there is not a specific area of Brazilian concentration in New Orleans, but Metairie and Kenner are popular neighborhoods due to apartment prices being lower than in New Orleans, the easy access to the interstate that makes getting to construction sites much easier, and the proximity to most of the other enclave spaces such as Brazilian stores, restaurants and evangelical churches.

community living in these neighborhoods.[54] This Catholic church was already familiar with multi-cultural Masses because Mass had already been offered here in Spanish and Vietnamese for several years.

Within the Brazilian congregation, there is great respect for Father Dufour. He has shown true altruism and dedication to the community. Father Dufour began learning Spanish and Portuguese when he was in seminary because he felt that if he were able to speak a little bit of Spanish and Portuguese, then he would be able to speak with almost all of the Catholics in the world. He never expected that he would use his Spanish or his Portuguese in his daily ministry, however. He developed his language skills simply to be able to communicate with other Catholics, not necessarily to preach to them. But because he is one of the few priests in New Orleans who speaks Spanish and the only priest who speaks Portuguese, his multi-lingual services were needed to preach within the New Orleanian post-Katrina social environment.

In 2007, Portuguese Masses were held once a month. Information about Brazilian Mass in New Orleans was spread mainly through word of mouth and through fliers handed out by core members in the congregation who were among the few Brazilian Catholic contacts that Father Dufour made through his Spanish Mass. The Mass was not advertised on Orkut, most likely because Father Dufour was not familiar with it. Even so, by 2008 the Brazilian Catholic community had grown large enough to hold a bi-weekly Mass, and, in August of 2008, Father David began a Portuguese Mass every Sunday with an average of 50 to 80 people in attendance. Father Dufour has performed Brazilian baptisms and holds weekly confessionals in New Orleans.

Pentecostalism Versus Catholicism in the Brazilian Community

Even though the Brazilian Catholic community has grown, it is notably smaller than the Protestant community. In 2009, there were six Brazilian evangelical churches and only one Catholic church offering a Brazilian Mass in New Orleans. There are several reasons that account for these size differences. One of these reasons is a difference in philosophy between the two. Father Dufour is not himself a Brazilian immigrant and is not involved with the Brazilian community

[54] 4640 Canal St., New Orleans, La.

except as a spiritual advisor. Also, as a priest who is paid through the archdiocese, the number of people who come to his services does not affect Father Dufour's personal income. He sees the Brazilian church as a space to provide a sense of community and to fulfill the spiritual need for catechism in Portuguese, not as a necessary means to his own livelihood. He will be a priest whether or not he provides services to the Brazilian community; he does not need the financial donations of his congregation to continue saying Mass and giving homilies, nor is the migration experience as omnipresent in his services since it is not part of his own lived experience, though he does his best to preach to the needs of his congregation.

Figure 18: Brazilian mass at St. Anthony Church, New Orleans

Advertising for the Catholic Masses has not been approached with the same sort of urgency as those services held by Pentecostal congregations. The outreach and promotion of the Catholic Mass finds difficulty competing with the Brazilian Pentecostal churches which are themselves Brazilian migrant spaces run by migrants whose livelihoods also depend on the size of their congregations. The pastors of the Brazilian Pentecostal churches work only with the Brazilian community, hold services in Portuguese several times a week, and usually do not work another job. All of their time is devoted solely to the Brazilian community. Because Brazilian pastors work almost exclusively to serve Brazilian migrants (and pastors are often dealing personally with migration issues themselves), migration is a constant theme in their preaching.

The Pentecostal Church has also had success in New Orleans because the pastors of the evangelical churches are very accessible. I found that setting up interviews with the pastors of the Pentecostal Church was surprisingly easy. I was able to set up an appointment for a meeting within a day or two of my phone call request. (In fact, most pastors invited me to continue to meet with them more frequently so that they could help guide my spiritual progress.) My meeting with Father David was more difficult to arrange because his work schedule is more hectic. He, too, was very open and eager to be of service to me, but he has responsibilities to three different Catholic communities and to the church parish. It took a week before we could set up a meeting and I am grateful that he was willing to make time for me. I also noticed that our conversation was much more driven by my scholarly questions about Brazilian demographics in the Catholic community and less focused on my own personal relationship with God. The opposite was true of my conversations with the Brazilian Pentecostal pastors and is probably a reflection of differences in approaches towards evangelism and difference in the levels of schooling required to become a religious leader in each community.

These differing conversation styles reflect the difference in existing relationships between religious leaders and the Brazilian community that they serve. It is much more likely that pastors from Brazilian Pentecostal churches in New Orleans will come to the doors of the immigrants. Pastors customarily make house visits to talk about spiritual issues. Brazilians in New Orleans who reported that they were Catholic before coming to the United States and later converted to Pentecostalism after arriving (either in New Orleans or in their previous city) reported that the accessibility of the Pentecostal churches and the lack of Catholic church options were factors that contributed to their decision to change their religious affiliations.

Freston has argued that one of the reasons that Pentecostalism has had such success among migrant communities is that Pentecostalism is a religion made to travel and, thus, is the ideal religion for migrants (261). Sociologists have long considered that immigrants may be self-selected to succeed because the act of immigration itself requires a certain personal drive and self-starter attitude (Borjas 29). Following this logic, it makes sense that self-motivated migrants would choose a religion in which they could proactively speak to, shout for, and finally receive direct benefits from their relationship with God, rather than choose a religion in which speaking to God happens mainly through the mediation of a priest.

The physical space of worship is also nearly irrelevant in the Pentecostal context, making travel easier. There are no special shrines or holy spaces that must be transplanted in order to worship God. Services can even be held in a hotel convention room or in an old warehouse. There is no national church or archdiocese that the church must follow as it opens a new Pentecostal congregation and the sermons of the Brazilian Pentecostal Church preach a direct connection between people and God. A Catholic Church requires consecrated space and authorization of the archdiocese in order to hold Mass, and there are a variety of saints, as well as the priesthood, that mediate people's relationship to God. While Father Dufour addresses issues of immigration during his homilies, these issues are not addressed in the direct and personal way that they are addressed in the Evangelical Churches, churches that are themselves products of immigration in both the literal and figurative senses.

It should also be noted that because there is less official financing of the Pentecostal church, there is also more room for corruption. In 2006, a Brazilian pastor in New Orleans began holding sermons from his house while he simultaneously worked in construction. After six months in New Orleans, he left town, owing thousands of dollars to workers whom he had employed in construction projects but never paid. Not all Brazilians I interviewed had positive opinions of the moneymaking practices in the Brazilian evangelical churches in New Orleans. In fact, some interviews expressed anger that particular churches were exploitive. One particular interviewee described a scene in which, during the height of the religious service, the pastor urged people to donate their personal belongings in order to have their souls saved. People donated watches, necklaces, and the shirts off their backs. One woman even donated her car, handing her keys over to the pastor. She did this even though she was a housecleaner and obviously was going to need her car for work. The interviewee commented that she felt that the church took advantage of the simplicity and the vulnerability of the immigrants who came in a desperate state in search of the church's protection and support.

The discourses that Brazilian pastors use to attract new members can be particularly powerful to people who are in a distressed state regarding their personal and financial goals. For example, in my interviews with Brazilian pastors, the pastors who talked with me about my faith tended to focus on how my own work and family life would greatly improve if I dedicated my life to God, often employing a fear tactic. If I were to keep resisting God, so I was told, my life projects would not succeed. One pastor went so far as to to tell me that, even though he saw that I was involved in spreading much goodwill within the Brazilian community through my volunteering and social activism, I was still going to hell unless I accepted Jesus into my life. Using the tactics of invoking the social utility of religion and manipulating by the threat of personal failure seemed common in conversations between pastors and potential church members. For immigrants who seek out the church under urgent circumstances when their lives are not going as they had planned, this discourse can be particularly compelling. Pastor Everton commented,

> In the evangelical church people talk directly with God. People are cured. They have their lives transformed. A person comes addicted to drugs or with some other affliction or addiction and the person is set free. They see God (Everton 30 June 2009).

The Pentecostal church is attractive to immigrants because the rhetoric assures that worshipping God can bring immediate financial and social benefits. The pastors preach in concrete terms about how afflictions and addictions and problems in work or in the home setting can be "cured" by believing in God. Alleged miracles are performed with the intensity of this belief. In my interviews, people spoke of religion as a catalyst that opened opportunities to migrate or brought about needed jobs. In almost all of these interviews, the higher power that guided the person was referred to as God or as Jesus Christ. Even those not involved in the church officially often attributed their opportunities for success (their post-migration survival as well as their upward mobility) to the influence of a higher power. Choices about religion are practical among the Brazilian immigrant community.

Even with the marked differences between the Catholic and Protestant communities, the space for community building offered by religious organizations are essential in creating a sense of stability for the Brazilian community in New Orleans. There are a proportionally larger number of families and children in the religious spaces in New Orleans in comparison to other Brazilian spaces in the city. And churches offer a more steady representation of the Brazilian enclave environment. Past researchers have noted that the birth of children and family unity in the U.S. means that Brazilian immigrants will be less likely to return to Brazil (Sales "Identidade Étnica…" 21). The appearance of united families and children in the Brazilian churches in New Orleans reveals pockets of Brazilians who do not envision migratory fluxes back to Brazil as part of their five-year plan.

Emergence of Brazilian Churches Motivate a Change in Brazilian Social Life

Involvement in Brazilian evangelical church circles often necessarily means a separation from other New Orleanian social outlets that are potential opportunities for cultural integration. The evangelical church asks its members, at least indirectly, to stay away from places where they will be tempted to drink alcohol or to dance to music that is not related to the worship of God. This means that Brazilians who become involved with evangelical churches begin to stay away from New Orleanian social spaces where Brazilians in the past found points of integration with locals. When I asked Brazilian Pastor Everton if it was acceptable for members of his congregation to enjoy the nightlife in New Orleans, for example, he tactfully responded, "Members are free to do anything that they want. But in the church they learn that not everything that they want is good for them" (Everton 30 June 2009). Pastor Everton remarked that being a pastor in New Orleans is similar to being a pastor in Brazil in that one must learn to coexist with a vibrant and diverse local culture. He then told me a parable about how, when dealing with the culture of New Orleans, his congregation should have two pockets: one pocket in which to keep the important things that they could learn from New Orleanian culture, and one pocket with a hole in it, so that they will not offend anyone when they throw the bad out by slipping it into the faulty pocket.

This story is revealing about the attitude that the Brazilian evangelical church has taken towards New Orleanian culture in general. Entering the evangelical church is a life decision that dictates many social relationships in the future. Some Brazilians who were once very involved in the social options of New Orleans found that the church offered them a more constructive sense of community to accomplish their goals in the U.S. By allying themselves with the church, however, they had to distance themselves from the previous social circles that they had frequented. A division exists within the Brazilian community between those heavily involved in church activities and those who are not. This division occurs in subtle ways from modifications in women's style of dress to accommodate differing concepts of modesty to changing attitudes about where church members should socialize—and with whom.[55]

To illustrate how Brazilian religious life has influenced the social lives of members of the Brazilian community in New Orleans, I want to return briefly to my interview with Álvaro, owner of "The Chat Room and Suingue Brazil." When I telephoned Álvaro in August 2009, requesting an interview about his 2006 business endeavor, it had been at least two years since I had seen him. He was no longer in Brazilian nightlife circles; in fact, I was not even sure that he was still in the New Orleans area. I was finally able to locate him, however, through the online community Orkut. My memories of Álvaro were of a man who loved parties and nightlife— an important personality trait for someone who was operating a Brazilian bar and dance club. One of my clearest memories of him was when he came to Rotolo's one Saturday night in 2006 with three women under his arms, telling Rogerio, owner of the pizzeria, that he wanted to buy drinks for everyone in the bar. In 2006, Álvaro was the type of guy who was always the center of every party. He bragged to me that night that he had just dropped $3,500 dollars on Bourbon Street paying for drinks and women.

In 2009, with these memories in mind, I suggested that we meet at Rotolo's for the interview because that is where I had remembered

[55] There are obviously differing degrees to which people who become involved with the Brazilian Pentecostal Church come to distance themselves from problematic social settings. I asked a woman who frequents the Brazilian World Revival Church of Louisiana (*A Família do Avivamento em New Orleans*) if she had ever been to Bourbon Street. She quickly responded that she would never partake in that sort of heathenry. But then she added, "Well, I have been on Bourbon Street before, but only to go into the sex shops, not to go out at night."

Álvaro being in his element; I thought he would feel more fully at ease to talk to me there. However, I was surprised to hear Álvaro say that he had joined the church and no longer went out at night. Instead, he suggested that we meet for a 9 a.m. breakfast on a Sunday morning. His social life now revolves around the church, and he has moved away from his house on animated Frenchmen Street to the quiet suburb of La Place, La.

Like Álvaro, many Brazilians in New Orleans involved with the evangelical church chose to live in a certain neighborhood based on their relationship to the church, either to be closer to the church or farther from the distractions of the French Quarter. The Brazilian religious life is particularly marking for the Brazilian community in New Orleans because it provides both a sense of community and support, yet it also can potentially be a point at which the Brazilian community experiences boundaries and divisions. A stronger Evangelical presence in the Brazilian community in New Orleans, in fact, has meant the emergence of a group of Brazilians less willing to integrate into New Orleanian social circles.

Private Brazilian gatherings, Orkut online communities, Brazilian stores, Brazilian bars and restaurants, and Brazilian churches are thus disparate social spaces that attract a majority Brazilian group; the groups differ in numbers, but each congregates with an outcome that consciously or unconsciously critiques and reinterprets what it means to be Brazilian in New Orleans. Immigrants seek out the spaces in which they feel most comfortable and supported, often finding their sense of community while moving between the diverse spaces outlined in this chapter. Brazilian enclave spaces in New Orleans illustrate the centrality of the construction market to the livelihood of the Brazilian community in New Orleans, the tendency of the Brazilian community to move back and forth between their created Brazilian enclave and their local New Orleanian community, and the fact that pioneer Brazilians to New Orleans post-Katrina earned a sense of agency over their communities by creating the enclave spaces themselves. The way that an immigrant understands his relationship to his Brazilian community through a night at Rotolo's Pizzeria may be very different from another whose relationship is expressed almost entirely through his spiritual connection to a Brazilian church. However, both are equally important representations of the Brazilian enclave in its unique and diverging performances.

While the idea of a Brazilian enclave community in New Orleans as a united and homogenous entity is an abstraction, it is a significant abstraction that manifests itself in those spaces that Brazilians mark as their own. Enclave spaces offer an alternative view of what it means to be Brazilian because performances of Brazilian identity within the enclave often challenge the categories or tropes people have come to accept as normative. When migrant identity performances put into question this hegemonic view of Brazil, the act itself questions our naturalized knowledge of Brazilian identity. The route towards understanding home and belonging takes different paths, but Brazilian enclave spaces recreate diverging imaginings of Brazil firmly planted in the New Orleans' local landscape. It is the constant push and pull between longing and renewal in intimate portraits such as eating Brazilian *churrasco*, buying *guaraná*, listening to *sertanejo* music, or worshipping in the Portuguese language that define the local, regional, and national characteristics of the Brazilian enclave in New Orleans.

Congregating with others to celebrate (and critique) these symbols is important for how migrants imagine their identities. Having other people who relate to the particular negotiations of identity, who share comparable economic struggles, who are in similar positions within the local social landscape, and who went through a similar rite of passage in order to get to New Orleans in the first place, is paramount for immigrants in forming a sense of who they are. Inventing oneself means becoming part of a group where immigrants can feel that they are "in this together." Enclaves provide this feeling of identity and belonging by both providing a space to talk about the cultural affinities across regional and national lines and also to discuss what makes them unique and different— as Brazilian immigrants in the U.S., as Brazilian immigrants in New Orleans, and as people.

Placing Brazilians in Mardi Gras Culture, New Orleans

In Episode II of the HBO television series "Treme," which documents the lives of New Orleanians after Hurricane Katrina, John Goodman's character makes reference to the fact that Tulane University cut many graduate programs after the storm in an effort to deal with the financial deficit spurred by hurricane damage to the university. He remarks snidely that Tulane did not, however, cut their Portuguese graduate program in the aftermath of Hurricane Katrina, noting that, Portuguese "could come in handy in case any Brazilians come up to New Orleans looking for Mardi Gras work." New Orleans, it turned out, did, in fact, become an attractive place for Brazilians, though instead of coming up from Brazil to look for work in the Mardi Gras world, they came down from other cities in the US to work in hurricane reconstruction and found themselves joining in with the Mardi Gras festivities along the way. In this final chapter analyzing the Brazilian enclave in New Orleans, I would now like to turn to the event for which New Orleans is best known: Mardi Gras.

Even though Brazilians themselves were not a significant presence in New Orleans until after Hurricane Katrina, representations of Brazilian culture have been performed on the local New Orleanian tourist circuit since 1985, first as a Mardi Gras krewe and then as the samba school and cultural organization, Casa Samba. Casa Samba, a Brazilian samba school run by African Americans in New Orleans, performs Brazilian cultural representations from Rio de Janeiro and, to a lesser extent, from Salvador and Recife. Being part of the tourist culture of New Orleans for over 25 years, Casa Samba performs Brazilian national culture representations in local New Orleanian settings, creating a hybrid cultural experience that represents a Brazilian-New

Orleanian worldview and becoming an important part of the way that Brazilian identity is constructed in New Orleans. The Brazil projected through Casa Samba performances inevitably becomes mediated through a New Orleanian worldview in what Director Curtis Pierre terms as an "Amerizilian" experience.

Migration creates new relationships between Brazilian immigrants and their understandings of their home in Brazil and abroad. Barbara Browning has said that public displays of Brazil are to be read as you would read a text; instead of words there are movements "written" by bodies of the performers. Performances, unlike objects or texts, cannot be detached from their performers, the local place (New Orleans), or the imagined community being performed (Brazil). Casa Samba, as a public performance group in New Orleans that invokes the image of Brazil, influences the flow of everyday life for Brazilian immigrants by calling attention to Brazilian identity(ies) in their global forms. Immigrants must constantly interpret these projected images in the context of their own local lives and experiences. The fact that Brazilian immigrants navigate these representations on foreign ground, within a community of Brazilians that is quite heterogeneous, marks the Brazuca migrant experience.

Though Casa Samba has open rehearsals and quickly became a place of contact for Brazilians who arrived post-Katrina to seek out contacts with Americans who were interested in Brazilian culture, Brazilian immigrants themselves are rarely performers with Casa Samba; this is mostly because they come from areas of Brazil where these cultural expressions are not representative of their local identity. As mentioned in previous chapters, in many of the sending communities from which Brazilians in New Orleans hail, the number of people attending the local rodeos often outnumbers the local soccer matches and the music playing on the local radio is *sertanejo* and not samba. However, whether or not they participate directly in Casa Samba as members, the existence of Casa Samba in New Orleans influences how New Orleanians view Brazilians. And, thus, Casa Samba becomes crucial in an immigrant's own construction of a Brazilian's place in New Orleans. The way that nation is displayed through theatrical performances of heritage gives life to what would normally be a static political border. This often means immigrants find their Brazilian identity in ways that they never have before migration. "Aprendi a sambar nos Estados

Unidos" (I learned to samba in the US), said a Brazilian immigrant in New Orleans.

Casa Samba finale, Howling Wolf, New Orleans, 2006

The History of Casa Samba

Samba schools abroad are examples of how images set forth by the global market influence how Brazilian culture is imagined on local stages. While samba schools in Brazil maintain ties to a specific culture revolving around Rio de Janeiro carnival traditions, US samba schools, though heavily based in Rio traditions, also tend to depict culture from Salvador and Recife with inevitable inflections of the US performance space. Culture from the coastal region of Brazil has also monopolized Brazil's nationalist discourse because 80 percent of Brazilians live within 200 miles from the ocean. (Wade and Harrison 332) The combination of Brazilian cultural traditions coming from these coastal urban centers is considered to be the most "authentic" and encompassing representation of Brazil as it is projected internationally. Casa Samba's performance of Brazil in New Orleans is an example of such a trend.

The interest in Brazilian culture in New Orleans that led to Casa Samba can be linked to the work of Bill Lennon, retired director of Tulane University's program of International Student Affairs. In 1984, three young black professionals looking for a carnival option rooted in Afrocentric concepts approached Bill with an interest in forming a Mardi Gras krewe based on Brazilian culture. After some initial research, the krewe members decided to name themselves Palmares after the legendary marooned slave community in seventeenth-century Brazil, and they beseeched Bill for additional information to provide historical meaning to their organization. Bill Lennon became the official historian for the Palmares carnival krewe and they began to collaborate with the Barthe Brothers, traditional Mardi Gras float builders, to develop their 1985 floats. The floats were self-propelled, a Mardi Gras first, built on top of a school bus chassis. The floats designed by the Barthe Brothers were based on the ideas of Bill Lennon and of a Brazilian graduate student at Tulane University named Sonia Daly. The two would go to the Barthe Brothers' den near NASA Michoud twice a week to consult with the builders in order to design the Brazilian inspired floats. There was a Zumbi[56] float, a Iemanjá[57] float, an Amazon float, a tropical fruit float, a parrot float, and a Saci Pererê[58] float in the Palmares parade line.[59]

The Palmares members were 95% African American. Bill himself is not African American, nor were many of the other participants who later joined the krewe, which attracted young professionals and foreign students of all races and ethnicities. Bill Lennon had spent time in Brazil both studying and working and was a resource for learning about Brazilian culture. Since Bill's arrival in New Orleans in 1979 (the 1980-1984 Mardi Gras seasons), he along with a small group of some 20 family and friends, had informally paraded behind the Rex krewe up Napoleon Avenue with a boom box inside a shopping cart blasting *samba de enredo*, the samba rhythm traditionally played during carnival in Rio de Janeiro. In an effort to reproduce a Brazilian carnival experience for the Palmares krewe, Bill convinced the Board of

[56] Zumbi is considered to be the last leader of the escaped slave community. Palmares is located in the interior of Alagoas and Bahia states.

[57] Iemanjá is the orixá, originally of the Yoruba religion, who was converted into a prominent figure in Brazilian candomblé. She is the essence of the sea and of motherhood.

[58] One of the most popular figures in Brazilian folklore, Saci Pererê is described as a young one-legged mulatto boy who wears a red cap and is able to miraculously appear and disappear. He is known as a prankster.

[59] Several years later the Iemanjá float supposedly went to the Smithsonian museum in Washington DC in an exhibit on Carnival traditions and the rest of the floats seem to have mysteriously disappeared.

Directors of Palmares that there needed to be an "on foot" presence to accompany the traditional Mardi Gras float riders. He recruited family and friends to be a *mestre-sala*, a *porta-bandeira*, and an *ala de foliões* that accompanied the krewe on foot dancing and merry-making.[60] This section of the krewe organization was a racially and ethnically diverse group. Due to Bill's position as Director of International Student Affairs, he was able to recruit a large number of international students and graduate students interested in being part of a Mardi Gras parade and a Brazilian cultural representation in New Orleans.

Bill Lennon was also interested in creating a *bateria* (drum line) to march with the Mardi Gras floats. He contacted local Brazilian musician, Edu Alves,[61] who in the 1980's had a band in New Orleans called Sounds of Brazil, to be the drum line leader for the group. Bill had a friend who worked for a lumber shipping company, so the Palmares krewe bought Brazilian percussion instruments from Belém, Brazil, the arrival port for the lumber company, and shipped them back to New Orleans on a Robinson Lumber Company Ship that made port in Chalmette, Louisiana. They bought 20 *surdus* (large bass drums), 20 *agogôs* (bell instruments), 20 *pandeiros* (large, heavy Brazilian tambourines) and 20 *tamborins* (a small hand drum played with a stick).

The krewe organizers decided that they still needed a powerful drum line and so they opted to use the drum sections of four New Orleanian high schools. The mission of the drum line project was to bring students together from different socioeconomic and racial backgrounds. They used Nicholl's High School (now Frederick Douglass high school in the Ninth Ward), Walter L. Cohen High School in Central City, Landrieu High School in the Fisher projects, and Heritage Academy in Metairie (an all-white post-integration academy). Edu Alves, Honduran Percussionist Miguel Banegas, and Bill Lennon visited these three schools every week for three months to practice Brazilian *carnaval* rhythms for the 1985 Mardi Gras season. At the

[60] The *mestre-sala* and the *porta-bandeira* are a couple that dance the first samba performance as the samba school enters the arena. *Mestre-sala* is a male samba dancer who is the official host of the samba school. It is the position of highest distinction among those who devote their careers to the samba world. He accompanies and protects the *porta-bandeira*, a female who carries the official flag of the school. Thus, the mestre-sala symbolically protects the samba school as well. The *ala de foliões*, is a wing of carnival-goers who accompany the carnival float as revelers often in matching shirts or costumes.

[61] Edu Alves is a musician from São Paulo who now lives in Japan.

first general rehearsal held in Congo Square one week before the parade, however, the band instructors from Heritage Academy, the only school in the group with white students, withdrew when they found out that they were the only white school in the drum line, thus revealing the racial divides still present in the city at the time. The Heritage students themselves were very disappointed to be pulled out of the parade. The next year, instead of using high school drum lines, Palmares recruited a group of amateur musicians who rehearsed with Edu Alves and Bill Lennon on Tulane's campus.

I asked Bill in our interview if he felt as if New Orleans is receptive to a Brazilian Mardi Gras krewe, and he responded,

> I think it is, but a big thing that we always had to deal with, especially with the Brazilians who came in, was that *Carnaval* has existed in New Orleans for 100 years without samba. So it didn't need it. That is why it couldn't be exactly the same [as in Brazil]. If we weren't in the parade they really wouldn't miss us. Like going faster all the time, we couldn't really add complicated steps because there really wasn't time. We were covering 6-7 miles. Not just the sambadrome. The cops were right behind us. 'Hurry up or we are going to kick you out of the parade.' It was hard… (Bill Lennon 11 May 2009)

Bill's comment speaks to the particularity of New Orleans as a space for Brazilian cultural performance. New Orleans creates a space for Brazilian *carnaval* performances to coexist with Mardi Gras performances. However, they must exist within the confines of the New Orleanian imagining of what carnival is. Dancing samba 6-7 miles with a parade is not easy. Samba shows are set up as sprints while Mardi Gras parades are marathons. Adjustments have to be made in the samba parade in order to cover the amount of ground necessary to fit within the cultural expectations of New Orleanian Mardi Gras traditions.

The Palmares krewe was a success in the 1985 and 1986 seasons. In 1985 the krewe was even covered on the Brazilian TV Show *Fantástico* and on the local Channel 12 production "Chappy Goes to Mardi Gras" that is still aired during Mardi Gras season each year. By the 1986 Mardi Gras season, the Jackson 5 (minus Michael) rode the floats along with the krewe as celebrity marshals. During these two years there were elaborate Palmares krewe carnival balls with more than 500 people in attendance held at the Sheraton hotel in New Orleans. Edu Alves' Sounds of Brazil band alternated with the Battiste Brothers Funk band, a great mixture of "Mamãe eu quero" and "Hey Pocky Way." Many black political and civic leaders attended, including the mayor to be, Sidney Barthelemy and congressman to be, William Jefferson.

But months after the 1986 Mardi Gras season, rumors floated that Palmares was in financial crisis after both the Sheraton Hotel and the Barthe Brothers complained about unpaid bills from the Mardi Gras season. According to Bill Lennon, there are several factors that led to the end of the krewe: Palmares needed 500 paying riders in order to meet budget, but the krewe could never quite meet that number. The oil recession of the mid-80s had left many people without the funds to join a new krewe. Also, the "Brazilianist" members of Palmares, that is, those people who were not interested in being riders in the Mardi Gras sense of the organization but, instead, wanted to be revelers on foot who would dance samba along with the floats, needed a lesser fee structure that was never sufficiently developed by Palmares. And, in terms of social pressures, the established krewes, both black and white, felt threatened by the multiracial emphasis of the Palmares krewe. Finally, there was only one person (the president of Palmares who had been a member of Zulu) with any Mardi Gras experience. Together, these factors led to Palmares' demise. After the money fiascos, the Captain of Palmares left town and the President of Palmares decided to return to Zulu (where he became the president of Zulu several years later). Thus, an official Brazilian Mardi Gras krewe in New Orleans ended abruptly after only two years.

The Brazilian-inspired Mardi Gras celebration may have faded into oblivion until the arrival of the post-Katrina Brazucas had it not been for the arrival of percussionist Curtis Pierre onto the local music scene. Two days after the 1986 Palmares parade, Curtis Pierre, current director of Casa Samba, returned to his hometown of New Orleans from

Los Angeles and contacted Bill Lennon about Palmares.[62] A Brazilian musician friend of Curtis's in Los Angeles who had played in New Orleans with Edu Alves in 1983-1984 had given Curtis Bill's contact information. Bill invited Curtis to accompany the Palmares *bateria* in two carnival shows: a carnival party at Touro synagogue and a parade with the Tucks krewe the following Saturday of Mardi Gras 1986. Curtis joined the Palmares *bateria* and by the summer of 1986, when Bill became aware of the organization's financial trouble, Curtis had taken on a vital role in continuing the promotion of Brazilian culture in New Orleans, which included warehousing the instruments in an effort to keep them safe from the debt collection agencies. Bill Lennon took a year sabbatical to Brazil and Edu Alves moved to Japan because he had received an offer to play with a band in Tokyo.

While the Palmares krewe had been primarily made up of Brazilian aficionados, a social group not trained as musicians or dancers, Curtis's goal as the new leader of the group was to transform the parade group into both a performance group and a social group; this structure persists today. Many of the musicians who marched with Palmares joined Curtis and he took it as his mission to train a professional-level drum line while his wife, Carol Pierre, whom he had also met through the Palmares Mardi Gras krewe, began to train a professional-level dance team. Curtis renamed his organization "Cosmopolitan Amigo Samba Association," hence CASA Samba to distance himself from the Palmares krewe fiasco. The old musical instruments from the krewe were appropriated by Casa Samba and, thus, began the first samba school in New Orleans in the fall of 1986.

Since the 1980s, Casa Samba has paraded each year with the Endymion "Super Krewe." Super krewes are the largest and most extravagant of Mardi Gras krewes, with celebrity rather than local kings. Curtis knew that parading with a super krewe was an important step in Casa Samba being able to insert itself within the New Orleanian tourist circuit. By 1987, Curtis had made connections with the Endymion and Zulu super krewes and the Casa Samba *bateria* was part of

[62] There have been other samba schools that have emerged in New Orleans. Most of them have broken off from Casa Samba because of personality or philosophical differences. Zabumba and Samba Rio are two samba schools that emerged but have disappeared since the 1990s. These break-off schools have not presented themselves as a rival to Casa Samba because they have not successfully inserted themselves into the New Orleans tourism industry as has Casa Samba.

their parade line up. It became obvious, however, that for Casa Samba to have an impact among the extravagant floats and riders of the super krewes, there needed to be a stronger street presence. Bill Lennon and his wife MaryAnn along with Curtis and Carol Pierre then organized a wing of eight to twelve marching *baianas* (women dressed in traditional Bahian clothing who are seen as the protectorates of the samba tradition in Rio) to accompany the band each year. They also coordinated a large non-professional parading group, the *ala de foliões* (75-100 each year, and mostly from the Tulane community given both Bill and Carol's contacts.) Original costumes were designed and created each year and the group held parade rehearsals to recorded samba *enredo* music on Tulane's campus on Saturday afternoons leading up to Mardi Gras. The *bateria* and *passistas* (the professional wing of Casa Samba) rehearsed in a separate space and the groups would join for a general rehearsal on the Mississippi River levee the week before the parade. The marching members who were not part of the professional team paid dues and had to come to three rehearsals in order to receive a costume. This structure lasted until 2003.

However, as Casa Samba professionalized its dancing and spent less time organizing and corralling members to parade in the *foliões* wing, it became physically impossible for dancers to put on a top-notch samba performance for a seven-mile parade route within the super krewe structure. Instead, Casa Samba began to perform its samba parades only at Endymion and Zulu Balls. Now Casa Samba meets the Endymion krewe in the Superdome after they arrive from their parade route and parade with the marchers in the congratulatory lap at the beginning of the ball. Later the group performs an elaborate floorshow on stage during the Ball itself. Zulu holds its ball before their parade and Casa Samba usually performs an opening dance to welcome the Zulu King and the Zulu Queen to the arena. Becoming part of the entertainment for these super krewes has meant that Casa Samba found itself a major performing group for New Orleanian Mardi Gras culture.

In an effort to both professionalize the group and to spread Brazilian culture to the community, Casa Samba has weekly open samba rehearsals that incorporate members of the community from all walks of life, and it organizes Brazil Camps where classes are taught not only in Brazilian music and dance, but also in capoeira, Brazilian history, and costume design. Curtis hoped to create Casa Samba in the spirit of samba schools in Brazil where the cultural organization is also a community center. He has taken under his wing many at-risk children and brought them into the samba school. These children with relatively unstable family lives find discipline, support, and a sense of community within the samba school.

The mission statement for Casa Samba says,

> Being a native of New Orleans and knowing the problems that kids face today, Curtis has adopted the same philosophy of the samba schools in Brazil in taking a social responsibility for safeguarding our children and providing them with creative and challenging opportunities and experiences other than what is found in the streets. It is our desire to provide a venue for getting the community, specifically children and young adults, interested in music and dance and providing them with a place to participate in supervised and structured activities, like residences, after school and during the summer months[63] (www.casasamba.com).

For Curtis Pierre, Casa Samba represents "the unfolding of his life path." Though he grew up in Killona, a small Louisiana town outside of New Orleans, Curtis spent time in Detroit and Los Angeles before returning to New Orleans to begin Casa Samba. Curtis was intrigued by percussion instruments and his travels in the United States were part of his search to find the type of percussion that best suited him. He became fascinated with the *berimbau* (a single-stringed musical bow used in capoeira consisting of a gourd as a resonator and a single wire stretched along a pole). "I played it (the berimbau) upside down for about a year before I knew. I had never seen one. I had just heard it on a record." (Pierre 7 November 2007) According to Jorge Alabe, Curtis's mentor, before meeting capoeira mestre Cobra Mansa, Curtis "played a capoeira that he had invented in his own head" (*fazia capoeira da cabeça dele*) (Jorge 23 December 2008).

Curtis reports that his love for Brazilian music began with a record of Brazilian percussionist Airto Moreira. When he listened to Airto Moreira's record for the first time, Curtis was in his mid-twenties and living in Detroit. One day at a practice for a percussion choir in Detroit, one of the directors of the group told Curtis that if he were really

[63] For more on *escolas de samba* as community centers in Brazil see Vianna, *The Mystery of Samba* and Guillermoprieto, *Samba*.

serious about making a career as a percussionist, then he needed to find a teacher. To be able to find a teacher, he had to find a style of music that truly moved him. Curtis realized that he had found that music style in the work of Airto Moreira. He "wore it [the record] out in a year and then he had the opportunity to go see him in concert." (Pierre 7 November 2007) Listening to the record and seeing Airto in concert were enough to convince Curtis to move to California to further his studies in Brazilian percussion, mainly in order to be closer to Airto who was living in Los Angeles at the time. Reminiscing about the critical role that Airto played in his musical development Curtis says,

> I went to the concert and went backstage and said 'Hey Airto, you remember me?' He said, 'Yeah, I remember you. Do you want to play with us tonight?'…I couldn't believe it! I didn't tell anyone what had just happened. It wasn't till years later that I was finally able to tell him how influential he had been in my life. And then the next day we got a-- he got—a review in the paper and it said that the two percussionists that played with him were great. I didn't know what the hell I was doing, you know? I mean I knew just a little bit. So after a year I was just like, 'Okay, well I'm going to drop everything that I'm doing here and I'm going to California to be around him wherever he is that is where I am going to be.' (Pierre 7 November 2007)

Curtis began developing his skills as a Brazilian percussionist in California. He took every opportunity that he could to meet and talk with famous musicians. One day Bill Summers, Curtis's first percussion teacher from New Orleans, walked into the rehearsal in LA. Bill Summers is a New Orleanian musician who specializes in African and Afro Cuban rhythms. In the rehearsal they were both playing the *cuíca*[64] side by side and Bill Summers gave Curtis the idea of returning to New Orleans to start a Brazilian carnival group.

Curtis said,

> Before that conversation I had never put the two things together! Samba music and carnival music!...never until he said it. And then a light just went off in my head. I was like 'Ha! That's right.'…It was just destined for me to do that. And when I came back…the

[64] A small sized drum with a thin rod attached to the drum skin on the inside that is rubbed to produce a squeaky sound.

destiny...one of the first people that I met in the group was my wife. (Curtis 8 October 2007)

Curtis: Migrant Hub for Brazilian Performers in New Orleans

In 1992, Curtis was back in New Orleans and beginning the performance group, Casa Samba. The Brazilian touring group Oba Oba came to New Orleans this same year. Just as Curtis had done with Airto Moreira, Curtis went to the show early and waited for the performers to arrive. He was interested in meeting Jorge Alabe, the director of Oba Oba and Cobra Mansa, the performing capoeirista in the group. The night of the Oba Oba concert, Curtis (and his wife Carol Barber-Pierre) sneaked the whole group out of the hotel and to their house for a party, strengthening their relationships with Jorge Alabe and Mestre Cobra Mansa (Carol 10 March 2008). This late-night encounter became important in the formation and development of Casa Samba. Jorge Alabe would later come back to New Orleans to live with Curtis for over 10 years and Cobra Mansa spent weeks at a time with Curtis's capoeira group for about two years during the group's formation. He still returns frequently to do workshops in New Orleans.

Jorge Alabe,[65] master drummer from Rio and Curtis's guru said, "Curtis is an American with a Brazilian soul..." (Jorge 23 December 2008). Curtis said that having Jorge with him was like having "a piece of Brazil there with him at all times" (Curtis 8 October 2007). Instead of Curtis needing to make constant trips to Brazil to learn, he brought Brazil to him. "Living with Jorge made me understand the culture. Performing Brazilian culture became a lifestyle for me." (Ibid) The relationship that developed between Curtis Pierre and Jorge Alabe has been essential to forming Casa Samba into the samba school that it is today. While there have been other Brazilian-inspired groups in New Orleans, none of them have had the longevity nor the commitment that Curtis has brought to Casa Samba; inviting a master drummer to live in your house for ten years shows major dedication. Jorge spoke no English when he first arrived and Curtis spoke no Portuguese. Today they are both bilingual.

For Curtis, his close connection with Jorge gives him a sense of le-

[65] Jorge Alabe spent 15 years touring with Brazilian performance company Oba Oba. He now lives in San Francisco and runs the samba school Quilombo.

gitimacy as an American playing Brazilian music. Curtis says that once he became involved with Jorge, Casa Samba became "more focused in their goal of the preservation of culture" (Curtis 7 November 2007). He says, "Today I can walk in different places now and have a lot more respect than I would if I had never met him…After living with Jorge I would go places and people would give me a lot more respect, where as before I was just, you know, somebody else learning." (Ibid)

Indeed, Curtis is now a respected figure in the Brazilian performance community not only in New Orleans but in the United States. He does yearly percussion workshops at Brazil Camp, an annual full-immersion Brazilian music and dance camp held in Cazadero, California in the Redwood Forest.[66] Brazil Camp is one of the most important national events for the promotion of Brazilian culture in the US, making Curtis Pierre one of the leading ambassadors of Brazilian culture in the US-Brazilian performance circle. Even more noteworthy, in December 2008, Curtis Pierre was invited to give a percussion workshop on Rio-style samba to *bloco afro* Ilê Aiyê in Salvador, Bahia. This workshop was organized through Curtis's connection to Marcio Peeter, an Ilê Aiyê member who, like Jorge, lived with Curtis for almost two years to help him develop the Bahian rhythms in the Casa Samba repertoire during 2008-09. The fact that Curtis Pierre was given the authority to teach Brazilian rhythms to one of the most famous percussion groups in Salvador is testament to the fact that the US cultural scene and the global market itself continues to be an influential aspect of Brazilian cultural production.

In a meeting for Casa Samba members in 2009 in which Curtis was discussing unsatisfactory elements of practice ethic, Curtis told members of the group that, if they had issues with the way that things were being run, perhaps it was because they were trying to view the organization from an American perspective. Curtis reminded the group that he has ultimate authority and is the decision-maker of the group because of his experience. In this speech Curtis said, "I've transcended myself to be a Brazilian. I don't see things the American way anymore. Sometimes I speak English and words come out in Portuguese. I love that. It means that I have transcended." (Pierre Rehearsal Field Notes 2 June 2009)

---

[66] Four of the faculty members at the Brazil camp have strong ties to Casa Samba in New Orleans—Curtis Pierre, Jorge Alabe, Carlinhos do Pandeiro, and Marcio Peeter.

Curtis' "transcendence" is associated with his position as the leader of the organization. Not only is he the leader in the sense that he is the founder of the organization, but he is also the "chosen" authority by having gone through this experience of "transcendence," which is talked about almost as if it were a spiritual rite of passage. Curtis's position as leader seems to rest on the fact that not just anyone can "transcend" to being a Brazilian, and in this rests his authority. Through the bodily practice of samba and his dedication to this experience, Curtis sees himself not as a person linked to where he was born, but to where he has chosen to be "reborn"; as his website and email alias tell us, he is now "the real samba man" through embodied experience rather than through the place of his birth.

To "transcend" something is to go to a place beyond what is considered our everyday temporal and worldly reality. Indeed, to be a Brazilian performer seems almost like a spiritual experience for Curtis. He explains his transcendence as moving beyond the "self" that was given to him by nature in order to inhabit another sense of being, independent of geographical boundaries. He has become someone else, someone who self-identifies (and should be identified by others) in different ways than the person that he was before beginning his journey into Brazilian performance culture.[67] The history of Casa Samba, most importantly Curtis Pierre's work and dedication to Brazilian performance, has provided a context in which Brazilian immigrants can visibly see aspects of Brazilian identity being celebrated on the New Orleanian stage by New Orleanians who have devoted their lives and careers to embodying Brazil, providing a space for Brazilian culture to be performed alongside the local Mardi Gras cultures of New Orleans.

Casa Samba performs around New Orleans at conventions, Mardi Gras balls, private events like weddings and birthday parties, cultural shows, and street festivals. Interestingly, New Orleans is as central as Brazil to Casa Samba's identity. In shows for the New Orleanian tour-

[67] The word "transcendence" also invokes religious connotations. In rehearsals, Curtis has mentioned that Casa Samba is his "church." This statement is philosophical in the sense that his morality, personal beliefs, and connection to the sacred have happened through drumming. But is also literal in the sense that Casa Samba has been the entry point to Curtis's religious life. When Jorge arrived in New Orleans in 1991, all aspects of Curtis's life began to revolve around the performance of Brazilian culture. Jorge Alabe initiated Curtis and his wife Carol into the Afro-Brazilian religion of *candomblé*. (Before this they had been followers of Cuban *palo*.) So Casa Samba has also provided Curtis with his spiritual foundation.

ist culture, Casa Samba is often contracted as a flashy interlude to the main event, performing samba parades to get audience members from one ballroom hall to the next. This is especially true for shows contracted at venues such as the Convention Center. These performances are often short, no more than 30 minutes, and usually involve a samba parade around a busy convention hall. Casa Samba has performed at Convention Center events as diverse as a neurologists' convention, a computer science convention, a swingers' convention, a sports management convention, and several Mardi Gras balls. The Convention Hall format calls for an abbreviated performance that can satisfy visitors who will quickly move on to experience another spectacle.

Brazilians in Casa Samba

When Brazilians began to move to New Orleans after Hurricane Katrina, Casa Samba rehearsals became a space where Brazilians could find local New Orleanians who were interested in Brazilian culture. A few Brazilians became integrated into the Casa Samba performance group, playing music, providing a vocal section to the band, and participating as dancers. The majority of Brazilians who moved to New Orleans, however, did not find a sense of community in Casa Samba because they were from areas of Brazil where samba culture was not a point of solidarity. The small numbers of Brazilian immigrants involved with Casa Samba on a regular basis has to do with the fact that the majority of Brazilians in New Orleans are not familiar with the culture of samba schools, much less with the particularities of Casa Samba because they do not come from areas of Brazil where a samba school tradition is strong. Rarely do you hear samba music played in the homes of immigrant Brazilians in New Orleans, for example. And almost never would you hear *samba enredo*, a type of samba reserved exclusively for carnival season, most notably in Rio de Janeiro. Also, since immigrants' main goal in New Orleans is to work, spending time on a regular basis with a samba school is not a priority, though they do sometimes frequent the performances on weekends.

However, when describing Brazil to Americans, Brazilians personally identify with a hegemonic national construction of Brazilian identity because it has a more privileged (and cosmopolitan) position in the minds of Americans. Allying oneself with this image is a way of strategically presenting and performing one's own identity to meet a locally determined representation of Brazil that is favorably viewed in New Orleans. Casa Samba becomes a vehicle for immigrants to connect to an understanding of the Brazilian nation that gives Brazilians cultural clout in the New Orleanian social scene.

Brazilians in New Orleans have frequently commented that carnival in Brazil is so much more exciting than Mardi Gras in New Orleans because of the dancing *mulatas*, the music in the streets twenty four hours a day, and the participatory nature of Brazilian carnival. They are playing into global images of Brazil with these commentaries since most of them hail from regions where carnival is not celebrated with dancing *mulatas*, if it is celebrated at all. Thus, they are auto-essentializing their own portrayal of Brazil when speaking with Americans. They critique the Mardi Gras floats in the parades and what they consider to be unanimated riders and compare them to the exuberant carnival processions from Rio and Salvador. Yet few of the immigrants have actually seen, much less participated, in these major carnivals in Brazil themselves. In their hometowns, they were much more likely to be dancing to *tecnobrega* or to *sertanejo* than to samba. But the positive images associated with the carnivals of Rio and Salvador give Brazilians immigrants a privileged position in the realm of culture on a global stage; thus, Brazilian immigrants often choose to emphasize these images when talking about Brazil to an international audience.

These same national images that are glorified by immigrants themselves are also the images that Brazilians in New Orleans invoke in their critiques of Casa Samba shows performed by persons who are, in their majority, New Orleanians and not Brazilians. This contradiction about the representation of Brazil by non-Brazilians is evident in the interview with Director Curtis Pierre, who found that allying himself and his group with actual Brazilian performers has been a way of providing legitimacy to his organization; he admits feeling that there is extra scrutiny of his musical and performance abilities because he himself is American. Even so, those Brazilians who learned of Casa Samba's existence were impressed by the fact that any representation of Brazil would be performed prominently on the tourist circuit of New Orleans. Casa Samba's performances of Brazilian culture became a means by which Brazilians who arrived post-Katrina viewed their acceptance already woven into the social fabric of the city.

Brazilian members who do frequent Casa Samba take on a position of leadership in the group. Curtis Pierre uses the presence of these Brazilians to legitimize his position as an American director of a Brazilian samba school. When asked in 2006 about how the Brazilian community has affected and been affected by Casa Samba, Curtis replied that, "Having a large Brazilian contingent in the community is something that [he has] always wanted to happen" (Gibson 2008, 117). Curtis calls on the head singer of the *pagode* band, an Afro Bahian from Salvador who arrived to work in post-Katrina reconstruction, to provide a Brazilian perspective on the way that Casa Samba practices are run "the way it is done in Brazil." Brazilians (and I would add Afro-Brazilians in particular) are given a position of prestige in the group because of their cultural heritage and this is self-affirming for those few Brazilian immigrants who have become involved with the group. Casa Samba has, thus, benefited from the legitimizing presence of native Brazilian performers at the same time that it has created a space for legitimacy and acceptance for Brazilian immigrants in New Orleans by providing festive and exuberant representations of Brazil within the New Orleanian tourist circles.

These immigrants that have arrived in New Orleans post-Katrina have also expanded Casa Samba's repertoire. There is now a vocal section to accompany the drumming performances and a *pagode* band (a subgenre of samba played mostly with hand drums) led by a post-Katrina migrant, which is marketed more specifically to the Brazilian audience and that plays at a wide array of local venues. *Pagode* band Som Brasil was developed specifically with the Brazilian community in mind. In most cases, when Som Brasil plays, the performers direct the show toward a Brazilian audience, giving announcements from stage solely in Portuguese.

Stage decisions such as language use represent how decisions about the Casa Samba repertoire have consciously taken into account the Brazilian immigrant community that arrived in New Orleans after Hurricane Katrina. As Casa Samba gains native Brazilian performers, and as their audiences include more Brazilian people, there are new decisions to be made about group marketing. Casa Samba is now in a position to appeal to tourists, New Orleanian locals, and Brazilian locals. There are often different expectations to negotiate depending on the context of the gig. The type of show that an American tourist is usually interested in, a flashy floorshow spectacle, does not have the same interest to a Brazilian who wants an interactive night out in a familiar Brazilian cultural setting where he himself can dance. When asked to describe the audience that *pagode/axé* band Som Brasil hopes to capture, the Bahian guitarist of the group said,

> The *pagode* repertoire seems to be trying to please the Brazilian audience. There is a preoccupation to choose famous songs that can entertain a Brazilian public. For example, Fundo do Quintal and Zeca Pagodinho are artists who are famous in Brazil. They are not famous here. For this reason, I conclude that the *pagode* band is more for a Brazilian audience. (Márcio 12 May 2009).

Som Brasil appeals to Brazilian audiences for several reasons. First, the music is dance music. *Pagode* and *axé* are not like the highly frenetic rhythm of *carnaval samba enredo* played in Brazil solely during the Rio de Janeiro carnaval parade. *Pagode* and *axé* are rhythms that are easier to dance to (and to fake the steps of for those who don't know how to dance). Second, the repertoire chosen for the group tends to be composed of popular songs that speak to the experiences of average people. The linguistic register of both *pagode* and *axé* are similar to the patterns of ordinary speech (Lima 2002, 5). The lyrics deal with concrete daily situations, with family and friends, and with relationship problems. These quotidian experiences expressed in *pagode* music are those that are being lived by the Brazilian immigrant community in New Orleans and these are the songs that they can more easily respond to and that answer their feelings of nostalgia for Brazil. Audience members interact with the band, singing along, clapping, and dancing. The arrival of Brazilian immigrants to New Orleans has, thus, meant that Casa Samba does not only perform Mardi Gras/Carnival music, but also has diversified to play a genre of music that is most popular among crowds of immigrant Brazilians.

Having an audience that could respond to Casa Samba's repertoire with both linguistic and bodily understanding was not a part of the Casa Samba show before Brazilian immigration to New Orleans in 2005. Brazilian immigration to New Orleans provided musicians who could sing in Portuguese and an audience who could respond to the lyrics. A Casa Samba *pagode* performance celebrates a particular representation of Brazilian national character that is tied to the working class and, thus, even more specifically approachable for immigrants.

Migrants interpret their own relationship with Brazil (and New Orleans) through that performance.

In an article on Brazilian immigration to New Orleans, I quoted a Brazilian member of Casa Samba who joined the group in 2006 post-Katrina who described Casa Samba as "nothing more than a piece of Brazil here in the United States" (Gibson 2008, 117). Gilberto enjoyed meeting and socializing with Americans who were interested in his culture. He felt a sense of home and community when he was with Casa Samba. When asked about the significance of the group to the newly-arriving Brazilian community he said,

> I think that the beginning of everything for the Brazilian community in New Orleans will be right here [Casa Samba]. As Brazilians start to discover this place, it is going to be the way in which Brazilian culture is shown to the rest of the New Orleanian community. The Brazilian and the New Orleanian musical culture have a lot in common, and this place is a place where everyone can communicate independently of language, color, or race. Here our culture is taken very seriously. (Gibson 2008, 117)

Despite Gilberto's optimism in this 2006 interview about the role of Casa Samba in the future of the Brazilian community in New Orleans, the reality in 2010 is that very few Brazilians seek out Casa Samba membership. For members of Casa Samba, dance and music classes are cost-free, yet there are currently only three Brazilian members in the samba school. Since Katrina motivated the migration of a large number of Brazilians to New Orleans to work in reconstruction, there have been only ten Brazilians who have come into Casa Samba and made an impact in the group either as musicians or as dancers, but, in most cases, their participation has been temporary. Some of these people have moved back to Brazil or have moved to other places in the United States where they could make more money participating in the Brazilian cultural scene or in construction work, whichever was most profitable. Some have remained in New Orleans, but the realities of their hectic work schedules makes attending practices too difficult.

Gilberto's interpretation of Casa Samba as a bastion of Brazilian culture is very positive, yet it should be taken in context. First, Gilberto is from Salvador, so he automatically feels more of a cultural affinity to the music and dance of Casa Samba than other immigrants in New

Orleans who would contend that *sertanejo* or *forró* are more representative of their own Brazil. Casa Samba has an especially strong connection with the Bahian *bloco afro*, Ilê Aiyê, because Curtis has brought choreographers and master drummers to teach workshops and even to live for extended periods of time with the group. Gilberto is familiar with the rhythms, songs, and the steps of his Bahian home, which also explains how he would describe Casa Samba as a "little piece of Brazil." The group is, in fact, performing *his* Brazil. The friends that Gilberto has brought to Casa Samba, in their majority, have also been Bahian. Thus, the majority of his friends view Casa Samba in a similar manner. When Gilberto has brought friends from Minas Gerais to Casa Samba, few of the visitors from Minas return regularly, nor do they seem particularly "at home" at Casa Samba rehearsals. In fact, their body language, the fact that they usually sit hidden in a corner and prefer not to participate in dancing or drumming, points to the fact that, while they may be interested, and even flattered, at the time and energy that Americans are willing to devote to performing Brazilian culture, they do not feel necessarily "at home" as direct participants in the making and performing of that particular audiotopic representation of Brazilian culture. It is not *their* Brazilian culture.

One Brazilian woman from Minas living in New Orleans who does like to dance samba commented to me that, though she likes to dance, she is deterred from getting involved with Casa Samba because she dislikes the representation of Brazilian women portrayed through *passistas* in Rio samba schools. *Passistas* is the Portuguese word for samba dancers, from the verb "passear" (to stroll), referring to the act of strolling through the sambadrome in Rio. Monica Rector defines *passistas* as,

> The dancers who "speak with their feet" They have the liberty to dance the samba and cut figures as they wish, with no prearranged choreography. The dance is characterized by the feet that move, the body that swings from one side to the other in perfect coordination. (53)

The Brazilian immigrant who criticized Casa Samba *passista* dancers did not criticize Casa Samba as falsely representing Brazilian samba culture, but she was not interested in being involved with this particular performance herself. While she interprets Casa Samba as a positive representation of Brazil in the sense that the shows draw a crowd of Brazil enthusiasts, are performed by Americans willing to devote their lives to representing Brazilian culture, and represent Brazil as culturally exciting, the shows also, for better or worse, she felt, represent Brazilian culture through the essentializing figure of the *carioca mulata* with which she herself did not self identify.

So how do Brazilian immigrants in New Orleans, the majority who are not members of Casa Samba, interpret its embodiment of a Brazilian national identity by a performance group that is composed in its majority by New Orleanian performers? Brazil and, thus, Brazilians, are celebrated as energetic, happy, sensual, and exuberant people through Casa Samba shows, drawing comparisons within the New Orleanian tourism market between Brazilians and New Orleanians themselves. Brazilians may reap the benefits or suffer the consequences as they see fit.

Different perspectives on what a Casa Samba show represents inevitably coexist and are dependent on where a person is from and what their relationship before coming to New Orleans has been to samba as an art form. As we have seen, many of the Brazilian immigrants who come to a Casa Samba show are just as much "outsiders" to the world of samba as the Americans present since they come from regions of Brazil where samba is not part of their daily life. They do have an advantage over Americans in interpreting the event because they can comprehend the Portuguese lyrics of the songs, but, beyond that, they are themselves viewing a spectacle that is usually foreign to them. Even so, the majority of my interviews show that Brazilians feel proud that the image of Brazil is regarded as desirable in New Orleans.

It is worth noting that an exoticized image of Brazil and Brazilians can be destructive if a cultural representation of the *carioca* samba school becomes seen as the normative, daily expression of being a Brazilian. (Though this argument could be made for almost any touristic display of heritage.) The majority of Brazilians living in New Orleans are hard-working immigrant laborers employed in the construction and housecleaning industries. Showing cultural excess as "naturally" Brazilian seems to imply that Brazilians don't have to work to achieve their skills. If Brazilians are seen only through this exoticized lens of being naturally "cool, laid-back, sexy," then these stereotypes seem to be in opposition to Brazilians as "hard workers," the image that is most favorable for Brazilian workers in New Orleans. Yet, historically, samba music and dancing are linked to a working-class culture where the trials and tribulations of the everyday are central samba themes. Samba performances are moments removed from everyday reality. "Hard workers" and "samba dancers" should not be seen in opposition. After all, Gari Renato Sorriso, a hard-working garbage collector for Rio de Janeiro, has achieved a mythical local status through dancing samba each year through the Sambadrome. He is even featured in the promotional video for Brazil as the host of the 2014 World Cup, thus becoming a celebrity of the Rio culture world.

The Casa Samba performance legitimizes certain forms of Brazilian expressive culture and appropriates them for the New Orleanian cultural scene through Mardi Gras parades, conventions, and music festivals where Casa Samba is hired to represent the local festive culture. Brazilians themselves, however, find Casa Samba to be a reimagining of their present social world as Brazilians living outside of the US rather than a representation of the Brazil that they left behind upon immigrating. Even if they critique certain representations of Brazil as essentializing, these Brazilian cultural products have been labeled as "cool," "rootsy," and "fun" on the global market and, in the context of New Orleans, are perceived as having similarities to New Orleanian culture itself--so much similarity, in fact, that Casa Samba is contracted to perform at venues for tourists where the group is a representative of New Orleanian Mardi Gras expression and *not* Brazilian Carnival. On the local stage where these images are performed, Brazilian immigrants receive social clout by being allied to a cultural representation seen as conversant with New Orleanian performance culture. Through this audiotopia, immigrants are put into contact with a culturally complex representation of Brazil that was foreign to them before living abroad, but that speaks to their social world as Brazilians outside of their home country.

When I asked, in my interviews with Brazilian immigrants in post-Katrina New Orleans, in what ways they thought New Orleanians were like Brazilians, Casa Samba was often referred to as being an example of the cultural parallel between the two places. That is, "New Orleans was like Brazil because both places like samba." (Chicão 29 December 2008) The fact that New Orleanians were the bearers of the samba culture in the city made Brazilians feel a sense of communion with people in New Orleans. This fact was independent of whether or not Brazilian immigrants were participating directly in Casa Samba or whether they personally liked samba. Brazilians see New Orleanians dedicating time and energy to recreating a Brazilian cultural experience, and for immigrants who are physically far from home-- yet emotionally and psychologically deeply connected to it-- Casa Samba performances offer a space for them to live out their longings for home viscerally even though their Brazilian identity is reinterpreted in new ways in New Orleans.

As Brazilians watch New Orleanians connect to, consume, and perform Brazilian national identity through samba within local social and tourist spaces, Brazilian migrants come to see New Orleans as an accepting city for Brazilian culture and to reimagine a new relationship to their Brazilian identity that is not inevitably comforting and affirming but that is, nonetheless, meaningful to how they reconceptualize their experience as Brazilians living abroad. The audiotopic space of Casa Samba may not provide a physical home for all Brazilians, but it provides room to enter imaginatively into their new social space as immigrants, engaging the contradictions and complexities of living in the performative city of New Orleans.

Brazilian Immigrant Engagement with Mardi Gras

Brazilian culture is, thus, imagined as desirable in the New Orleans context because of its malleability to fit within constructs of New Orleans performative culture, most specifically, into its carnivalesque culture. Whether Brazilians themselves become involved in these representations or not, performances of their national identity are given cultural clout. Besides Casa Samba performances, however, Brazilian immigrants themselves have created their own performative representations of Brazilian culture within the Mardi Gras setting that express their diverging understandings of Carnival celebrations in both Brazil and New Orleans.

Brazilian sociologist Fred Goés, a Rockefeller Scholar at Tulane University in 2003-2004 who was researching carnival traditions in New Orleans, wrote that his research revealed to him a universal carnival citizenship. Carnival "no matter where, allows us to experiment with other forms of more universal citizenship, where excess, anarchy and orgy rule, always under the scepter of Momo or Rex" (Goés 146).

This notion of carnival citizenship is similar to the sentiment that Brazilian immigrants express when describing their connection to Mardi Gras in New Orleans.

Not only is Brazilian culture performed formally with Casa Samba during Mardi Gras in New Orleans, but Brazilian immigrants themselves have begun to celebrate Mardi Gras incorporating their past lived experiences of *carnaval* in Brazil. The experience of carnival in New Orleans is seen as asserting a New Orleanian ethos that situates the city and its people apart from the rest of the US. While Mardi Gras is obviously different from the celebrations of *carnaval* in Brazil, the experience, nevertheless, serves as a ritual of integration for Brazilians with their New Orleanian world. Participating makes them feel a part of the city. The fact that they can understand the revelry of carnival through the context of Brazilian *carnaval* (in all the diverse ways of celebrating it as well as critiquing it) allows them to feel culturally adept in New Orleans.

De Certeau states that "to walk is to lack a place" (103). Yet to walk is also to gain an experience of a cityscape, mapping the emphasis and contradictions between one's imagined sense of place and the space that one is walking through. This is the experience that Brazilians undergo when making cultural comparisons with New Orleans as migrants who theoretically always feel a sense of "lacking a place." Brazilians become part of the cityscape during Mardi Gras time by "walking through it." The city is not their own space, yet they read meaning onto the cityscape anyway. Mardi Gras is a walking performance spectacle, which falls outside of the time-space continuum of everyday life yet intensifies the experience of "walking." Walking through the Mardi Gras spectacle, thus, becomes an action of "making a place." As people take over the streets, preconditioned to act, mask, gesture, revel, and walk in certain ways, Brazilians compare and contrast this with their Brazilian experiences in order to plant themselves in their local place.

A Brazilian interviewee commented (about things that he missed after leaving New Orleans) that he had spent four sleepless days and nights on Bourbon Street during Mardi Gras 2006, and that, in those four days, he had spent $1,500! His favorite part of the whole carnival experience, he said, was when women would lift up their shirts for beads. Needless to say, he describes a characteristic tourist, not local, experience of New Orleans. In 2005 and 2006 when Brazilians reported making significant earnings in construction, some reported spending up to five nights a week on the tourist mecca of Bourbon Street. In interviews with return post-Katrina migrants, Bourbon Street was often mentioned as one of the places that Brazilians who had left New Orleans missed the most. Now that reconstruction work has slowed and Brazilian immigrants report that they have less money to spend, those still living in New Orleans say that they go out to Bourbon Street much less often. Its novelty has also run out. But even so, Bourbon Street remains the most visited public nightspot where Brazilian immigrants actively mix with Americans.

Brazilians tend to prefer Bourbon Street to Frenchmen Street, which is considered to be a more local hangout for nightlife. Frenchmen Street is walking distance from Bourbon Street. It is a three-block section of bars and clubs that play live local music seven days a week. In general, Frenchmen Street is more relaxed and casual; it lacks the anonymity and the anything-goes, year-round carnivalesque atmosphere of Bourbon Street. People who frequent Frenchmen usually come with a group of friends with the specific purpose of listening to music or dancing. It is less "wild" and thus, according to Brazilians, harder for them to feel as if they "fit in" on a regular night-- and harder for them to "hook up" with women. During festivals and Mardi Gras, however, Frenchmen Street is a prime destination for Brazilians because the atmosphere changes with the large influx of tourists to the city. On Bourbon Street, year round, the nightlife is set up for partiers to experience local culture from the outside and feel welcomed. It is the ultimate "outsider-insider" experience. Although local New Orleanians may argue that Bourbon Street is a crude representation of New Orleans' culture, it is a place that creates ample opportunities for contact with Americans, has rules about socializing and alcohol consumption that are more similar to Brazil than the rest of the United States, and highlights Louisiana musical culture and performance in an easily accessible way.[68]

During the 2009 Mardi Gras season, Vesgo and Bola (Rodrigo Scarpa and Mauros Chiesa), hosts of Brazil's comedy show TV Pânico, came to New Orleans to record a special segment on Mardi Gras in New Orleans. They made fun of the subdued atmosphere along the parade routes, the lack of excitement among Americans watching the marching bands, and the tradition of throwing beaded necklaces. Where was the craziness they were used to seeing during *carnaval* in Brazil? (TV Pânico 1 March 2009) During the second segment of the show, however, they went to Bourbon Street, where they apparently and ironically did discover the *real* Mardi Gras according to their standards.

While Vesgo and Bola's show is satirical and exaggerates how a Brazilian might critique the Mardi Gras experience, there are elements of it that seem to speak true from the perspective of Brazilians

---

[68] Brazilian musicians, however, who have come to New Orleans have had a hard time making money on Bourbon Street because of the centrality of New Orleanian music styles in this space. New Orleans centers itself around the French Quarter as the enshrined homage to the romantic Creole past. Brazilian music does not necessarily fit into this context unless it can become blendable with Louisiana beats to become part of the illusion of the image of New Orleans—a cultural and timeless anomaly that allows tourists a sense of freedom and independence not allowed in other parts of the country.

Ale, a Brazilian bassist (and construction worker) who spent two years living in New Orleans from 2007-2009 said (and many New Orleanian musicians would agree), "Working as a musician in New Orleans is like dying of hunger." (Ale 20 March 2009) According to Ale, New Orleans is the best city in the US for a musician to come to learn about music, but is a hard place to start your own band. (He had the chance to play with various different soul and R&B groups in New Orleans and Mississippi while living in New Orleans.) Through the connections that he made playing New Orleanian music with other groups, he had hoped to be able to begin a Brazilian night on Bourbon Street with some of his old band members from Atlanta.

However, his group, Ale & Cia, soon learned that musicians in New Orleans were paid very little in comparison to what they earned playing in Atlanta. During a two-hour set on Bourbon Street they usually made between $70-150 a person. In Las Vegas, he now makes $500 for the same show. Ale preferred living in New Orleans for the music culture there, but Las Vegas has been a better place for him to make a career out of music.

The difficulties Ale faced largely resided in the fact that he was trying to break into the Bourbon Street industry, an industry that feeds on the New Orleanian touristic culture of putting Louisiana heritage on display.

living in New Orleans. Brazilians enjoy carnival time in New Orleans not only because it reminds them of Brazil, but because it also reinforces the unique character of New Orleans in relation to other cities in the US. They do not interpret Mardi Gras as identical to *carnaval* in Brazil. In fact they often concentrate on its differences, but they are able to recreate a hybrid Brazil-New Orleans carnival experience by drawing such comparisons. Brazilians who have truly embraced the Mardi Gras tradition have figured out ways to work within the Mardi Gras environment to make a Brazil-New Orleans experience. They ironically use the very anonymity of carnival time to feel more intimately a part of the local culture.

The following excerpts are Brazilian immigrant descriptions of Mardi Gras:

> *Carnaval* in New Orleans is a 10 (on a scale of 1-10). Very fun. There aren't many differences between *carnaval* in New Orleans and *carnaval* in Brazil. The way that people have fun there is great. I spent three straight days on Bourbon Street. We danced until the sun came up. (Frank 3 January 2009)

> The *carnaval* in New Orleans is like the carnival in Brazil—Really good. I wouldn't miss carnival for anything. We were always there. I participated every day, especially during the period when work was slow. During Carnival time in New Orleans, work stops, only after carnival. So I was there every day. I spent the days on the streets and then went to Bourbon at night. It was awesome! (Vazinho 29 December 2008)

> Here [in New Orleans] Carnival is like the old Carnival (in Brazil) with the French march of the 16th century. The floats that pass by seem funny to me because they seem so old-fashioned. The difference in Brazil is that now you see *trio-elétricos* that are as big as this building! In both places, Carnival is the party of the flesh, but people manifest this in different ways. (Ale 20 March 2009)

Brazilians Organize their Own Space within Mardi Gras

Brazilians participate in Mardi Gras in a variety of ways. For example, some choose to view only neighborhood Mardi Gras celebrations in their own neighborhoods in suburban Metairie; others choose to spend the weekend on Bourbon Street with the thousands of tourist revelers who flock to the city each year. But, most interesting to me, a substantial group of Brazilians have also begun, since 2007, to organize their own Brazilian "bloco-krewe" that meets along the Mardi Gras Parade route in the Garden District of New Orleans, at the heart of the local Mardi Gras celebration, and to commemorate carnival time in a hybrid Brazil-New Orleans fashion. Brazilians have become familiar enough with New Orleans to reinvent and record their experience as Brazilians within the local tradition of Mardi Gras.

Each year the organization of the Brazilian version of Mardi Gras has become more elaborate as their knowledge of local traditions has grown. In 2006, in the first year after the storm, the African American-run Brazilian performance group, Casa Samba, held a small Brazilian event in the house of Directors Curtis and Carol Pierre. The Brazilian contingent of the party was organized by a pre-Katrina Brazilian resident who had worked in event planning in Brazil before immigrating to the US. This event was significant because Brazilians and New Orleanians worked together to celebrate Brazilian culture within the context of Mardi Gras.

The organizers made shirts for the event to give the party the feel of a Brazilian *bloco*-style party. *Blocos de rua* in Brazil are often put together by a group of friends who decide on a color, a name, often even a banner, and plan a parade route for the group. Members will hit the streets dancing, singing, and merry-making. Casa Samba's *bloco,* which has continued into the present, creates a parade that joins the Zulu (an African American krewe) parade route at St. Charles Avenue near Terpsichore. Back at the Casa Samba house after the parade, there is free food available for those who bought *bloco* t-shirts. And the Som Brasil *pagode* band, a band formed as a break-off of Casa Samba after Brazilian musicians moved down to work post-Katrina reconstruction, performs Brazilian *carnaval* music.

However, as Brazilian immigrants became more comfortable with Mardi Gras traditions, some wanted to be able to celebrate Mardi Gras along with the local New Orleanian community. The Casa Samba house can only hold a limited number of people, and this party is not open to the general public. Although the Casa Samba parties at Mardi

Gras have continued, another sector of young Brazilians have begun a new Brazilian *bloco*. The organization of this bloco, Bloco Mardi Folia, was spontaneously organized by Brazilians in the community who came to New Orleans as construction workers. They have begun to organize their community around the festive culture of New Orleans that they feel holds affinities with Brazil.

Douglas, the main organizer of the new Brazilian *bloco,* has lived in New Orleans since 2005. He moved to New Orleans with his uncle when he was 18 years old, less than a month after Hurricane Katrina devastated the city. As he became familiar with Mardi Gras, he wanted to be able to have a Brazilian-style carnival that fit within the context of New Orleans. So, in 2009, he and his friends began to make t-shirts for his Mardi Gras group "*Bloco* Mardi Folia," and they sold them within the Brazilian community in the months leading up to carnival. Douglas went to a mechanic's garage run by a Brazilian friend and spent the three days before carnival installing a powerful speaker system into the back of his car. He worked at his construction job during the day and spent nights until 2-3 a.m. preparing his car for Mardi Gras day.

Lundi Gras night, he and his friends staked out a prominent place on the parade route and pulled a trailer into a parking spot along St. Charles Avenue. They arrived in the middle of the night to ensure that they would find a parking place immediately adjacent to the parade route. Mid-day on Mardi Gras Tuesday, all the people who had purchased shirts converged at the trailer on St. Charles Avenue. They rolled the speaker-loaded car onto the trailer and began their own Brazilian *bloco* party right on the Mardi Gras route. As they waited for the Mardi Gras parade to approach, the Brazilian crowd opened the car doors and blared their Brazilian and American music. They, thus, created their own carnival party that they shared with all who were with them on the parade route, Brazilians and New Orleanians alike.

The Brazilians even sold their remaining t-shirts to anyone along the route who wanted to buy them and cooked out of the back of their trucks on small grills. However, instead of hamburgers and hot dogs, the Brazilians grilled steaks in the customary Brazilian fashion, making friends with their neighbors by offering a cut of meat. Once the parade started to roll by, they enjoyed the New Orleanian custom of grabbing beads. Part of the fun of the event was also being able to celebrate carnival in the New Orleanian fashion.

The Brazilian *bloco* style carnival party is ideal for the parade route because it is essentially a block party, and Brazilians revealed their familiarity with the different community blocks in New Orleans in the placement of their *bloco*. For the last two years, the *bloco* has been held near Saint Charles and Amelia Streets, one block past the restaurant Superior Grill. This section of the parade route is Uptown, New Orleans, the local neighborhood of the Brazilian organizers, and also an area where many young people, especially students, gather to enjoy Mardi Gras. Superior Grill, two blocks away, has speakers set up with music playing and the crowd tends to be more rambunctious than on other sections of the Uptown parade route. Deciding on the location to set up the speakers was not random. Brazilians had participated in Carnival since 2005 and had become familiar with the different spectator cultures along the parade route.

Brazilians are unconsciously interpreting New Orleans through a Brazilian lens and creating a hybrid New Orleans-Brazil Mardi Gras tradition by making an effort to intermingle socially with Americans on the Mardi Gras route. Indeed, Brazilians and Americans interact through the festivities of the Mardi Gras *bloco* to a heightened degree. There is obviously a certain amount of cultural assimilation and integration occurring in such a scenario since Brazilians are participating in a New Orleanian social event, but they also bring their own Brazilian understandings of *carnaval* with them.

Brazilians choose locations for their *bloco* party where they know their Brazilian-New Orleanian celebration will be best accepted. They are, thus, more free to celebrate carnival their own way. The Brazilian Mardi Gras *bloco* is a performance of identity through which Brazilians communicate collective solidarity to a diverse set of Mardi Gras observers. Through participation in Mardi Gras in their own Brazilian style, Brazilians are able to remember their homeland and perform local belonging simultaneously through the time and space allotted to the Mardi Gras tradition.

After the parade ends on Saint Charles Avenue, the Brazilian *bloco* enacts an even more-heightened performance demonstrating their comprehension of the New Orleans Mardi Gras landscape. They next relocate their loaded car and all the Brazilian partiers in the *bloco* to Frenchmen Street, another area in New Orleans famous for its street party atmosphere during Mardi Gras. Unlike Bourbon, which is blocked to cars, Frenchmen Street is a place where Brazilians can park their speaker-loaded car in the middle of the street where the Mardi Gras celebration will actually take place. Again, this is a decision that only those familiar with local New Orleans culture could make, because Frenchmen Street is considered much more of a local hangout than a main tourist attraction.

As Brazilians continue their Mardi Gras celebrations on Frenchmen Street, a neighborhood with a carnival tradition alternative to the major krewes, the Brazilians again become part of the Mardi Gras attraction for onlookers just as they were for the people on Saint Charles Avenue. People cruising the street take their pictures and ask the Brazilians what New Orleanian krewe they belong to, revealing that the Brazilians are interpreted by onlookers as an organized part of the Mardi Gras celebration. The immigrants respond by simply saying that they are Brazilian, yet feeling accepted as such within the Mardi Gras world of New Orleans. After Mardi Gras 2010, one of my former students from a Tulane class on Brazilian immigration came up to me and said, "I know that we read that Brazilians are an invisible minority in the US, but they sure weren't on the parade route." She had been at the big Mardi Gras party at Superior Grill but said that the party improvised by the Brazilians drew more attention, had louder

Brazilian Mardi Gras Celebration on Frenchmen St, New Orleans 2010

music, involved people jumping and dancing on top of their car (all wearing yellow t-shirts), and upstaged the passing Rex parade. The New Orleanian performance context has not only allowed Brazilians, most of whom are undocumented, to feel accepted and visible—but has even given them center stage within their carnival *bloco* space.

Mardi Gras in New Orleans has become so popular among Brazilians that there are now Brazilian immigrants who come down from other cities to visit their friends living in New Orleans during Mardi Gras. Some of the visitors are Brazilians who have lived in New Orleans and moved back to other areas of the country, and some are Brazilians who have never been to New Orleans before but who have heard about New Orleans' carnival from friends. Because construction work is often slower during the winter in the Northeast, Brazilians in Boston are sometimes able to take off a week to go visit friends in New Orleans. There have been Brazilians who come down for Mardi Gras and end up staying in New Orleans because they were able to secure a job through a friend.

The way that Brazilians are interacting to create a Brazilian space within the New Orleanian Mardi Gras is a particularly significant and visible example of Brazilian acculturation into the city through performance. I have not observed a similar example of such identity-making among any other immigrant group in New Orleans. While other immigrant communities do attend carnival celebrations, no other group has set up hybridized carnival traditions within the New Orleans Mardi Gras setting. Brazilians have shown an informed understanding of how carnival traditions work in New Orleans—knowing where to position their car, when to turn the music down, where to move their car to continue the party once the parade passes by. And they have figured out how their own cultural traditions of carnival can best fit within the New Orleanian cultural space. By performing "*Bloco* Mardi Folia," Brazilians are performing their own relationship to the city of New Orleans.

The emergence of hybrid Brazil-New Orleans performances represents a new sense of identity for Brazilian immigrants that grounds them in their New Orleanian space. These performances remind observers that Brazilian immigrants cannot be excluded from the understanding of the New Orleans social culture today. New dialogues are created for conceptualizing belonging, closing gaps between the distant locales of a Brazilian migrant's understanding of home and allowing Brazilians to feel visible while remaining the invisible immigrant community that rebuilt New Orleans.

Afterword

This book began with an epigraph of the song "Iracema Voou" by the Brazilian singer Chico Buarque. In 1998, Chico Buarque released the song "Iracema Voou" (Iracema Flew Away) on his disk "As cidades." The song invokes the Brazilian novel *Iracema,* by Jose de Alencar (1865). Set in Ceará, Alencar's novel is the story of a beautiful indigenous woman, Iracema, whose physical splendor is metaphorically compared with the magnificence of the landscape of Brazil itself. But, unscrambling the letters of her name, the reader sees that Iracema is an anagram for "America." In the plot of the novel, Iracema's union with Portuguese explorer Martim results in the birth of Moacir, in an allegorical encounter of two civilizations during colonization— indigenous and European— leading to the birth of a new Brazilian nation. The exaltation of indigenous culture, known as *indianismo,* has been part of Brazilian nationalist discourse since the nineteenth century and Iracema has become part of popular imagination as a foundational Brazilian figure.

I would like to return to Chico Buarque's musical reenvisioning of Iracema as a way of concluding this study of the experience of Brazilian immigration to New Orleans. In Buarque's version, instead of Iracema being the Indian heroine who is passively encountered by the Portuguese explorer, she is the agent in a new Brazilian encounter experience caused by Iracema's immigration to North America. This song provides various clues to reveal that this new Iracema is living in North America illegally, as her daily activities seem to fall in line with those of Brazilian immigrants who have come to the U.S. undocumented in search of a better future: "She does not speak English/ She washes the floors in a tea house/ She doesn't fret the police." Whereas in Alencar's novel Iracema misses Ceará when she leaves the *sertão* (dry backlands) to follow Martim to the coast, the Iracema of Chico Buarque, instead, follows the dream of earning money in North America. As the lyrics explain, she feels longing for her home of Ceará while she is abroad, but not enough to return to Brazil, at least, not yet.

Buarque's "Iracema of América" represents the invention of the Brazilian community as increasingly transnational. Iracema's attitude towards her experience of migration in Buarque's song lyrics resounded throughout my own interviews with Brazilian immigrants living in New Orleans. Taking the initiative to migrate is a liberating experience, though difficult, and the immigrant experience is not often what immigrants had expected before migrating. Without English, they often feel themselves "talking with mimes" as Iracema does when trying to communicate with those around her. Like Iracema, immigrants make phone calls home to friends and family when the longing for home is strong. However, if asked to do it all over again, most of them would. The feeling of longing for home is always present, but so is the spirit of adventure and freedom that comes with earning a living in North America. Living with the realities of having to move or the fantasies of wanting to move, Iracema is yearning to be somewhere else at the same time that she chooses to stay rooted in her new place. Brazilian immigrants to the U.S. seek migration in order to be able to invest back home, ironically coming to feel more Brazilian along the way.

This is the transnational dilemma of the Brazilian migrant who is the new Iracema of America. The narratives I have told in this book reveal the stories of those Iracemas who have reconstructed who they are in the context of post-Katrina New Orleans at the same time that they have built homes in Brazil and rebuilt a city in the U.S. A Brazilian immigrant who I interviewed in New Orleans, and then again in Brazil when he returned home after four years working construction in New Orleans, has a tattoo on his arm with an American and a Brazilian flag side by side; the name of his mother is tattooed above the Brazilian flag and his father's name is tattooed above the American flag. This tattoo is a visual reminder of a lived tension between a longing for home (represented by the mother figure) and a desire to earn a living in the U.S. (represented by the providing father) described in almost all of my interviews with Brazilian immigrants in New Orleans.

According to Rosivan, he decided to get this tattoo because there are now two countries that define him: Brazil and the U.S. The fact that he returned to Brazil is a direct result of his love for his aging parents and testimony to the fact that migration decisions are often made by and for the family unit. The number of ways in which both New Orleans and Brazil have been inscribed on the bodies of migrants is very telling of the intensity of the experience of living between two worlds.

Just as Buarque's Iracema flew to América, Rosivan and many more before and after him, flew as well. And this flight complicated definitions of home, of belonging, and even of Brazilian identity. There are now two places and a diverse group of people that come to represent home for Rosivan. The tattoo, drawn on his skin at a tattoo parlor on Bourbon Street months before returning to Brazil, is a representation of the new "Rosivan of América" described in the voices of this book.

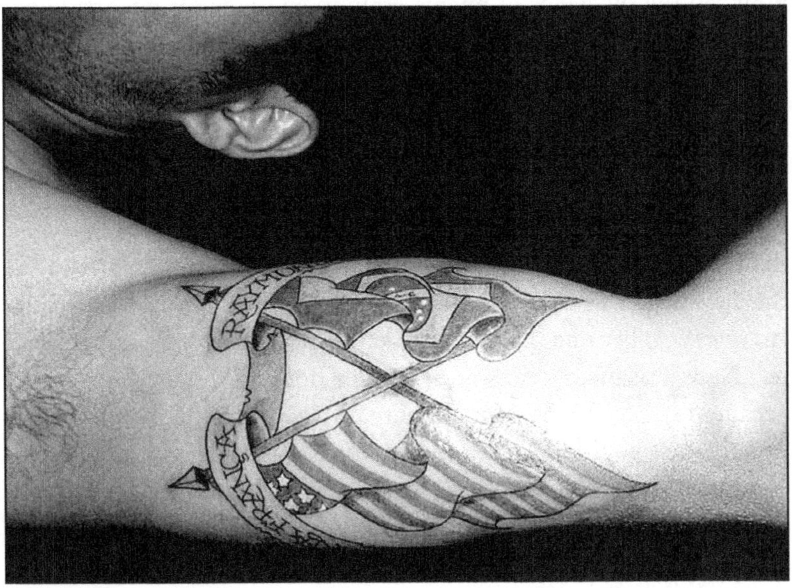

Figure 19: Rosivan of América

The act of migration is an act of self-invention. As New Orleans rises again from the Katrina disaster, Brazilians respond to this new New Orleans by learning their place within a fluid system of social, cultural, and economic interactions, reinventing themselves within this new context. Brazilians in New Orleans have imagined their sense of place in relationship to New Orleans post-Katrina, to communities in

Brazil, and to other communities in the U.S. Enclaves are formed from mediating experiences through the customs of migrants' own home cultures, through the global images of their nation, and finally through the local context in which they find themselves.

There have been many "uniques" about the narratives you have read: Brazilians are an understudied minority in the U.S., Hurricane Katrina was a national disaster without precedent, and a large Brazilian immigration to New Orleans had never happened before. But I would also like to remind the reader that when I talk about the invention and imagination of migrant identity, the researcher herself has been one of those self-inventors.

This book project began as a dissertation. All graduate students can argue that their dissertations become their lives. This was literally true for me. I found myself at the right time in the right place, and my life provided the substance of my dissertation and now for my first book. In many ways, my own evolving history was the glue that holds the chapters together. Because of circumstance, I found myself in a unique position. I experienced Hurricane Katrina first-hand as a displaced person. And when I returned to New Orleans, not only did I witness the first Brazilians arrive, but I became inextricably linked to their arrival. My telephone number was passed around for people to call when they needed help finding a job, getting out of jail, or even translating at the morgue and sending loved ones home to Brazil in a casket. Brazilian *churrascos* became my social world for the months when there were few New Orleanian spaces open besides Bourbon Street. Immigrants became my best friends. One eventually even became my boyfriend, and then ex-boyfriend when he returned to Brazil. As a dancer, my picture was on the posters of the Casa Samba Brazilian Independence Day parties. And because I was able to travel back and forth from New Orleans to Brazil, I became a physical link for some Brazilian immigrants to imagine closeness between New Orleans and their homes and families left behind in Brazil. The chapters of this book and the invention of the Brazilian enclave identity in New Orleans are also my story— though the heroes of the story are the Brazilians who braved an unknown physical and social world to try their luck in a devastated city, thereby helping to re-make New Orleans.

When I returned to New Orleans to restart my graduate career at Tulane University six months after Hurricane Katrina and I noticed the new Brazilian community in the city, I remember feeling both excited by the new Brazilian presence and inquisitive about whether or not Brazilians would be a permanent addition to New Orleanian demographics. Five years later, as I convert the narratives of my dissertation into a book, my impulse is to say that the Brazilian community in New Orleans is here to stay, even if individual members of the community come and go. My reason for saying this is because the Brazilians in New Orleans have imagined a sense of place for themselves within a more normalized post-Katrina world. While the New Orleanian Brazilian community is still in a process of settlement and formation and has not reached its point of stability, early markers of a permanent enclave seem to exist.[69]

Even as recovery work slows and the Brazilian community in New Orleans is shrinking due to the fact that there are not as many construction jobs, the community is far from disappearing. Perhaps it is not at the same size that it once was in the first year after Katrina, but it is at a size that is more realistic for the new New Orleans as the city falls into its post-storm normalcy and as the United States faces the current economic crisis. Those who stay continue to believe that they are living in a place that allows them social liberties to be both more Brazilian than they could be in other areas of the country but also be more "New Orleanian," grounded in their local context more than they are in other enclaves. Feeling as if they are becoming part of a community that is both culturally distinct from their own and linked to some shared cultural symbols in Brazil, Brazilian immigrants have formed a Brazilian enclave that is uniquely grounded to New Orleans.

The Brazilian enclave in New Orleans is different from those in other parts of the country because of the direct role Brazilians played in rebuilding New Orleans. The sense of who they are as a group is very much contingent on the moment in history when they arrived—in the aftermath of Hurricane Katrina. While I am sure that there

[69] There are many Brazilians who have begun to start families, buy houses, and think of New Orleans as a permanent residence. But the immigrant enclave business world shows much volatility. Every few months a new Brazilian store or restaurant opens in New Orleans at the same time that another closes. There are two Brazilian stores and six Brazilian churches for a population that is probably somewhere around 3,000-5,000 people. At the time of writing the first draft of this chapter, there were two stores; at the time of the second draft, there were three; and now, as I make these final revisions, there is only one. This is all in a time frame of less than a year.

are similar historically significant moments that have marked other enclaves, Hurricane Katrina produced the largest displaced diaspora of citizens that the U.S. has ever seen. The flooding, the deaths, the destruction, the way that this disaster was framed in the media, and the rebuilding and renewal of a social landscape, were experienced first-hand by the Brazilians in these narratives.

The emotional connection that Brazilians feel to New Orleans through their involvement in the rebuilding process became a marking emotion behind the enclave identity. Immigrants rebuilt New Orleans. This is a fact. They are the people who gutted houses and put roofs back on again. They witnessed destroyed neighborhoods come back to life as a result of their labors. Many of them feel personal investment in the city. Brazilian immigrants found that their work and sacrifice were not only to make money, but were also opportunities to see their visible impact on the community for which they were working. Seeing the direct and dramatic positive effects of their work as immigrants was empowering for them.

Traveling through New Orleans with Brazilians, I am constantly shown buildings that immigrants have taken pride in bringing back to functionality. They take time to explain to me the paint job, the texturing, or the sanding that they toiled over so that a restaurant could open again. Or they look proudly at the Super Dome when they go to see a monster truck event there, knowing that they are the ones who put the roof on after Hurricane Katrina blew the panels off. When they come by to visit me at work at Tulane University, they point out the lawn that they landscaped and reminisce about the days that they lived through a hurricane disaster zone. Indeed, for anyone who experienced Hurricane Katrina, it was an emotional time. Bonds were created between people and a city in a way that only happens during times of crisis. And who knows what the city would look like today if those immigrants had not been brave enough to come and work in a recovery zone without any idea of what they might find? These intangible emotions are part of the foundation of the Brazilian immigrant enclave in New Orleans that makes the community unique and different from other diaspora populations.

The particulars of the work environment post-Katrina also instilled a new myth among the Brazilian migrant community of New Orleans as the new immigrant El Dorado. New Orleans was imagined as a place where work was plentiful, where no one checked immigration status, and where there was little anti-immigrant sentiment. In truth, this context was a short-lived window of time. But the imagination of this "Katrina Time," which continues to be told and retold among the Brazilians who lived through it, has allowed New Orleans to maintain its mythical status that has outlived the ebbs and flows of the construction market and the local policies surrounding immigration. We have yet to see what the future holds. When these pioneer immigrants leave, will the myth play on among newer immigrants who did not experience Katrina first hand? Perhaps without another hurricane it will not.

But anyone who has found solace in a rebuilt New Orleans must be thankful for the workers who made it possible for the city to be reborn after Hurricane Katrina. These Brazilian (and Latino) workers were the real first-responders to the city. These are the people who invented ways to help, to work, and to live when there was no infrastructure to do any of these things. When we remember the stories of Katrina, we should not overlook the voices of the Brazilian immigrants who made a home and rebuilt a city in New Orleans.

Bibliography

Ana Carvalho, and Florencia Costa. "Um Jeito Brasileiro De Ser." *Isto é* January 19, 2005: 39.

Anderson Benedict. *Imagined Communities: Reflections on the Origin & Spread of Nationalism*. New York, NY: Verso, 1983.

Andrade, Oswald de. *Obras Completas: Ponto de Lança*. Rio de Janeiro: Editora Civilização Brasileira. Vol 5. 1972.

Appadurai, Arjun. *Modernity at Large: Cultural Dimensions of Globalization*. Minneapolis: University of Minnesota Press, 1996.

Armstrong, Piers. "Songs of Olodum: Ethnicity, Activism, and Art in a Globalized Carnival Community." In *Brazilian Popular Music and Globalization*. Ed. C. Perrone & C. Dunn. New York: Routledge, 2002. 177-191.

Assunção, Mathias Rohrig. *Capoeira: The History of an Afro-Brazilian Martial Art*. London: Routledge. 2005.

Attali, Jacques. *Noise: The Political Economy of Music*. Minneapolis: University of Minnesota Press, 1985.

Augé, Marc. *Non-Places: Introduction to an Anthropology of Supermodernity*. Translated by John Howe. London: Verso, 1995.

Azevedo, Kathleen de. *Samba Dreamers*. Tucson: University of Arizona Press, 2006.

Bartolomei, Marcelo. "Autora Defende Brasileiro Ilegal Em 'Sonho'." *Folha de São Paulo*, 4 November 2005, Sec. Culture/Entertainment.

Barthes, Roland. *Roland Barthes*. Translated Richard Howard. Berkeley: University of California Press, 1994.

Bashi, Vilna. *Survival of the Knitted: Immigrant Social Networks in a Stratified World*. Stanford, Ca: Stanford University Press, 2007.

Bastos, Dau. *Clandestinos Na América: O Romance Dos Imigrantes Brasileiros na Busca do Sonho Americano*. Rio de Janeiro: Relume Dumará, 2005.

Baum, Dan. "What It Means." *New Yorker*. Condé Nast Digital, 1 June 2007. Web. 13 Mar. 2009. http://www.newyorker.com/online/blogs/neworleansjournal/.

Béhague, Gerard. "Rap, Reggae, Rock, Or Samba: The Local and the Global in Brazilian Popular Music (1985-95)." *Latin American Music Review* 27.1 (2006): 79-90.

Bernstein, Nina and Elizabeth Dwoskin. "For Brazilians, Now It's Home That's a Land Of Plenty." *New York Times* 04 Dec. 2007: 1. Newspaper Source. EBSCO. Web. 17 Jan. 2010. http://query.nytimes.com/gst/fullpage.html?res=9B0DEFDD143BF937A35751C1A9619C8B63&sec=&spon=&pagewanted=2.

Beserra, Bernadete. *Brazilian Immigrants in the United States: Cultural Imperialism and Social Class*. New York, NY: LFB Scholarly Publishing, 2003.

_______________. "In the Shadow of Carmen Miranda and the Carnaval: Brazilian Immigrant Women in Los Angeles." In *Becoming Brazuca*. Ed. Clémence Jouët-Pastré and Leticia Braga. Cambridge: Harvard University Press, 2008. 57-80.

Bhabha, Homi. *The Location of Culture*. London: Routledge, 1994.

Bicalho, José Victor Pires. *Yes, Eu Sou Brazuca Ou A Vida do Imigrante Brasileiro Nos Estados Unidos Da América*. Governador Valadares, MG: Fundação de Serviços de Educação e Cultura, 1989.

Blair, William. *Cities of the Dead: Contesting the Memory of the Civil War in the South, 1865-1914*. Chapel Hill, NC: University of North Carolina Press, 2004.

Bolin, Robert and Lois Stanford. "Constructing Vulnerability in the First World: The Northridge Earthquake in Southern California, 1994." In *The Angry Earth: Disaster in Anthropological Perspective*. New York: Routledge, 1999. 89-112.

Bollig, Ben. "White Rapper/Black Beats: Discovering a Race Problem in the Music of Gabriel o Pensador." *Latin American Music Review* 23.2 (2002): 159-78.

Borjas, George. "Immigration and Self Selection." In *Immigration, Trade, and the Labor Market*. Ed. John Abowd and Richard Barry Freeman. Chicago: University of Chicago Press, 1991. 29-76.

Bourdieu, Pierre. "The Forms of Capital." In *Handbook of Theory and Research for the Sociology of Education*. Ed. J. Richardson. Westport, CT: Greenwood, 1986. 241-258.

__________. *The Logic of Practice*. Stanford, Calif.: Stanford University Press, 1990.

Bourdieu, Pierre, and Loïc J. D. Wacquant. *An Invitation to Reflexive Sociology*. Chicago: University of Chicago Press, 1992.

Braga, Letícia and Clémence Jouet Pastré. "Interdisciplinary Perspectives on Becoming Brazuca." In *Becoming Brazuca: Brazilian Immigration to the United States, Impacts on Economies, Identities, and Cultural Practices.* Ed. Clémence Jouet Pastré and Leticia Braga. Cambridge, Ma: Harvard University Press, 2008. 1-24.

Braziel, Jana Evans, and Anita Mannur. *Theorizing Diaspora: A Reader*. Malden, MA: Blackwell Publishers, 2003.

Bretas, Angela. *Sonho Americano*. Boca Raton, FL: A. Bretas, 1997.

Brody, Jennifer DeVere. "The Yankee Hugging the Creole." In *Creole: The History and Legacy of Louisiana's Free People of Color*. Ed. Sybil Klein. Baton Rouge: Louisiana State University Press, 2000. 101-116.

Browder, John. "Surviving in Rondônia: The Dynamics of Colonist Farming Strategies in Brazil's Northwest Frontier." *Studies in Comparative International Development (SCID)* 29.3 (September 1994): 45-69.

Brown, Katrina, and David W. Pearce. *The Causes of Tropical Deforestation: The Economic and Statistical Analysis of Factors Giving Rise to the Loss of the Tropical Forests*. London: UCL Press, 1994.

Browning, Barbara. *Samba: Resistance in Motion*. Indianapolis: University of Indiana Press, 1995.

Butler, Judith. *Gender Trouble: Feminism and the Subversion of Identity*. New York: Routledge, 1999.

Byrne, David. "I Hate World Music." *New York Times*, Arts & Leisure, October 3, 1999: 1.

Calvani, Carlos Eduardo Brandão. *Teologia e MPB*. São Paulo: Edições Loyola, 1998.

Canclini, García. *Hybrid Cultures: Strategies for Entering and Leaving Modernity*. Minneapolis: University of Minneapolis Press, 1995.

______________. "Rewriting Cultural Studies in the Borderland." In *Postborder City*. New York: Routledge, 2003. 277-286.

Capoeira, Nestor. *Galo ja Cantou: Capoeira para Iniciados*. Rio de Janeiro: Editora Rasteira, 1985.

______________. *O Pequeno Manual do Jogador da Capoeira*. São Paulo: Editora Ground. 1981.

______________. *A Street-Smart Song: Capoeira Philosophy and Inner Life*. Berkeley: Blue Snake Books, 2006.

Castles, Stephen, and Mark J. Miller. *The Age of Migration*. New York:

Guilford Press, 2003.

Caulfield, Carlota, and Darion J. Davis. *A Companion to US Latino Literatures*. Woodbridge, UK; Rochester, NY: Tamesis; Boydell & Brewer, 2007.

Cepeda, María Elena. "'Columbus Effects': The Politics of Crossover and Chronology within the Latin(o) Music Boom." *Discourse*. 23.1(2001): 242-267.

Chastles, Stephen and Mark Miller. *The Age of Migration*. London: Macmillan, 1994.

Chvaicer, Maya Talmon. "The Criminalization of Capoeira in Nineteenth-Century Brazil." *Hispanic American Historical Review* 82.3(2002): 525-547.

Clark, Emily. "How American is New Orleans? What the Founding Era Has to Tell Us." Washington, D.C.: Kenan Institute. Paper 301 (2006): 27-34.

"Com "América", brasileiros batem recorde de imigração ilegal." 25 Aug. 2005. Web. 1 July 2009. <http://www.guiadoimigrante.com/artigo.php?idPublicacao=2359>.

Crawford, Matthew B. *Shop Class as Soulcraft: An Inquiry into the Value of Work*. New York, NY: Penguin Press, 2009.

Crook, Larry. *Brazilian Music: Northeastern Traditions and the Heartbeat of a Modern Nation*. Santa Barbara, CA: ABC-CLIO Inc, 2005.

Cunha, Maria Clementina Pereira. *Carnavais e Outras Frestas: Ensaios de Histórias Social da Cultura*. São Paulo: Editora da UNICAMP, 2002.

Da Matta, Roberto. *Carnavais, Malandros e Heróis: Para uma Sociologia do Dilema Brasileiro*. Rio de Janeiro: Zahar Editores, 1978.

________________. *O qué é o Brasil?* Rio de Janeiro: Rocco, 2004.

Davis, Darién. "Racial Parity and National Humor: Exploring Brazilian Samba from Noel Rosa to Carmen Miranda." In *Latin American Popular Culture*. Ed William Beezley and Linda Curcio-Nagy. Oxford: SR Books, 2000. 183-200.

Davis, Wade, K. David Harrison, and Catherine Herbert Howell. *Book of Peoples of the World: A Guide to Cultures*. Washington, D.C.: National Geographic, 2007.

De Certeau, Michel. *The Practice of Everyday Life*. Berkeley: University of California Press, 1984.

Dear, M. J., Gustavo Leclerc, and Jo-Anne Berelowitz. *Postborder City: Cultural Spaces of Bajalta California*. New York, NY: Routledge, 2003.

Degler, Carl N. *Neither Black nor White: Slavery and Race Relations in Brazil and the United States*. New York, NY: Macmillan, 1971.

Dennison, Stephanie and Lisa Shaw. *Popular Cinema in Brazil*. Manchester: Manchester University Press, 2004.

Dent, Alexander Sebastian. "Country Brothers: Kinship and Chronotope in Brazilian Rural Public Culture." *Anthropological Quarterly* 80.2 (2007): 455-95.

______________________.*River of Tears: Country Music, Memory, and Modernity in Brazil*. Durham: Duke University Press, 2009.

Desmond, Jane. "Embodying Difference: Issues in Dance and Cultural Studies." In *Everynight Life: Culture and Dance in Latin America*. Durham, NC: Duke University Press, 1997. 33-64.

Donato, Katherine. "Reconstructing New Orleans After Katrina: The Emergence of an Immigrant Labor Market." In *Sociology of Katrina: Perspectives on a Modern Catastrophe*. Ed. David Brunsma, Davido Overfelt, and J. Steven Picou. Lanham: Rowman and Littlefield Publishers, Inc, 2007. 217-234.

Donnelly, Brian. "Nestor Capoeira (Interview)." *Planet Capoeira* June 13, 2002: 14. Web 3 November 2006. http://www.planetcapoeira.com/index.php?id=P14.

Douglas, Frederick. *My Bondage and My Freedom*. New York, NY: Arno Press, 1968.

Downey, Greg. *Learning Capoeira: Lessons in Cunning from an Afro--Brazilian Art*. New York. Oxford University Press. 2005.

Duany, Jorge. *The Puerto Rican Nation on the Move: Identities on the Island and in the United States*. Chapel Hill: University of North Carolina Press, 2002.

Dunn, Christopher. "Black Rome and the Chocolate City: The Race of Place." *Callaloo* 30.3 (2008): 847-61.

________________. "A Roma Negra e o Big Easy: Raça, Cultura e Discurso em Salvador e Nova Orleans." *Afro-Ásia* 37 (2008): 97-118.

Dynes, Russell and Havidán Rodriguez. "Finding and Framing Katrina: The Social Construction of Disaster." In *The Sociology of Katrina: Perspectives on a Modern Catastrophe*. Ed David Brunsma, David Overfelt, and Steven Picou. Plymouth, UK: Rowman and Littlefield Publishers, 2007. 23-34.

Eco, Umberto. *Travels in Hyperreality: Essays*. London: Pan Books in Association with Secker & Warburg, 1987.

Farrell, Patrick. "Portuguese *Saudade* and Other Emotions of Absence and Longing." In *Semantic Primes and Universal Grammar: Empi-*

rical Evidence from the Romance Languages. Ed. Bert Peeters. Amsterdam: John Benjamins, 2006. 310-340.

Fernandes, Florestan. *A Integração do Negro à Sociedade de Classes.* Rio de Janeiro: M.E.C, 1965.

Flaherty, Jordan. "New Orleans' Culture of Resistance." In *What is a City: Rethinking the Urban After Hurricane Katrina.* Ed. Steinberg, Phil and Rob Shields. Athens: University of Georgia Press, 2008. 30-55.

Fleischer, Soraya Resende. *Passando a América a Limpo: O Trabalho de "Housecleaners" Brasileiras Em Boston, Massachussets.* São Paulo: Annablume, 2002.

Freston, Paul. "The Religious Field among Brazilians in the United States." In *Becoming Brazuca: Brazilian Immigration to the United States.* Ed. Clémence Jouët-Pastré and Leticia J. Braza, Cambridge, Mass: Harvard University Press, 2008. 255-270.

Freyre, Gilberto. *Sobrados e Mucambos.* São Paulo: Companhia Editora Nacional, 1936.

Fryer, Peter. *Rhythms of Resistance: African Musical Heritage in Brazil.* Hanover, Mass: Wesleyan University Press, 2000.

Fussell, Beth. "Hurricane Chasers: Latino Immigrants as a Source of a Rapid Response Labor Force." 2006. Web. 5 June 2007. http://www.allacademic.com/meta/p_mla_apa_research_citation/2/4/2/5/8/p242583_index.html.

______________. "Constructing New Orleans, Constructing Race: A Population History of New Orleans. *Journal of American History* 94:3 (2007): 851-862.

Galinsky, Philip. "Co-option, Cultural Resistance, and Afro-Brazilian Identity: A History of the "*Pagode*" Samba Movement in Rio de Janeiro." In *Latin American Music Review: Revista de Música Latinoamericana*, 17:2 (1996): 120-149.

Gannon, Martin J. *Understanding Global Cultures: Metaphorical Journeys through 23 Nations.* Thousand Oaks, Calif.: Sage Publications, 2001.

García Canclini, Néstor. *Hybrid Cultures: Strategies for Entering and Leaving Modernity.* Minneapolis: University of Minnesota Press, 1989.

Gates, Henry Louis, Jr. *The Signifying Monkey: A Theory of African American Literary Criticism.* Oxford: Oxford University Press, 1988.

Gaynor, Tim. "Brazilians using Mexico to Enter the U.S Illegally." *San Diego Online* 22 April 2005. Web. 4 September 2008. http://legacy.signonsandiego.com/news/mexico/20050422-1537-mexico--immigration.html.

Gibson, Annie. "Brazuca in NOLA: A Cultural Analysis of Brazilian Immigration to New Orleans Post-Katrina." *Latin American Journal of Popular Culture* 27 (2008): 103-128.

_________________. "Parading Brazil Through New Orleans: Brazilian Immigrant Interaction with Casa Samba of New Orleans." *Latin American Music Review.* 33-2. December 2012.

_________________. "Performing Cultural Visibility: Brazilian Immigrants, Mardi Gras, and New Orleans." in *Performing Brazil.* Ed. Severino Albuquerque and Kathryn Sanchez.

Gilroy, Paul. *'There Ain't no Black in the Union Jack': The Cultural Politics of Race and Nation.* Chicago, Ill.: University of Chicago Press, 1991.

Goés, Fred. *Antes do Furacão: O Mardi Gras de um Folião Brasileiro em Nova Orleans.* Rio de Janeiro: Língua Geral, 2008.

Goldstein, Donna. *Laughter Out of Place: Race, Class, Violence, and Sexuality in the Rio Shantytown.* Berkeley: University of California Press, 2003.

Gomes, Laura Graziela Figueiredo Fernandes. *Novela e Sociedade no Brasil.* Niterói, RJ: Editora da Universidade Federal Fluminense, 1998.

Gotham, Kevin Fox. *Authentic New Orleans: Tourism, Culture, and Race in the Big Easy.* New York: New York University Press, 2007.

Gramsci, Antonio. *Selections from the Prison Notebooks of Antonio Gramsci.* Ed. and trans. Quintin Hoare and Geoffrey Nowell Smith. London: Lawrence and Wishart, 1971.

Guillermoprieto, Alma. *Samba.* New York: Vintage Books, 1991.

Guimarães, Antonio Sérgio Alfredo. *Classes, Raças, e Democracia.* São Paulo: Editora 34, 2002.

Hall, Gwendolyn Midlo. "The Formation of Afro-Creole Culture." In *Creole New Orleans: Race and Americanization.* Ed. Arnold Hirsch and Joseph Logsdon. Baton Rouge: Louisiana State University Press, 1992. 58-90.

Hay, Andrew. "Soap Opera Lures Brazilians to United States." 25 August 2005. Web. 13 Sept 2007. <http://www.redorbit.com/news/general/219723/soap_opera_lures_brazilians_to_united_states/>.

Heathcott, Joseph. "Urban Spaces and Working-Class Expressions Across the Black Atlantic: Tracing the Routes of Ska." *Radical History Review* 87 (2003): 183-206.

Holloway, Thomas H. "'A Healthy Terror: Police Repression of Capoeiras in Nineteenth-Century Rio de Janeiro," *Hispanic American Historical Review* 69:(1989): 637-674.

Hirschman, Charles, Philip Kasinitz and Josh DeWind. *The Handbook of International Migration: The American Experience.* New York: Russell Sage Foundation, 1999.

Joana, Angélica. "Samba Guerrilheiro: O *Pagode* Cresce e Distribui Discos de Ouro." *Isto É.* 18 June 1986, 58-59.

Kirshenblatt-Gimblett, Barbara. *Destination Culture: Tourism, Museums, and Heritage.* Berkeley: University of California Press, 1998.

Kubik, Gerard. "Ethnicity, Cultural Identity, and the Psychology of Cultural Contact." In *Music and Black Ethnicity: The Caribbean and South America.* Ed. Gerard Béhague. Miami, Fl: North-South Center Press, 1992. 17-46.

Kun, Josh. *Audiotopia: Music, Race, and America.* Berkeley: University of California Press, 2005.

LaChance, Paul F. "The 1809 Immigration of Saint Domingue Refugees to New Orleans: Reception, Integration, and Impact." *Louisiana History* 29 (1988): 109-141.

LaStrapes, Lauren. "Casa Samba: Twenty One Years of Amerizilian Identity." Unpublished Paper from the New Orleans: Cultures of Rebuilding Conference, 7 November 2008. Used with Permission of the Author.

Lefebvre, Henri. *Critique of Everyday Life.* London; New York: Verso, 1991.

________________. *The Production of Space.* Oxford: Blackwell, 1991.

Leon, Thales de. *Clandestinos: Aventuras Verídicas De Um Guia De Imigrantes Ilegais Nas Fronteiras Americanas.* Rio de Janeiro, RJ: Domínio Público, 1996.

Lima, Ari. "Black or Brau: Music and Subjectivity in the Global Context." In *Brazilian Popular Music and Globalization.* Ed. Charles Perrone and Christopher Dunn. New York: Routledge, 2002. 220-232.

Linger, Daniel. "Brazil Displaced: Restaurant 51 in Nagoya, Japan." *Horizontes Antropológicos* 5 (1997): 181-203.

Lipsitz, George. *Dangerous Crossroads: Popular Music, Postmodernism, and the Poetics of Place.* New York: Verso, 1994.

Lopes, Nei. *Bantos, Malês, e Identidade Negra.* Rio de Janeiro: Forense, 1988.

_________.*Sambeabá: O Samba que não se Aprende na Escola.* Rio de Janeiro: Casa da Palavra/Folha Seca, 2003.

Lowe, Lisa. *Immigrant Acts: On Asian American Cultural Politics.* Durham: Duke University Press, 1996.

Mahar, Denis and Robert Schneider. "Incentives for Tropical Deforestation: Some Examples from Latin America." In *The Causes of Tropical Deforestation: The Economic and Statistical Analysis of Factors Giving Rise to the Loss of the Tropical Forests.* Ed. Katrina Brown and David Pearce. Vancouver: UBC Press, 1994. 159-171.

Marcus, Alan. *The Contexts and Consequences of Brazilian Transnational Migration Processes: An Ethnic Geography in Two Countries.* Dissertation. University of Massachusetts Amherst, 2008. Dissertations & Theses: ProQuest. Web. 20 Jan. 2009.

___________. "Once again: Brazilians are Not Hispanic." Oct. 2003. *Brazzil.* Web. 46 May 2009. http://www.brazzil.com/2003/html/articles/oct03/p112oct03.htm.

Margolis, Maxine L. *Little Brazil: An Ethnography of Brazilian Immigrants in New York City.* Princeton: Princeton University Press, 1993.

_____________. "Na virada do Milênio: A Emigração Brasileira para os Estados Unidos" In *Fronteiras Cruzadas: Etnicidade, Gênero, e Redes Sociais.* Ed. Ana Cristina Braga and Soraya Fleischer. São Paulo: Paz e Terra, 2003. 51-72.

______________. "Becoming Brazucas: Brazilian Immigration to the United States." In *The Other Latinos.* Ed. Falconi, Jose Luis, Jose Antonio Mazzotti , and Michael Jones-Correa. Cambridge: Harvard University Press, 2007. 213-230.

______________. "September 11th and Transnationalism: The Case of Brazilian Immigrants in the United States." *Human Organization: Society for Applied Anthropology* 67.1 (2008): 1-11.

Martes, Ana Cristina Braga. "Neither Hispanic, Nor Black: We're Brazilian". In *The Other Latinos.* Ed. Falconi, Jose Luis, Jose Antonio Mazzotti , and Michael Jones-Correa. Cambridge, Mass.: Harvard University Press, 2007. 231-256.

Martes, Ana Cristina Braga and Ruth Cardoso. *Brasileiros Nos Estados Unidos: Um Estudo Sobre Imigrantes Em Massachusetts.* São Paulo, SP: Paz e Terra, 2000.

Massey, Douglas. "Why does Immigration Occur? A Theoretical Synthesis." *The Handbook of International Migration: The American Experience.* Ed. Charles Hirschman, Philip Kasinitz, and Josh DeWind. New York: Russell Sage Foundation, 1999. 34-52.

Massey, Douglas S., Jorge Durand, and Nolan J. Malone. *Beyond Smoke and Mirrors: Mexican Immigration in an Era of Economic Integration*. New York: Russell Sage Foundation, 2002.

Mattias, Rohrig Assunção. *Capoeira: The History of an Afro-Brazilian Martial Art*. New York: Routledge, 2005.

McCann, Bryan. "Blues and Samba: Another Side of Bossa Nova History." *Luso-Brazilian Review* 44.2 (2008): 21-49.

McDonnell, Patrick J. "Brazil's Bahia a Link for African Americans: The state, where black customs are kept up, is a draw for US tourists hungry for tradition." *Los Angeles Times*, 23 September 2007: A6.

McGowen, Chris and Ricardo Pessanha. *The Brazilian Sound: Samba, Bossa Nova, and the Popular Music of Brazil*. Philadelphia: Temple University Press, 1998.

McLaughlin, Ken and Mike Swift. "Recession Seen Deterring Illegal Immigration." *San Jose Mercury News* (CA) 22 July 2009: Newspaper Source. EBSCO. Web. 17 Jan. 2010.

Merrell, Floyd. *Capoeira and Candomblé: Conformity and Resistance in Brazil*. Princeton, NJ: Markus Wiener Publishers, 2005.

Miguel, Antônio C. "Jobim no Tom de Armstrong." *Revista: O Globo* September 24, 2006, sec. Internacional: 14-17.

Millman, Joel. "America the Irresistible: Conditions at Home Improve but Foreigners Still Want to Come Here." *The Wall Street Journal* April 2005. Web. 23 March 2007.

Millman, Joel, and Geraldo Samor. "Changing Face of Immigration." *Wall Street Journal* - Eastern Edition 24 Jan. 2005: A16. Web. 18 Jan. 2010.

Mitchell, Reid. *All on a Mardi Gras Day: Episodes in the History of New Orleans Carnival*. Cambridge: Harvard University Press, 1995.

Moehn, Frederick. "Music, Citizenship, and Violence in Postdictatorship Brazil." *Latin American Music Review* 28.2 (2007): 181-219.

Moeller, Susan. "'We had to take the risk' Brazilians Gamble Future, Lives in Illegal Border Crossings." *Cape Cod Times* 25 February 2003. Web. 29 January 2007. http://archive.capecodonline.com/special/brazil03/wehad25.htm.

Morales, Ed. *The Latin Beat: The Rhythms and Roots of Latin Music from Bossa Nova to Salsa and Beyond*. Cambridge, Mass: Da Capo Press, 2003.

Mota, Kátia María Santos. "Two Languages at Play: Language Boundaries in the Speech of Second-Generation Brazilian Immigrants." In *Becoming Brazuca: Brazilian Immigration to the United States*. Ed. Clémence Jouët-Pastré and Leticia J. Braza, Cambridge, Mass: Harvard University Press, 2008. 313-338.

Moura, Milton. "World of Fantasy, Fantasy of the World: Geographic Space and Representation of Identity in the Carnival of Salvador, Bahia." In *Brazilian Popular Music and Globalization*. Ed. C. Perrone & C. Dunn. New York: Routledge, 2002. 161-176.

Ness, Sally Ann Allen. "Being a Body in a Cultural Way: Understanding the Cultural in the Embodiment of Dance." In *Cultural Bodies: Ethnography and Theory*. Ed. Helen Thomas and Jamilah Ahmed. Malden, Ma: Blackwell Publishing, 2004. 123-144.

Neto, Belchior. *Aventureiros do Dólar : Romance de Amor Entre Os Emigrantes Para Os Estados Unidos*. Belo Horizonte: Imprensa Oficial de Minas Gerais, 1990.

Nolan, Bruce. "Brazilian Boom; Attracted by Construction Jobs and an Easygoing Lifestyle, More and More Brazilian Immigrants are Settling in New Orleans. But it's too soon to say whether the enclave will put down permanent roots." *Times-Picayune* 20 Jan. 2008, National sec.: 1-2.

Perrone, Charles, and Christopher Dunn. "Chiclete Com Banana: Internationalization in Brazilian Popular Music." In *Brazilian Popular Music and Globalization*. Ed. Charles Perrone and Christopher Dunn. New York, NY: Routledge, 2001. 1-38.

Pierson, Donald. *Cruz das Almas: A Brazilian Village*. Washington, DC: Smithsonian Institute of Social Anthropology Publication No. 12, 1948.

Pinho, O. A. "Fogo na Babilônia: Reggae, Black Counterculture, and Globalization in Brazil." In *Brazilian Popular Music and Globalization. Ed.* Charles Perrone & Christopher Dunn. New York: Routledge, 2002. 192-206.

Piore, Michael J. *Birds of Passage: Migrant Labor and Industrial Societies*. Cambridge; New York: Cambridge University Press, 1979.

Porter, Eduardo. "Katrina Begets a Baby Boom by Immigrants." *New York Times* 11 December 2006, sec. A20.

Powers, Michael. "A Matter of Choice: Historical Lessons for Disaster Recovery." In *There is No Such Thing as a Natural Disaster: Race, Class, and Hurricane Katrina*. Ed. Chester Hartman and Gregory Squires. New York: Routledge, 2006. 13-36.

"Public funds drive slow recovery in New Orleans." *Washington Times - Politics, Breaking News, US and World News*. 27 June 2009. Web.

16 Aug. 2009. <http://www.washingtontimes.com/news/2009/jun/27/public-funds-drive-slow-recovery/?feat=article_related_stories>.

Pravaz, Natasha. "Brazilian Mulatice. Performing Race, Gender, and the Nation." In *Journal of Latin American Anthropology*. 8:1 (2003): 116-146.

Rainey, Richard. "38 Nabbed in Immigration Raid." *Times Picayune* 17 May 2007.

Rector, Monica. "The Code and Message of Carnival: 'Escolas de Samba'." In *Carnival!* Ed. Thomas Sebeok. New York: Mouton Publishers, 1984. 37-165.

Reed, Susan. "The Politics and Poetics of Dance." *Annual Review of Anthropology*. 27(1998): 503-532.

Reis, Rossana Rocha, Teresa Sales, and Ana Cristina Braga Martes. *Cenas do Brasil Migrante*. São Paulo, Brazil: Boitempo Editorial, 1999.

Rheda, Regina. *First World, Third Class – and Other Tales of the Global Mix*. Austin: University of Texas, 2005.

Rich, Bruce. *Mortgaging the Earth: The World Bank, Environmental Impoverishment, and the Crisis of Development*. Boston: Beacon Press, 1994.

Roach, Joseph. *Cities of the Dead: Circum-Atlantic Performance*. New York: Columbia University Press, 1996.

Robertson, Campbell. "In New Orleans, Recovery is Not Enough." *New York Times*. 31_August 2009, A:8.

Rodrigues, Alan, and Sônia Filgueiras. "Guerra Ao Tráfico Humano" *Isto é*. 9 March 2005: 53.

Rodrigues, Alan. "Operação Tequila." *Isto é* 30 March 2005: 38.

Rosende, Rosana. "Brasileiros no Sul da Flórida – Relatos de uma Pesquisa em Andiamento." In *Fronteiras Cruzadas: Etnicidade, Gênero, e Redes Sociais*. Ed. Ana Cristina Braga. São Paulo: Paz e Terra, 2003. 139-156.

Sales, Teresa. *Brazilians Away from Home*. New York: Center for Migration Studies, 2003.

_________."Constructing an Ethnic Identity: Brazilian Immigrants in Boston, Ma." *Migration World* 16:5 (1999): 15-21.

_________. "Identidade Étnica entre Imigrantes Brasileiros na Região de Boston." In *Cenas do Brasil Migrante*. Ed. Rosana Reis and Teresa Sales. São Paulo: Boitempo Editorial, 1999. 17-44.

Sanson, Livio. *Blackness Without Ethnicity*. New York: Palgrave Mac-

Millan, 2003.

Santos, Jocélio Teles de. *O Poder da Cultura e a Cultura no Poder: A Disputa Simbólica da Herança Cultural Negra no Brasil*. Salvador, Bahia: EDUFBA, 2005.

Savigliano, M. *Tango and the Political Economy of Passion*. Boulder, CO: Westview, 1995.

Schmink, Marianne and Charles Wood. *Contested Frontiers in Amazonia*. New York: Columbia University Press, 1992.

Schwarz, Roberto. *Ao Vencedor as Batatas*. São Paulo: Editora 34, 2000.

Sered, Susan Starr. *Religious Healing in Boston: Reports from the Field*. Cambridge, Mass: Center for the Study of World Religions, Harvard University, 2002.

Silva, Nelson do Valle. "Updating the Cost of Not Being White in Brazil." In *Race, Class, and Power in Brazil*. Ed. Pierre-Miche Fontaine. Los Angeles: Center for Afro-American Studies, University of California, 1985. 42-55.

Simonett, Helena. *Banda: Mexican Musical Life Across Borders*. Middletown, Conn.: Wesleyan University Press, 2001.

Siqueira, Sueli. "Emigrants From Governador Valadares: Projects of Return and Investment." In *Becoming Brazuca*. Ed. Clémence Jouët-Pastré and Leticia Braga. Cambridge: Harvard University Press, 2008. 175-194.

Skidmore, Thomas. "Race and Class in Brazil: Historical Perspectives" In *Race, Class, and Power in Brazil*. Ed. Fontaine, Pierre-Michel. Los Angeles: Center for Afro-American Studies, University of California, 1985. 11-24.

________________. *Black into White: Race and Nation in Brazilian Thought*. Durham, NC: Duke University Press, 1993.

Soares, Carlos Eugênio Líbano. *A Capoeira Escrava e Outras Tradições Rebeldes no Rio de Janeiro (1808-1850)*. Rio de Janeiro: Editora da Unicamp, 2001.

Stanonis, Anthony. *Creating the Big Easy: New Orleans and the Emergence of Modern Tourism*. Athens: University of Georgia Press, 2006.

Stark, Oded and David Bloom. "The New Economics of Labor Migration." *The American Economic Review*. 75:2 (1985): 173-178.

Stewart, Douglas Ian. *After the Trees: Living on the Transamazon Highway*. Austin: University of Texas Press, 1994.

Sublette, Ned. *The World that Made New Orleans: From Spanish Silver to Congo Square*. Chicago: Lawrence Hill Books, 2008.

Telles, Edward. *Race in Another America: The Significance of Skin Color in Brazil.* Princeton, NJ: Princeton University Press, 2004.

Topolnicki, Denise. "Why We Still Live Best in the USA." *Money Magazine* October 1991: 86-93.

Tosta, Antonio Luciano. "American Dream, *Jeitinho Brasileiro*: On the Crossroads of Cultural Identities in Brazilian-American Literature." In *A Companion to US Latino Literatures.* Ed. Carlota Caulfield and Darién J. Davis. Rochester, NY: Tamesis, 2007. 140-157.

_______. "Between Heaven and Hell: Perceptions of Brazil and the United States in Brazuca Literature." *Hispania: A Journal Devoted to the Teaching of Spanish and Portuguese* 88.4 (2005): 713-25.

_______. "Latino, Eu? the Paradoxical Interplay of Identity in Brazuca Literature." *Hispania: A Journal Devoted to the Teaching of Spanish and Portuguese* 87.3 (2004): 576-85.

Turner, Victor. *The Anthropology of Performance.* New York: PAJ Publications, 1986.

___________. *From Ritual to Theatre: The Human Seriousness of Play.* Vol. 1. New York City: Performing Arts Journal Publications, 1982.

Vaca, Nick Corona. *The Presumed Alliance: The Unspoken Conflict between Latinos and Blacks and What it Means for America.* New York: Rayo, 2004.

Varney, James. "40 Jailed in Raid on Immigrants; but Legal Groups Say City Needs Workers." *Times Picayune* Saturday, March 18, 2006.

Veloso, Caetano. "Carmen Mirandada" In *Brazilian Popular Music and Globalization.* Ed. Charles Perrone and Christopher Dunn. New York: Routledge, 2002. 39-45.

Vianna, Hermano. *The Mystery of Samba: Popular Music & National Identity in Brazil.* Chapel Hill: University of North Carolina Press, 1999.

Vilas Boas, Sergio. *Os Estrangeiros do Trem N.* Rio de Janeiro: Rocco, 1997.

Wade, Peter. "Rethinking Mestizaje: Ideology and Lived Experience." *Journal of Latin American Studies* 37 (2005): 239-257.

Waldinger, Roger David and Michael Ira Lichter. *How the Other Half Works: Immigration and the Social Organization of Labor.* Los Angeles: University of California Press, 2003._

Walsh, John. "Labor Pains: Immigration Reform Could Ease Employment Strain." *BNET.* CBS Interactive, Inc. 16 Feb 2004.

Web. 29 May 2009. http://findarticles.com/p/articles/mi_m3072/is_3_219/ai_113860171/.

Weber, Soares. "Emigração e (I)mobilidade Residencial: Momentos de Ruptura na reprodução/ Continuidade da Segregação Social no Espaço Urbano." In *Cenas do Brasil Migrante*. Ed. Rossana Rocha Reis. São Paulo: Boitempo, 1999. 167-192.

Wierzbicki, Susan K. *Beyond the Immigrant Enclave: Network Change and Assimilation*. New York: LFB Scholarly Publishing, 2004.

Yúdice, George. *The Expediency of Culture: Uses of Culture in the Global Era*. Durham NC: Duke University Press, 2003.

Yu, Bin. *Chain Migration Explained: The Power of the Immigration Multiplier*. New York: LFB Scholarly Pub, 2008.

Index

BIOGRAPHY

Annie Gibson was born in Princeton, N.J. and grew up in Davidson, N.C. She received her BA from Dartmouth College in 2003 and her Ph.D. in 2010 from the Stone Center for Latin American Studies at Tulane University. Her areas of specialization include Brazilian and Cuban performance cultures and Brazilian immigration to the United States. Her resume includes dancing samba for the Zulu Mardi Gras King and being a piranha fisherwoman. She currently teaches at Tulane in both the Departments of Latin American Studies and of Spanish and Portuguese.

Available from
UNO PRESS

General Titles

**The Not Yet* by Moira Crone, 978-1-60801-072-1 (2012)

A Baltic Anthology Book 1: Contemporary Latvian Poetry, edited by Inara Cedrins, 978-1-60801-050-9 (2012)

A Baltic Anthology Book 2: Contemporary Estonian Poetry, edited by Inara Cedrins, 978-1-60801-052-3 (2012)

A Baltic Anthology Book 3: Contemporary Lithuanian Poetry, edited by Inara Cedrins, 978-1-60801-051-6 (2012)

**The Astral Plane: Stories of Cuba, the Southwest and Beyond* by Teresa Dovalpage, 978-1-60801-078-3 (2012)

**The Man Who Wanted to Buy a Heart* by Leonard S. Bernstein, 978-1-60801-073-8 (2012)

Post-Katrina Brazucas: Brazilian Immigrants in New Orleans by Annie McNeill Gibson, 978-1-60801-070-7 (2011)

New Orleans: The Underground Guide (2nd Edition) by Michael Patrick Welch & Alison Fensterstock, 978-1-60801-079-0 (2011)

The Saratoga Collection, edited by Terrence Sanders, 978-1-60801-061-5 (2011)

**The Garden Path: The Miseducation of a City,* by Andre Perry, 978-1-60801-048-6 (2011)

Before (During) After: Louisiana Photographers Visual Reactions to Hurricane Katrina, edited by Elizabeth Kleinveld, 978-1-60801-023-3 (2010)

**Beyond the Islands* by Alicia Yánez Cossío, translated by Amalia Gladhart, 978-1-60801-043-1 (2010)

**The Fox's Window* by Naoko Awa, translated by Toshiya Kamei, 978-1-60801-006-6 (2010)

Black Santa by Jamie Bernstein, 978-1-60801-022-6 (2010)

Dream-crowned (Traumgekrönt) by Rainer Maria Rilke, translated by Lorne Mook, 978-1-60801-041-7 (2010)

**Voices Rising II: More Stories from the Katrina Narrative Project* edited by Rebeca Antoine, 978-0-9706190-8-2 (2010)

**Rowing to Sweden: Essays on Faith, Love, Politics, and Movies* by Fredrick Barton, 978-1-60801-001-1 (2010)

Dogs in My Life: The New Orleans Photographs by John Tibule Mendes, 978-1-60801-005-9 (2010)

New Orleans: The Underground Guide by Michael Patrick Welch & Alison Fensterstock, 978-1-60801-019-6 (2010)

Understanding the Music Business: A Comprehensive View edited by Harmon Greenblatt & Irwin Steinberg, 978-1-60801-004-2 (2010)

**The Gravedigger* by Rob Magnuson Smith, 978-1-60801-010-3 (2010)

Portraits: Photographs in New Orleans 1998-2009 by Jonathan Traviesa, 978-0-9706190-5-1 (2009)

**I hope it's not over, and good-by: Selected Poems of Everette Maddox* by Everette Maddox, 978-1-60801-000-4 (2009)

Theoretical Killings: Essays & Accidents by Steven Church, 978-0-9706190-6-8 (2009)

**Voices Rising: Stories from the Katrina Narrative Project* edited by Rebeca Antoine, 978-0-9728143-6-2 (2008)

On Higher Ground: The University of New Orleans at Fifty by Dr. Robert Dupont, 978-0-9728143-5-5 (2008)

The Change Cycle Handbook by Will Lannes, 978-0-9728143-9-3 (2008)

Us Four Plus Four: Eight Russian Poets Conversing translated by Don Mager, 978-0-9706190-4-4 (2008)

The El Cholo Feeling Passes by Fredrick Barton, 978-0-9728143-2-4 (2003)

A House Divided by Fredrick Barton, 978-0-9728143-1-7 (2003)

William Christenberry: Art & Family by J. Richard Gruber, 978-0-9706190-0-6 (2000)

The Neighborhood Story Project

New Orleans in 19 Movements by Thurgood Marshall Early College High School, 978-1-

60801-069-1 (2011)

The Combination by Ashley Nelson, 978-1-60801-055-4 (2010)

Between Piety and Desire by Arlet Wylie and Sam Wylie, 978-1-60801-040-0 (2010)

The House of Dance and Feathers: A Museum by Ronald W. Lewis by Rachel Breunlin & Ronald W. Lewis, 978-0-9706190-7-5 (2009)

Beyond the Bricks by Daron Crawford & Pernell Russell, 978-1-60801-016-5 (2010)

Aunt Alice Vs. Bob Marley by Kareem Kennedy, 978-1-60801-013-4 (2010)

Signed, The President by Kenneth Phillips, 978-1-60801-015-8 (2010)

Houses of Beauty: From Englishtown to the Seventh Ward by Susan Henry, 978-1-60801-014-1 (2010)

Coming Out the Door for the Ninth Ward edited by Rachel Breunlin, 978-0-9706190-9-9 (2006)

Cornerstones: Celebrating the Everyday Monuments & Gathering Places of New Orleans edited by Rachel Breunlin, 978-0-9706190-3-7 (2008)

The Engaged Writers Series

Medea and Her War Machines by Ioan Flora, translated by Adam J. Sorkin, 978-1-60801-067-7 (2011)

Together by Julius Chingono and John Eppel, 978-1-60801-049-3 (2011)

Vegetal Sex (O Sexo Vegetal) by Sergio Medeiros, translated by Raymond L.Bianchi, 978-1-60801-046-2 (2010)

**Wounded Days (Los Días Heridos)* by Leticia Luna, translated by Toshiya Kamei, 978-1-60801-042-4 (2010)

When the Water Came: Evacuees of Hurricane Katrina by Cynthia Hogue & Rebecca Ross, 978-1-60801-012-7 (2010)

**A Passenger from the West* by Nabile Farès, translated by Peter Thompson, 978-1-60801-008-0 (2010)

**Everybody Knows What Time It Is* by Reginald Martin, 978-1-60801-011-0 (2010)

**Green Fields: Crime, Punishment, & a Boyhood Between* by Bob Cowser, Jr., 978-1-60801-018-9 (2010)

**Open Correspondence: An Epistolary Dialogue* by Abdelkébir Khatibi and Rita El Khayat, translated by Safoi Babana-Hampton, Valérie K. Orlando, Mary Vogl, 978-1-60801-021-9 (2010)

Gravestones (Lápidas) by Antonio Gamoneda, translated by Donald Wellman, 978-1-60801-002-8 (2009)

Hearing Your Story: Songs of History and Life for Sand Roses by Nabile Farès translated by Peter Thompson, 978-0-9728143-7-9 (2008)

The Katrina Papers: A Journal of Trauma and Recovery by Jerry W. Ward, Jr., 978-0-9728143-3-1 (2008)

Contemporary Poetry

Sheer Indefinite: Selected Poems 1991-2011 by Skip Fox, 978-1-60801-080-6 (2011)

Atlanta Poets Group Anthology: The Lattice Inside by Atlanta Poets Group, 978-1-60801-064-6 (2011)

Makebelieve by Caitlin Scholl, 978-1-60801-056-1 (2011)

California Redemption Value by Kevin Opstedal, 978-1-60801-066-0 (2011)

Dear Oxygen: New and Selected Poems by Lewis MacAdams, edited by Kevin Opstedal, 978-1-60801-059-2 (2011)

Only More So by Tony Lopez, 978-1-60801-057-8 (2011)

Enridged by Brian Richards, 978-1-60801-047-9 (2011)

A Gallery of Ghosts by John Gery, 978-0-9728143-4-8 (2008)

The Ezra Pound Center for Literature

Modernism and the Orient, edited by Zhaoming Qian, 978-1-60801-074-5 (2012)

The Poets of the Sala Capizucchi (I Poeti della Sala Capizucchi) edited by Caterina Ricciardi and John Gery, 978-1-60801-068-4 (2011)

Trespassing, by Patrizia de Rachewiltz, 978-1-60801-060-8 (2011)

**The Imagist Poem: Modern Poetry in Miniature* edited by William Pratt, 978-0-9728143-8-6 (2008)

Contemporary Austrian Studies

Global Austria: Austria's Place in Europe and the World Volume 20, Günter Bischof, Fritz Plasser (Eds.), Alexander Smith, Guest Editor, 978-1-60801-062-2 (2011)

From Empire to Republic: Post-World-War-I Austria Volume 19 edited by Günter Bischof, Fritz Plasser and Peter Berger, 978-1-60801-025-7 (2010)

The Schüssel Era in Austria Volume 18 edited by Günter Bischof & Fritz Plasser, 978-1-60801-009-7 (2009)

*Also available as E-book

Contemporary African Studies